Marilyn Taft Horn

Leadership in the Arts

An Inside View

by

Marilyn Taft Thomas

authorHOUSE®

AuthorHouse™
1663 Liberty Drive, Suite 200
Bloomington, IN 47403
www.authorhouse.com
Phone: 1-800-839-8640

First published by AuthorHouse 3/11/2008

ISBN: 978-1-4343-6888-1 (sc)

Library of Congress Control Number: 2008901670

Printed in the United States of America
Bloomington, Indiana

This book is printed on acid-free paper.

DEDICATION

This book is written for those who have headed an arts program, those who are presently doing so, those who think they'd like to do it, those who want to know more about the people who do this sort of thing, and for those who just need a good laugh.

Purpose In Writing This Book

This book is based upon the premise that running an arts organization is counter-intuitive. The skills needed to get the job in the first place are often the same attributes responsible for the undoing of the leader's sanity:

- in-depth knowledge and a passion for the profession is needed to lead an arts organization, but the person running such a program seldom has enough time to keep his/her own art going;

- organizational skills are a strong requirement for the position, but the person doing the job has to adjust to nearly continuous disorder as the myriad of arts activities overlap one another on a daily basis;

- highly developed interpersonal skills are a must, but there are never enough of these to keep the large number of artistic temperaments from exploding;

- logic and clear thinking are vitally important, but the people with whom you must deal are seldom operating with logic—emotion is the commodity in greatest abundance;

- strong leadership is critical to doing the job, but the stronger the leader, the more apt the artists are to resent somebody (anybody) telling them what to do;

- decisive people have the best shot at getting something accomplished, yet they have to somehow learn to run in circles while everyone reacts to each change in terms of what it will mean to number #1;

- and, oh yes, everyone in the place needs to believe (s)he is #1—all the time.

Now, if that description doesn't scare you off, read on. There are no answers in this book, but there is a lot of descriptive information about what it's really like to run an arts program. If I had known some of this going into my first administrative job, perhaps it would have taken me a lot less time to figure out why I couldn't move forward in a much straighter line. With proper warning, maybe new leaders of arts programs can enjoy those first few months without worrying about the things they have not yet been able to accomplish. Getting through the day is sometimes a major achievement.

I remember attending a round-robin meeting of new women executives of music programs at the annual conference of the National Association of Schools of Music. Each person was to stand up and introduce herself, telling the group how long she had been head of her music unit and briefly describe the circumstances under which she assumed the responsibility of the directorship. One woman stood up and told us she had only been head of her music school for four months, and had assumed the job on very short notice when the previous head had a nervous breakdown. So there you are. Obviously, the job isn't for everybody.

TABLE OF CONTENTS

ACKNOWLEDGMENTS

It takes a lot of courage, determination, and moral support to bring an author's words into print. This book is no exception. In fact, you wouldn't be holding it in your hand right now if it were not for the encouragement of the late Richard M. Cyert, former President of Carnegie Mellon University, who insisted that I "not give up" before it was published.

To his memory, I dedicate this book.
Everything I learned about leadership was inspired by his dynamic example.

To Author House, and especially to Lisa Metcalf, my Author Services Representative, I extend my deepest gratitude for helping me erase the guilt of many years of ignoring Dr. Cyert's advice.

Day after day, I sat in my pink bathrobe, well into the afternoon, capturing the thoughts that ended up in this book. I appreciate the quiet understanding of my husband, Harry, who had every reason to run off and find better company that year, but didn't. And speaking of family, our three grown children, Marshall Thomas, Michele Thomas McGregor, and Lauren Thomas Hraber, provided all the loving support and feedback any author needs during the evolution of a new book.

Some of my extended family managed to wade through the original manuscript, which was more than twice the length of the final product. Special thanks to my daughter Lauren, to my brother Donald Taft, to my sister-in-law Judy Horgan and brother-in-law John Horgan, and to my cousin Dwight Patton. Each of them went well beyond the call of duty.

Other friends and colleagues also read that early version, and to each of them I offer my deepest gratitude: Benno Bernt, Margaret Guchemand, Kenneth Keeling, the late Akram Midani, Frederick Miller, Robert Page, Ceci Sommers, and Kerry Walk. Their insightful comments and observations guided my massive editing process and contributed significantly to the final form of the book. I hope they see every one of their suggestions embedded in these pages.

Finally, I wish to thank three special colleagues who read excerpts of the book and gave me the advice I needed: Marilyn Posner, Dan Martin, and James A. Mercolini.

The names and professional identity of each of the artists cited in this book, except for me, have been camouflaged to avoid embarrassment. All of the anecdotes, however, did actually happen as I have described them. I freely admit to my role in handling these situations—often with exactly the wrong approach, sometimes getting lucky and doing it right. I leave it to the reader to draw whatever lessons may lurk within these pages.

Chapter #1:   Working With People In The Arts

Leadership will determine the future of the arts. It is central to the health and stability of every arts organization in existence today. Yet, exciting, dynamic leadership in the arts is as rare as the perfect diamond. Why? Well, running an arts program is anything but a day at the beach, and most of the challenges come from the people themselves.

Keeping a large group of professionals on the same train, headed in the same direction, can be a major managerial challenge. Keeping them feeling involved and personally supported is even tougher. Personnel issues are a continual challenge for the director of the arts unit.

Effective leadership begins with a deep understanding and appreciation of the people you must lead. So, let's step inside the job and explore the complex dynamics of the people who work there.

She was not very tall—five-foot four, maybe—but she had that sturdy girth of the professional singer. Performing had been her life's work; now, it was developing young talent. For her students, she would go to the ends of the earth! No one cared more. No one worked harder to make it happen for each of them. She was a professional, clear through to the core of her being.

The week was not going well. She had been to rehearsal last night; the drama director was not handling the voices right. He wanted more and more sound from them. . . pushing too hard. . . not healthy for young singers. . . time to step in. . .

She was headed down the hall to see him. Even in this massive two-story hall of marble, students moved well out of the way, probably in reaction to her crisp, purposeful stride,

1

or maybe to the look in those deep-set hazel eyes. They could bore a hole right through a person. She was a woman on a mission. Anyone could see that.

Quite by accident, her adversary happened out of his office at that very moment. He, too, was short, and quite stocky. They met. She unleashed her venom, right there in the middle of everything. Faculty and students within range all turned toward the sound of the voices, rapidly growing more and more strident.

And then it happened! To this day, no one knows just what he said to her. But somewhere from the depths of her soul came a clenched fist. The director dropped to the marble floor with a thud. Ever mindful of his audience, he looked up at the faces of shocked spectators, and with the consummate skill of decades of theatrical training, wrapped up the scene in a single wail: "She Hit Me!"

UNDERSTANDING THE ARTIST

Of greatest importance is the personality profile of the "typical" artist. Once, at an annual conference of heads of music schools I overheard someone quip, "We have 112 artist faculty and they're all crazy!"— an exaggeration, to be sure, thrown into the conversation for the laughter it drew; however, the concept of an artistic temperament is not fictional.

Highly qualified leaders, who have many years of experience working with artists of all sorts, seem to agree that:

- Artists tend to be either up or down, and their moods shift with incredible speed;
- Problems are catastrophes;
- Needs are immediate;
- Attention and praise are necessities of life; the need for applause is real;

- A basic insecurity is nearly always present. Perhaps, the continual threat of being overshadowed by the next artist in line feeds this insecurity, but the need for reassurance that they are still valued is universal among artists;

- There is a real desire to be #1. With a large roster of artists, the head of the arts unit has a huge job just keeping people on board and feeling good about their work. Yet, every one of them has to feel (s)he is #1.

If they don't, they just may quit.

What Makes An Artist Quit?

Here are some direct quotes from artists who left various arts organizations:

- "I could never get in to see the Executive Director. I had maybe two-three meetings with her the whole time I was there. The only time I got her attention was when I quit."

- "I negotiated my contract, and was all ready to sign it, when the guy told me he couldn't make the salary any higher, because Artist Longevity, who had been there for a hundred years, would "have a fit" if somebody made more money than he did. That was it. I handed back the contract and left."

- "The Dean kept referring to me as Junior Faculty; I had just won a prestigious international competition and I expected that achievement to mean something to the institution. It obviously didn't; so, I quit. That was too bad, because I liked working there. My own teacher still taught there, I had some terrific students, but I had really had it with that woman!"

So, why not just let them quit if they aren't happy? Well, the people quoted above are some of the finest artists in the country; they are the "cream of the crop." Each of them was well worth that leader's effort to reach out and attempt to understand and support their needs, whether artistic or personal. The needs were real.

Dealing With Insecurity

An arts organization is a very personal environment. Forget thinking about it in terms of a typical office or place of business. The artists need to know that everyone recognizes their worth. They have proven themselves in the profession, or are in the process of doing so, and they need you to recognize and acknowledge their achievements. Even some artists in the middle of brilliant careers may need periodic fixes in their self-esteem—perhaps continual reassurance—because deep down, they may not be sure they are good enough. In fact, in these professions, nobody is ever quite certain just when they will become obsolete, and the shadow of this inevitability hangs overhead like a cloud. There are always youngsters coming along who shine like stars on the horizon.

So, at the least little indication from the boss that somebody is perceived to be better, or more valuable, or more successful—well, it just could be curtains. If the artist can't quit, for whatever reason, the outcome can be even worse. Bitterness, frustration, hostility may build until the person explodes. It may be a blowup at a colleague or a member of the staff. (It is seldom a direct hit on the person who caused the problem.) It may even be days or weeks away from the initial incident or remark that triggered the emotional freight train. This time lag makes the blow-up totally unpredictable, and the person or group of people on the receiving end of the tirade may be baffled or, worse yet, feel responsible, guilty, and inadequate. The insecurity can spread like a plague, infecting everyone around who is susceptible to flashes of self-doubt, which is probably all of us.

It would be a mistake to assume that you can put a stop to this kind of a problem. Fortunately, a great many artists do learn how to handle their occasional insecurities; and, thankfully, the vast majority of artists are outwardly strong and highly competent. When the difficult exception surfaces, it would appear that all you have to do is reinforce that person's self worth, but, keep in mind, there may be more than a hundred artists in the organization. (Or it may just seem like there are a hundred.) It is virtually impossible to treat them all with an equal amount of admiration and respect. The real bad news is that even if you could, that, too, would be a problem, because a lot of them need to feel superior, not equal.

That brings us back to the concept of making everybody feel (s)he's #1. The most successful way to interact with an artist is by keeping in mind the image of the grinning football player, who has just scored a big one. All you see on the screen is that index finger raised to the heavens, and a mouth full of teeth. The words "I'm Number One" may or may not be there, but you can be sure he's thinking them. Make no mistake, those are the words that drive that grin, and for the moment, at least, that player has earned the title.

Remember, these are brilliant artists. They are the best at whatever it is that they do. It is the leader's job to reinforce these strengths, to remind them of their value to the institution they serve, and to make certain the insecurities that hover overhead, those vultures of self esteem, do not swoop down and smother the creative environment.

One of the interesting things about running an arts organization is that the person in charge is usually an artist as well, and probably comes to the job with the same type of personality outlined above. If so, that leader will need to adjust, and fast, because nobody worries about the psyche of the boss. In fact, there is often a rather debilitating attitude coming from the artist/faculty, especially in the performing arts, that has nothing at all to do with who is in charge. I call it the Conductor Syndrome.

The Conductor Syndrome

The professional musician matures with an image of leadership very often built around his/her experience working with conductors; for the actor, it is the director. Seldom is this image completely positive.

As an ensemble performer, the musician/actor must learn to play a single part as perfectly as humanly possible, while the overall success of the performance depends upon the way in which the conductor/ director molds and shapes the individual parts into the whole. The player becomes a single color on the canvas; the conductor/director gets to choose how prominent or how subtle to make that color, how much attention to draw toward it, and even how it should be shaped and presented. The player always has an opinion, but doesn't always get to voice it. The conductor/director is the boss—all the time, unequivocally. (S)he who challenges this authority doesn't last long in the profession.

Carry this image into the administrative arena, and the boss becomes the one to resent. Breaking through that preconceived notion to build a team is exceedingly difficult. The phrase, "it's lonely at the top," certainly applies to heading a performing arts program.

Yet, working together is a concept every performer should be able to handle. After all, music and drama are both professions of colleagues. Any ensemble, whether it be a major symphony orchestra, an acting company, a string quartet, a Broadway cast, or a jazz combo, is built on the ability to work as a team. The sum is nearly always greater than its parts. Why, then, is it so difficult to maintain a sense of collegiality within the arts unit? I suspect the answer can be found in the individual artist's personality profile mentioned above.

In an artistic setting, everyone is in competition for the #1 spot, and most of the professional artists are used to being #1. They don't know how to be #2; any indication that someone else is regarded more highly by the boss is all that is needed to set off all sorts of troublesome behavior. Keeping 30 or 60 or 100+ superstars feeling they are each #1 is a talent that instantly qualifies a person for eternal leadership among artists. After all, only God would have the patience to issue harps to all those angels. (I suspect He has since taken more than a few of them back.)

They Are what they Do

The focus required to excel as a performer, sculptor, composer, painter, or conductor nearly guarantees a personality in which the identity is tied to the work. Typical artists see themselves first and foremost as artists. That is who they are, it is not just what they do. Consequently, the entire identity is tied to being an artist. The more successful the career, the longer the person remains active in the profession, the stronger this connection becomes. Often, professional artists turn to teaching as their performance careers begin to ease, and quite frequently, their identities then shift to that of master teachers. The performer becomes the teacher of the next generation of performers; the painter becomes the role model for the next generation of painters; the actor becomes the mentor for the next generation of actors. An inability to see themselves as people separate from their roles as artists and master teachers can cause artists to over-personalize absolutely everything. This can create some special challenges for the head of the arts organization.

With so much of the artist's self esteem linked to his/her work, any sort of on-the-job evaluation process can be extremely threatening. Retirement presents yet another problem for the artist faculty who are what they do. Not all artists remain as effective as they once were; some actually continue to grow more effective the older they get. With no mandatory retirement age, it can be tricky, indeed, to encourage someone to retire. Since they are what they do, retirement can be devastating. A caring leader needs to use a healthy mix of logic and compassion to ease the pain of this transition.

Recognizing the Need for Applause

There is one additional facet of the artist's personality not yet mentioned: the need for applause. Let's face it, the performer needs to hear that applause, and the performing artist who becomes a master teacher needs to be revered by his/her students. Therein lies problem number 1,001, which on a typical day at the office can pop into first place faster than you can say, "Oh, no!" It's nobody's fault, really; that's part of the problem. Artists, like most people, can't help needing to be loved, but in a professional organization, this need can present all sorts of complications.

When we step back and consider the reality of the artist, we have to realize that in the organizational setting, the administration is the conductor or the director, who really controls the artist's ability to gain applause—the person capable of making or breaking their careers. Seen in this light, the need for applause, which has been developed and reinforced through years and years of successful performances, cannot just be ignored. It is there, inside the performer, and it is going to drive the emotional reactions of this person through all sorts of situations.

In reality, the artists' relationship to the arts leader can be fraught with problems carried away from the world of performance and of conductors and directors. Suffice it to say, this is a serious dilemma that must be understood and anticipated in order to be dealt with in some reasonable fashion.

Good news: anyone who can be helped to feel (s)he is #1 will settle down and do the job. Bad news: it is next to impossible to keep all those people feeling they are each #1.

Managing People in the Arts

A complex organizational structure is like a bowl of Jell-O; you can't touch any part of it without setting the whole substance into reactive motion. Working effectively with highly emotional people requires a stepping back, an objectivity and a calmness that is difficult to achieve. If you allow your own emotions to get involved, the situation will most assuredly be worsened.

Weeks of work and anxiety had gone into this one. It was clearly a triumph. The hall was packed, the playing was exquisite, and Mr. Famous Cellist seemed truly happy to be performing with the faculty quartet. Intermission came and the audience burst into the hallways, chattering with excitement and sheer joy following the smashing conclusion of the Schubert.

I couldn't have felt better. This was a high profile event, and a lot could have gone wrong. The worry system set up in my stomach to handle such times was just beginning to ease up, and my professional smiles were beginning to feel honest.

Charles, professor of viola, saw me and hurried over—to join in the celebration of our success, I assumed. I greeted him with a grin of sheer pleasure as he barked, "When are you going to get the water fountain fixed?"

Keep in mind, with creative, artistic temperaments, reactions can never be fully anticipated. Further, reactions can be delayed or hidden to the point that it is even difficult to determine their source. Emotions are very much a part of the day-to-day work place, no matter what you do.

Contributing Factors

This is not meant to imply all artists are the same. In fact, the degree to which the problems outlined above play out is greatly influenced by such factors as: the individual age of the artist; the level of success in the profession; his/her ability to relate to colleagues; and the depth of the love for the profession. When an artist has enjoyed wide-spread acclaim as a professional, there is no good reason for insecurity. That, of course, does not mean it won't be there. You, as the leader of the arts organization, will absolutely have to deal with insecurity, in great abundance—which takes us right back to where we started: the personality profile of the artist. The artist is a very interesting species.

Something was wrong. As I shook hands with my guest, the sound of voices managed to permeate the heavy wooden door that ordinarily keeps the inner office private. I dawdled a bit with the closing of the meeting, exchanging some casual anecdotes with Rebecca, trying to give the problem outside a few extra minutes to subside. As I reached for the doorknob, another door slammed emphatically, marking the end of whatever was going on out there. The public relations rep smiled knowingly as we chatted our way into the outer office.

Karen, the office manager, had obviously seen better days. Her voice was just a bit tight as she greeted our guest, her face flushed with a shade of pink I hadn't seen since the day they installed the new computers. As Rebecca reached the hall, I turned to Karen. "So, you don't seem to be having a good day. Who won?" She didn't laugh—another very bad sign. As the tirade unleashed, it gradually became clear that the art history professor had chewed her out royally. "Wait a minute, Karen. What exactly was his problem?"

"There's no soap in the men's room."

SUPERVISING THE STAFF

The day-to-day life of an arts organization is driven by the underlying premise: "The show must go on!" Consequently, staff need to develop a willingness to do "whatever it takes" to help the artistic process reach its highest possible level of excellence. An ideal staff person for any arts organization is the individual who is committed to the mission of that institution. No matter what the job description says, or what the responsibilities of the position may entail, the most essential characteristic of an effective employee in the arts is dedication. Every person in the operation has to care about the quality of the arts program and must have a desire to contribute to that quality.

This attitude applies to the educational programs as well as to the public presentations. The spirit of unity and camaraderie that can develop among the cast of a successful theater company, for example, is the same type of teamwork that is essential to support a healthy arts program of any type. Each person on board must be able to see the big picture and know (s)he is making a vital contribution to that artistic product—whether it be the education of young artists, a large-scale concert, an important art exhibit, or an institutional board meeting.

The Problem of Hierarchy

Remember that all the people problems encountered by the head of the arts unit are also right "in the face" of each member of the staff, and the staff lack the institutional power to hold the artists in check. When someone important blows his/her top, it will probably be at a staff member, not at the boss. Consequently, it is essential that the person at the top keeps a sharp eye on the artists, in particular, and makes certain to provide the kind of personal support the staff need to do their jobs. The power structure, being what it is, leaves the staff on a lower rung of the ladder than just about anyone around them. It is vitally important that they be protected from abuse. It may even become necessary from time to time to step in and make artists aware of the need for a kinder approach to the staff who are attempting to work with them.

Whoever is higher on the totem pole has a tendency to dump on the guy below. (It is the old story of kicking the dog.) Whenever problems arise, it is important for the leader of the arts unit to give sufficient support to the one on the bottom—not to the detriment of a fair outcome—but to at least recognize the separate levels of power involved in the situation. Staff need to feel a certain sense of service to the people around them—all the people. Their skill in coping with this service orientation will help determine their relative success in these jobs.

The Need for Advanced People Skills

The staff person who can cope with manic-depressive behavior, who at least appears to be unruffled by temper tantrums, is ideal. Someone who has raised a two-year-old may actually be better qualified for the job than the more likely candidates with lots of professional credentials. Why? Because the artists with whom they must deal can be exceedingly difficult, especially to the staff whose job it is to support their activities.

All of the topics discussed in this book relate to the special problems inherent in working with artists and dealing with the artistic process. It requires a great deal of maturity and patience to work in this type of environment. The person who brings both qualities to the office each day has a better than even chance of going home in one piece at the end of the day, provided (s)he also has a healthy sense of humor to help push through the rough spots.

Every job has its ups and downs. For the person at the front desk, well, let's just say, "The downs have it." This is the person who handles three phones all day long, answers questions, solves problems, routes calls to eighty-seven faculty, attempts to keep track of keys to facilities in three different buildings, matches space to teachers at a hysterical pace (when there are usually many more of the former than the latter,) and still manages to wear a frozen smile for a continuous stream of walk-in customers—students, faculty, visitors, administrators, whomever happens to wander into the office. At least, that's what the job description says this person does.

If the truth were known, it's actually a whole lot worse than that, because hardly ever does someone come in the door without a problem. These are artists, remember, so each problem is the most important problem in the entire universe. It requires immediate attention, usually by the one person who is unavailable to deal with it at that moment—me.

For awhile the position was called "receptionist." Then, we switched it to "office manager" in the attempt to get stronger candidates into the pool. It is no surprise that this particular job is, more often than not, up for grabs.

During one such cycle, we decided to hire a "temp." Katie was a small, thin lady of about 50, maybe 55. She arrived bright and early, looking fit and ready for whatever we assigned her to do. She was, apparently, a dynamo typist, filer, dictation taker—all the things we had absolutely no use for. As I described the routine and as much of the necessary information as possible, she nodded knowingly, and assured me she would have everything in hand in no time at all. I remember feeling a vague sense of impending doom as I walked into my office and closed the door.

12

It was a jam-packed morning of non-stop appointments. By noon, I emerged to find Stan, our Assistant Head, at the desk. "Where's Katie?" I asked. He laughed and said, "Oh, she went out the door about an hour ago crying. Haven't seen her since."

The Ability to Deal with Chaos

This arts stuff is messy business. People who need to do one thing at a time, and finish it perfectly before going on to the next task—well, this is just not the place for them. An arts environment is chaotic, in part, because each person in that environment is engaged in his/her own arts activity. Then, there are groups working together with different artistic and organizational needs. Deadlines abound. Anxiety runs amok in all directions. Needs bump into each other. Emotions spill over the boundaries of mature behavior with surprising frequency. There is a climate of continual crisis. Staff simply need to learn how to roll with the punches.

We once had an ensembles manager who burst into tears every time there was a problem. Needless to say, this was not a helpful response. The last thing you need in the midst of all these artistic temperaments is more emotion. The staff need to be strong, well organized, yet able to adjust to continual shifts in their day. More often than not, their "To-Do List" will become their "To-Do-Just-As-Soon-As-This-New-Crisis-Is-Over-List."

Understanding that Jobs Spill Over

The only true nine-to-five job I can think of in an arts environment is the position of receptionist, the person who answers the phones during business hours. Nearly all the other positions related to the management of artistic activity are as difficult to box up neatly as a bunch of newborn puppies. Arts activities absolutely peak at the time of public presentations; the need for administrative support, therefore, will ebb and flow depending on these mounting pressures. There are times when staff jobs may be almost manageable, such as in the middle of the summer or perhaps the middle of the night.

Most of the time, there is more to be done than anyone has hours to do it.

This presents a myriad of difficult problems:

- Employees can easily grow frustrated by their inability to finish things during normal working hours;
- They may become more and more self-protective and refuse to do one thing more than is required;
- They may, on the other hand, work far too much, trying to do a perfect job, and eventually feeling over-worked and under-paid;
- They will probably resent their lack of control over their own jobs.

There is not a whole lot you can do about the cycling of pressures brought on by artistic work, but you can and should take steps to help the staff cope with these cycles. Of primary importance is the effort to control the hours spent doing the job. Most staff can deal with extra work if they know there will be extra down time to balance it. Staff who must go to evening performances or weekend presentations need to be able to trade some time off during normal office hours. Perhaps the person who works evenings should not start work until noon. Or an extra day on the job should be balanced by an extra day off. Flexible hours are essential when staff are expected to work overtime. If you engage the staff member in the process of defining this schedule, there will be a very positive sense of power over the job and control of his/her own time. This will go miles toward avoiding some of the problems listed above.

Even one member of the staff with odd working hours can create a morale problem among all the other staff, who notice the absence, but are not there to see the extra work after hours. For this reason, it is of paramount importance to have clear guidelines for managing the flexibility of staff time and to make sure all staff have equal access to this policy of flexibility. It is human nature to believe the grass is greener over there. It is also human nature to believe the world is dealing us a bad hand. So, staff need to be treated with the utmost care; nothing is more critical than a sense of equity within the system. If someone is perceived to be ducking responsibilities and still getting paid, the resentment in the air will be thicker than snow in a blizzard.

The Need for Buy-In

If you really want people to buy into the mission of the institution, there has to be a sense of fulfillment in helping to make things happen. The dedicated staff person has to be able to see the results of his/her labor, and recognize the value of this contribution to the institution (s)he serves; and of more immediate importance, the staff need to see that you, the boss, recognize the value of their work. It is impossible to give staff too much praise, provided, of course, that praise is honest, deserved, and truly felt by the person giving it. Blanket praise means little. Individual words of appreciation from the boss, delivered face to face, are by far the reward of choice. Raises in salary and promotion are not to be overlooked, but they cannot possibly happen frequently enough to keep a person going through the day-to-day pressures of a stressful job, feeling appreciated.

Provided the staff do receive sufficient support from the boss, there is a much greater likelihood of their buying into the needs of the organization they serve. This requires that the big picture is obvious to them, and that they see how their own work contributes to this big picture. It is the primary responsibility of the leader of the arts organization to make explicit to everyone working in the environment just what the goals are and the quality of work needed to achieve these goals. If the leader is unable to help each member of the staff see just how (s)he personally fits into the institutional mission, no amount of back patting will suffice. You can't fake it. A person knows when the job (s)he must do is vital to the organization and when it is less so. It is only when there is a clear sense of purpose, of being a part of the outcome, that people are willing to go beyond the call of duty. Commitment to the institution comes with the desire to help make it better. If you can get this going at the staff level, you will have an engine that runs right up the mountain.

Shaping the Job to Fit the Person

Your chance of getting that engine going is greatly enhanced by your willingness to be flexible. People bring themselves to work every morning. If they have to spend half their day pounding themselves into square holes, they will either lose their own sense of self or they will actually become that square shape you are requiring them to assume. Either way, you have lost the essence of the person you hired.

Why not go with what you've got? If you hired a staff person to answer the phones, and you discover that person has real skill in proofreading, for heavens sake, give him/her the latest newsletter to read in between calls. If your business manager has great people skills, as well as sharp accounting talent, perhaps (s)he can absorb a little fund-raising activity. Even if you thought you wanted your student advisor to keep the student data base up-to-date, maybe your office manager has a real love for computers and is detail-oriented, whereas the head of advising hates both. As long as everybody is happy with the switch, move the tasks around a bit until you find the best fit.

Obviously, you can't go too far with this musical chairs game, or you just may have two people doing one thing and nobody doing something else. You might also create some resentment, if a staff person feels (s)he is doing more than his/her share, or another person feels bad about losing a particular responsibility. It's usually important to keep the job looking like the job the person applied for in the first place. If it gets too far from home, you will need to sit down with the employee and work out a new job description that may or may not require a promotion, as well. Beware: any time you add responsibilities to a job, rather than trading them for others, the person is bound to feel entitled to some sort of reward. Wouldn't you?

The goal is to maximize job satisfaction, not to squeeze every ounce of life out of the people on your staff. As far as possible, let each person's innate strengths and weaknesses shape the way they do their jobs, instead of expecting them to stand on their heads, or turn inside out, in order to accomplish the tasks at hand. If you have a really bad fit, with a person totally unsuited to the job for which (s)he was hired, you need to move that person out of that job. You also need to examine rather closely just how you managed to get into this untenable situation. (More on this in the section on "Hiring and Firing.")

Inability to Do the Job

It is rare for an arts institution of any sort to have extra employees. Arts organizations are normally "lean and mean" operations, because there is seldom enough money to satisfy everyone's artistic (or just greedy) appetite for bigger and better art. As a result, it becomes absolutely essential that every employee give 100% to the task at hand. You simply can't afford to have people who don't do their jobs. So, what do you do with staff who either can't or won't do what is expected of them?

The obvious answer is to fire them, but that may not always be the best solution. If you are in the middle of an academic and/or performance season, it can be horribly disruptive to change staff. There is just so much specific knowledge involved—tiny little nuts and bolts of information holding the whole operation together. Changing staff means somebody, probably you, will have to absorb the details of that job while it is in transition. There is rarely enough time in your day to pick up the pieces of another person's job, plus launch an intensive search for the "right" person to fill that job, while still doing everything else you have to do. Firing someone needs to be regarded as a last resort. From the human relations side, it is obviously better to help the person you already have on your staff succeed.

There is no question that this, too, takes time. Your time. Supervising an ineffective employee requires close supervision and continuous feedback. You need to be up front with the person; you have to make it clear that certain aspects of the work are unsatisfactory and that you want to help correct these problems. You also have to be able to articulate the steps needed to make the improvements. You probably need to set a time frame for correcting the insufficiencies, after which you will have to terminate the contract, if the problems still exist. Putting all of this in writing is highly advisable, so there can be no misunderstanding.

It is exceedingly difficult to deal with such a situation calmly, since ineffective staff can make a terrible mess of things. Whatever responsibilities they are supposed to be handling are, no doubt, right in the middle of some very important arts activities. There is undoubtedly serious fallout from their inadequacies, and you certainly don't need additional problems on your plate. Still, losing your cool will only make things worse. The sinking staff is already full of anxiety and perhaps more than a little resentful toward you for being such a pain-in-the-neck. Be careful you don't provide additional cause for them to blame you instead of taking full responsibility for their own improvement.

In today's litigious society, it is doubly important to move carefully, documenting your attempts to help the employee correct the inadequacies. Remember, lawsuits abound in cases just like yours. Blow it, and you will have problems that make these look like a day at the beach.

A Lack of Clarity in the Job Description

Nothing creates more havoc than a job description that fails to describe the job. If you hire someone with certain expectations, and that person does not fully understand those expectations, there is trouble ahead. Clear communication is difficult under the best conditions, and the circumstances surrounding the hiring process are not conducive to clarity. You, the hirer, need this job to be filled—yesterday. The hiree wants the job. You describe the position in glowing terms; (s)he hears your words all wrapped up in a cloak of optimism. Everybody is sifting information like mad, latching onto the good stuff, letting the nebulous negatives swim around in the atmosphere—never quite landing on the table.

Consequently, the groundwork is laid for future dissatisfaction on everybody's part. How much better it would be for the employer to say, "This is a terrible job. Long hours. Impossible people. Too much work. Not enough time. Inadequate pay. High stress. If you still want it, it's yours, but don't say I didn't warn you." The prospective employee then responds, "That's OK. I'm a no-good worthless bum, who hates to get up in the morning, has a million excuses for not getting the job done, brings a truck load of personal problems to work every day, takes long lunch hours, and likes to leave early. But, if you want me to do the job, I'm available."

No, this is not exactly the way the interview plays out. Weeks later, maybe months later (if you are lucky) you begin to hear things like, "But nobody told me I would have to do "X!" or "I thought I would be able to leave at 5:00," or "I can't just sit here all day answering phones!" or "But 'Staff W' doesn't have to deal with XYZ! Why do I?" Life is too short to engage in these kinds of discussions. It's so much easier to just pull out the job description and point. Hopefully, you have something suitable in those files, just waiting for your index finger. If you don't, the next time I bet you will.

The Use of Artist Staff

It makes perfect sense: the job requires continual immersion in artistic endeavors, and intense dealings with professional artists and young "wannabe" artists; so, the staff probably need to have artistic backgrounds. Right? Wrong. If you can possibly avoid it, don't hire staff with serious training in the arts area you lead. Why? There are several reasons:

- If they want to be artists, they will no doubt find it frustrating to facilitate other people who are actually doing what they originally set out to do. The job will be perceived as a step backward for them, or worse yet, will be taken with the hope of turning it into a stepping-stone toward the career they really want. You know and I know, a person hired as supportive staff in an arts organization is not going to be able to work up to a faculty position or suddenly become one of the performers. Yet, it is amazing how many people think this will happen. Ideally, you need to hire people who are fulfilled by the job itself, not people who actually want to be doing something else. Unhappy staff are a nightmare!

- If they were trained as artists, they may possess the dreaded artistic temperament. (We will make an exception here for those who found the field totally unsuitable—a sure sign that the personality does not fit the profession.) The last thing you need on your staff is someone who wants to be #1. This person will have battles with the artists—all the time. You also need to avoid the staff person who is an emotional wreck. Calmness and logic are a real asset in the supportive staff; your chances of finding either of these in the trained artist are a little below that of hitting the lottery. It can happen, but don't count on it.

- If they really want to be artists, they will leave the minute they get an opportunity somewhere else to do that. Unlike traditional job changes from one office to another, a leap back out into the profession will usually occur with very little warning. Opportunity strikes, and your staff person is out the door faster than you can say, "But your contract says. . . ." You shouldn't be totally surprised. Hiring an artist on your staff should be done with your eyes wide open. If you need that much artistic expertise, then go for it, but don't plan to hold onto that person forever. A real artist has to do what an artist has to do. You know that. You are probably one yourself.

This is not to say that the ideal staff person is totally clueless about the arts.

We once had a concert manager, whose job it was to produce all the programs for our public concerts, recitals, and master classes. She had absolutely no background in music, but since she was normally just printing what music faculty and students gave her, we figured it would be OK. I invited her to ask me about anything she was unsure of, and gave her a copy of the definitive Groves Dictionary, with the instructions to look up whatever she needed in that.

Well, one memorable day I was sitting in the audience of an in-house (thankfully) performance of the trumpet students. One of the pieces on the program was arranged for brass by the famous Leroy Anderson. Apparently, the students had handed Shirley the information with L. Anderson as the composer. She had dutifully looked up the name in Grove's Dictionary and somehow came up with the name Lucy. So, there in bold type was Lucy Anderson's "Holiday for Brass."

In fact, the ideal person is probably someone with a deep interest in the arts area, but only as an avocation. This is the best of both worlds; you can count on the artistic knowledge being there, without paying the price of having a high-strung disgruntled wannabe artist on your hands.

The Combat Zone

Oh, if only we could achieve peace on earth, good will toward men (and women), at least in the work place. To understand this problem, let's take a look at the major causes of war in general: territorial disputes, battles over essential resources, major cultural differences, power struggles, and just downright aggressiveness. Look around and you will find every one of these seeds of destruction right in your own artistic back yard. So, how do you handle major feuds between two members of your staff?

By a major feud, I mean a situation that transcends the occasional disagreement between two employees who otherwise get along just fine. Here, we have two people who absolutely hate each other, and they both happen to be on your staff, supposedly working on the same team. Except for this problem, they are excellent employees, performing essential functions within your otherwise peaceful artistic operation. (This is a hypothetical situation, remember.) Not only do they refuse to work together, they actively take shots at one another whenever the opportunity arises. What do you do?

Step back, and try to figure out exactly what is going on. Perhaps all hell broke loose when you hired the second person, "Staff Vinegar." Before that, "Staff Oil" was happy as a lark. Now, before you jump to any conclusions, it is not necessarily "Vinegar's" fault. "Oil" just may resent anybody on his/her turf. Or maybe "Vinegar" ruffled "Oil's" feathers needlessly upon arrival. Whatever the case, if you determine that only one person is behaving badly, you will want to work with that person to change the behavior.

But, more often than not, the problem runs deeper than that. Both people are probably contributing to the conflict—maybe unintentionally, but contributing nonetheless. You may be able to ease the tension by separating them physically. If the major cause of this war is territorial, get them out of each other's way. If the problem is resources, try to address each of their needs individually. If the difficulty is cultural differences, go for a higher level of tolerance; forget the more ideal solution of acceptance. If the primary problem is a struggle for power, make sure everyone knows who sits where on the hierarchical chart; they both need to accept this reality or give up the job. But if the real cause of the difficulty is downright aggressiveness, this may be transformed into a more positive assertiveness directed toward their jobs, which could make both of them exemplary employees.

The goal is to contain the problem. You are not going to turn these people into bosom buddies, but warfare is disruptive. It is, at the very least, a distraction from the real business at hand. At its worst, people get hurt, the climate is charged with negativity, and productivity falls through the floor. As the leader of the arts unit, you cannot tolerate a civil war. So, don't. Bottom line: make it clear to everyone involved that people don't have to like each other; but they do have to work together—peacefully and productively. If they cannot, one or both have to go. (More on hiring and firing in Chapter #7.)

The Ultimate Problem

Money! Unless your arts organization is a whole lot richer than most, you probably have difficulty paying your employees as much as they are really worth. It stands to reason that if salaries are too low, you will lose some very good people. It takes a tremendous commitment to an organization to hang in there, when you could be making more money somewhere else.

This problem is particularly acute in the arts, because so much is expected of the staff in charge of implementing arts projects, policies, and programs. As discussed earlier, staff in the arts have to deal with difficult people, simultaneous streams of complex activities, high levels of stress, and continual crises. This takes enormous maturity, wisdom, patience, and skill. You don't find that combination of personal attributes on the bottom of the employment ladder; yet, far too often the pay scale for a staff position in the arts is akin to an entry-level position in a different professional environment. On paper, the job may appear to be appropriate for someone with a high school diploma and no prior work experience; in reality, you need a wizard with four hands and a magic wand in each.

The trick is to find the wizard who is willing to work for nothing. Good luck!

Holding onto the Wizard

So, you found one, did you? Well, now, just how do you intend to hold onto him/her? Wizards need lots of elbowroom; after all, they have all those magic wands to wave around. The first rule of thumb is to give them space—not physical space, although that is desirable, too—but operational space. Never over-supervise a wizard. If the responsibility is theirs, step back and let them do their thing. The more abilities you see, the more tasks you should turn over to their capable hands; remember, wizards have four hands, you only have two.

Another basic tenet of wizard-watching is to go easy on the criticism. Wizards are used to doing things right. If they screw up, you don't have to say a thing; they will be so distraught, they will most certainly fix that blooper faster than you can say "Abracadabra", and don't worry—it will never happen again. Wizards never make the same mistake twice.

If you do blow it, and react to the mistake, even in your facial expression, you will have shot an arrow straight through the heart of the wizard. Wizards care deeply about their "master's" state of mind; they also want desperately to please you. They are sensitive to the slightest little twitch of the face or the shoulders or even the feet. Walk away from the situation, and they will infer your displeasure. Wrinkle your nose, and they will see your tension. Even a dilation of the pupils in the eyes will be read as unhappy surprise.

So, what do you do in the unlikely event of a wizardly slip up? Probably the best reaction is to commiserate with the wizard. Make it obvious that you recognize how bad the wizard feels about the mistake, that you know (s)he will take care of the problem, that you also know it wouldn't ever in a thousand years happen again, and that you will be happy to help, but only if (s)he actually needs you. Convey your complete and utter confidence in the wizard's continued wand waving and make sure (s)he knows that nobody in this world or in the world of wizards could do a better job than this particular wizard. Then, forget it ever happened. Wizards do not enjoy being reminded of their blunders.

Yet another guideline on wizard management is to make sure they have the ability to succeed. Nothing discourages a wizard faster than repeated failure to implement their magic. Give them whatever they need to work their miracles. Wizards need physical space, budgetary support, and time. Don't expect them to lower their own standards of wizardry. If they can't wave their wands in public, give them privacy. If they have trouble saying the magic words without a cell-phone, hey, phones are cheap enough. If they need five or ten bucks to implement a miracle, give it to them. Don't expect them to practice their most elegant wizardness instantly; even wizards need time to think and plan their strategies. After all, special potions may need to be mixed—just so.

If your wizard is given the support (s)he needs to succeed in doing top-of-the-line wizardry, and if the wizard knows you know magic when you see it, this wizard just may grow old in the job. Wizards are, above all, the most loyal of creatures, and they don't work for just anybody.

Knowing When a Wizard is a Wizard

You know you have a wizard in your midst when problems you intend to handle tomorrow disappear before you even get to them. (You have grown accustomed to problems getting worse while they sit there waiting for your attention, so this is highly unusual.) You know there's a wizard at work when the number of crises per day seems to be declining. Crises never diminish! So, somebody else must be heading them off before they get to your door. You know there is a wizard close by when you delegate something and it actually disappears, without bouncing back once or twice like a boomerang. Wizards do everything you ask them to do, and then some things you haven't thought of just yet. You know you are in the presence of a wizard when you go home at the end of the day feeling better than when you got there. Somebody must be helping.

Find that wizard and put your "Wizard Protection Policy" into effect immediately. Never take a wizard for granted. Anyone else who tries to hurt your wizard or stand in his/her way should be shot. You just can't afford to lose this one.

Letting Go of your Wizard

If, as luck will have it, your wizard outgrows the job, or needs new challenges, and if you have no way of providing a more exciting position, then you have to do the noble thing: let go of your wizard. I know, I know, you need that wizard, you can't imagine life without him/her, you've said over and over, "If (s)he ever quits, I'll go, too." But, you didn't really mean that. Let's face it, you have grown fond of that old wizard. How could you not love the person who helps get you through the day? Because you love your wizard, you do want the best for him/her. So, with a tremendous sense of loss, you set your wizard free.

Now, what? Well, you are not going to find another wizard like the one you just lost. Don't even try. Sit down and figure out just what aspects of the job the wizard was actually handling; it was probably far more than you originally outlined in the job description. Revise the job description to include whatever you can't live without, and start your search. If you are extremely lucky, you may find somebody who does all of those things really well. This person's no wizard, mind you, but then, you didn't expect to find another one just yet.

Besides, you still have your own special wizard friend out there in the world, working his/her special magic. If you did a good job of setting your wizard free, most likely (s)he's still holding some small piece of concern for the old "master." Every now and then, you will reconnect, and feel good about your friendship and your past work together. One of life's greatest joys is in knowing you have left someone better than you found them. This goes for wizards, too.

CHAPTER #2   BECOMING A LEADER

Much of this book deals with the management issues and administrative challenges faced on a daily basis by leaders in the arts. This is essential. The arts executive must be able to handle the myriad of complexities inherent in the arts environment, and must be able to work effectively with the rich tapestry of people found within that environment. Always, behind these discussions, lies the overriding concern that skillful management is not enough, competent administration is just the beginning. Leadership demands so much more of us!

Leadership vs. Management

I looked these words up in two different dictionaries and discovered the following: associated with the term *management* were the words handling and controlling; for *leadership*, the descriptive words used were guiding and directing.

If you are the employee, there is certainly a huge difference between being handled or controlled and being guided or directed. Take my word for it, with artists, you had better plan to guide and direct, and forget you ever heard the word "control." Knowing full well this is an issue primarily of style, it is, nevertheless, of the utmost importance. Artists are traditionally a cantankerous lot. They have earned their credentials through years of arduous study and personal achievement; they possess an inordinate amount of expertise. They deserve your respect and admiration and they better get it.

> *"You have to do something about Theodore! He's splitting the whole department!" These words had a real familiar ring. Just this morning Theodore had said the same thing about Fred. "You have to do something about that Fred. He's driving a wedge right through the acting program."*
>
> *I managed to mask the smile, but it spread through my gut, soothing the bite of the problem I faced. "Wait a minute,*

Fred. There's no reason for you two to get into each other's faces. You run the acting program; he runs production. You are both world-class. You know I'd go to the mat supporting your work. Now, let's try to find a rehearsal schedule that you can both live with."

And so it goes. There's no short cut. You have to listen to each of them. You have to reassure both that their work is valued. You have to get into the middle of the problem like a referee, and make the final call. Then, you have to deal with the fall-out. Everybody's mad, because nobody got exactly what (s)he wanted.

Alternatives? Try shrugging and letting them fight it out, and you will have, without a doubt, a shooting match which every student in the program will remember for years to come. You may even have to cancel a show in the process. Probably not, but that is always the threat; and that brings the public into the picture, and the flurry of cancellation announcements, parents, and who knows what else? So, it's far better to diffuse the situation as best you can.

Stupid? Yep! But, that's why they pay you the big bucks.

The Artists' Perspective

Except for scenes like this one, for the most part, artists would prefer not to have a boss at all, and they usually produce their best work when they are permitted to feel self-employed. The problem, of course, is that each of them has a slightly different view of the ideal artistic environment. This view emanates outward in all directions from—guess what? Yep, the individual artist's personal needs, desires, and opinions. Every artist's view of the world has you-know-who in the center.

To visualize this situation, take each person in your organization and make them a dot on the page. Around every dot, draw a circle or a squiggly line resembling a box or oval or crooked circle representing his/her beliefs, needs, goals; make sure to keep each person in the center of his/her structure. Now, if the page represents your organization, the more artists you have, the more likely it is that a lot of these wiggly structures will overlap one another. These can be considered areas of similarity or agreement in needs or goals. In real life, there will probably be sub-groups of artists who stick together most of the time, out of a perceived similarity in viewpoint or vested interest.

The challenge is to get all of these wobbly circles acting like wheels, moving in more or less the same direction. Some are undoubtedly aimed in opposite directions. Just for fun, let's put an arrow inside each person's circle to signify the way that artist wishes to travel. We'll make sure these arrows are pointed every which way, just as in real life. The difference between management and leadership can be easily demonstrated by assuming the manager goes from circle to circle attempting to cajole, order, or physically force each circle into the desired position, with the arrow pointing in the direction the manager wishes to go. Or, perhaps, the manager is willing to go in any direction at all, provided (s)he can get all those wheels headed in a single direction.

The leader, on the other hand, recognizes that each arrow has a metal point. By raising a powerful magnet overhead, the leader, in one magnificent gesture, causes all arrows to turn toward him/her. Once accomplished, that leader jolly well better know where (s)he is taking them, because this kind of opportunity doesn't come along every day.

What it Takes to be a Leader

I am not speaking of manipulation or control here, but of motivation. The effective leader is a master of motivation. (S)he understands to the core how people feel, why they feel as they do, and what it would take to move them beyond their personal needs toward the greater good of the group or the organization. (S)he cares deeply about these individuals, yet understands clearly the relationships of the various parts to the whole. The leader has a passion for the organization and its mission that can be seen and felt by everyone with whom (s)he comes in contact.

Expertise in the field is imperative to gain the credibility you need to run the organization and to recognize the things that should be done. Doing things right is essential. So is doing the right thing. Deciding just what is the right thing to do is obviously the trick. The inspiring leader has the depth of character and the global vision to take the arts organization beyond its current limitations, to motivate the people within the arts environment to reach for a higher level of excellence.

We, as managers and as administrators, are in the thick of things, watching over all the details, solving problems as they arise, arbitrating disputes, putting out forest fires, making things happen. It is vitally important that we do this well. But as leaders, we are called upon to go out in front like a minesweeper, getting rid of obstacles so that everyone else can do their work. It is the leader in each of us that sets the vision for our arts unit, inspires others to follow us, and steers the ship on a path toward a better future for the arts.

Our greatest challenge as arts executives is to dig out of the day-to-day details of the implementation process, to find sufficient time to exercise our leadership abilities—to step back and reflect, to actually see where we are headed and to make sure this is really where we want to be going. The management and the administrative aspects of our jobs can easily consume us; far too often, our leadership skills remain virtually untapped. Yet, it is our role as leaders that will ultimately determine our importance to the institutions we serve.

If being a director of an arts organization meant just making sure the trains run on time, I suspect none of us would be interested in the job. It means much more than that. Being in charge of an arts program is an opportunity to further advance the arts themselves. It is also an opportunity to excite new audiences and encourage more active supporters for the arts. If a door opens into the world of fund raising for your arts unit, or of recruitment for your programs, or of advocacy for the cause of the arts in general, open that door and find time to do it. If more trivia comes your way, more paper-pushing, memo-writing, more meetings, more reports, just duck. Do whatever you can to resist getting chewed up by the junk in your job. Delegate it. Dig out of the details. Climb up to the important stuff, and don't be afraid to deal with it. We desperately need strong leaders in the arts.

SETTING A VISION

While not everyone will agree with me on this point, I fervently believe that, while a strategic plan needs to be developed hand-in-hand with the people within the organization, the vision should be set at the outset by the leader. In other words, I believe you, as a leader, must assume the helm with a clear picture of where the institution needs to go. Often, this means taking big risks and putting yourself on the line.

Developing a Vision

A new vision for an organization may be created in part through the hiring process itself. As you learn about the arts unit, its place in the professional field, and its current state of internal operations, you will undoubtedly form impressions of the organization's current direction. It should soon become clear to you whether the arts unit is on track or in trouble. These initial impressions need to be tested further in conversations with the Board or other influential and knowledgeable people in the organization. It is only after you have a clear picture of the organization and its current direction that you are in a position to decide whether or not you are the appropriate person to lead that organization forward. It is assumed that those hiring the new leader are simultaneously making the same assessment as to your fit with the institution.

Your vision may initially be no more than a general sense of direction. There may be a gut-level feeling that the arts unit can become much greater than it presently is, just by staying on course and working on the issue of excellence. Or your vision may be that the current direction of the arts unit is wrong; that it will inevitably lead to a dead-end; that a new direction is desperately needed for the long-term survival of the organization. Sometimes, there is no current direction; the organization is stuck and needs someone to restore a sense of purpose and direction. Anyone considering a new position as leader of an arts unit must know going into the job which of these scenarios is presently in place and how far you, as a leader, might be able to take the organization. This is the vision we are speaking about.

Ideally, your vision for the arts unit should be in consonance with the administration or the Board's image of its future. If this is not the case, the discrepancies between these two disparate concepts of leadership need to be resolved before you are hired. This requires that you, as the potential leader, are able to articulate the general direction toward which you intend to steer the organization. If this is not what the people in charge want to hear, you will probably not be hired. This is better than taking the job and winding up unable to accomplish what you set out to do.

When a Vision Isn't Obvious

What if you took the job, but you still can't find the vision you need? What if the place is pretty good just the way it is? Nonsense! It can always be better. You don't have to go for a totally new organization. The current direction of the arts unit may be just what it should be. You might be wise to "buy into" an already established vision for that organization. Yet, still there is much to be done. You might envision a program that functions more smoothly, an environment that is more positive, with higher morale, better management of facilities, perhaps more adventurous programming. Do artists need to work together more effectively? Is the balance of innovative and conservative thinking where it should be? Could you be recruiting stronger artists? What is your niche in the market place? Is there a clear and accurate perception out there of who you are and what you are about? How do your programs rank nationally, internationally? Where do you want them to be?

Nobody who seeks to lead an arts organization should step into a job without first giving some serious thought to the future of that organization. Where is it today? What are the dangers it faces? What are the needs? The challenges? The problems? The obstacles? If all of those could be addressed, what could the organization ultimately become?

If you can see a picture of the organization in the ideal world, without all those problems and obstacles holding it back, then you have your vision. If it seems unattainable, great! You really do have your vision. Puny little goals cannot be called vision. You need to be driving toward utopia in order to make the kind of progress that will be even noticeable. If your destination is too close at hand, nobody will feel inspired to work very hard to get there. Conversely, if it is so far out of reach that nobody but you can imagine it, you will need to keep some shorter-term goals clearly in front of everyone else until they also begin to glimpse the potential of the organization. Either that, or be an incredible cheerleader with the ability to inspire confidence in otherwise "Doubting Thomases."

Whatever you decide upon as the vision for your unit, you have to be able to articulate it to your colleagues. Remember, without a vision, you have no magnet to wield, and those arrows will remain in helter-skelter positions forever. Have you heard the analogy that running a complex organization is like trying to herd squirrels? Double that effort, if your squirrels happen to be artist-squirrels.

DEVELOPING A STRATEGIC PLAN

So far, we have been talking as though the leader alone sets the vision and single-handedly drives the ship toward that destination. In reality, you can't even begin to leave the dock without a crew who is willing and eager to go where you want to go. Nor is it feasible to just point in the general direction of your vision without a detailed map to get you there. The map for your organization is called the strategic plan.

Now, if you don't have enough information to answer the questions about current problems, obstacles, challenges, and needs, your first order of business is to acquire this data. I highly recommend going straight to the source: the artists. They are the folks you need to be getting on board. Whether their information is correct or not doesn't matter; it is all about perceptions. If the artists think such-and-so is a problem, then it most assuredly is, and sometimes that problem will come as a total surprise.

The strategic planning retreat was going well. Discussion was lively and intense. Spirits were high as we talked about our strategic plan for technology. The first goal was to purchase a powerful computer system for every faculty office. We explored the possibilities of networking, communicating with students, and of finally catching up to the rest of the campus. There had been so many other priorities; but now, we were ready.

Then, it occurred to me. Wait! Slow down. Maybe I'm ready, and they're not. So, I asked. "Before we move forward to try to get the funding for this project, let me just ask all of you if this is something you really want to do. Maybe you don't want a computer in your office. Could I see a show of hands, please? How many of you actually want a computer?"

Hands just shot into the air. Not only did they want them, they were excited, absolutely exuberant. Even the older faculty—some in their seventies—all had their hands up, faces beaming with the sheer joy of a new experience. I laughed out loud at their zeal. Then, just as the hands were coming down, one climbed even higher. Rising to his feet, to be sure of being seen and heard, Professor Veteran, who had been with us for decades, spoke out in his most impressive scholarly voice. "Could I have an office?"

Collecting Data for the Strategic Plan

When you are ready to actually shape a strategic plan for the future, you will need all of the various constituencies included in the process. The more you know about the people involved—their individual biases, ethics, goals, allegiances—the better able you will be to handle a large-scale planning process. So, the strategic plan will need to take shape rather gradually.

There are numerous methods of gathering information and perceptions from the people within your organization. One is to get to know each of the individuals one-on-one. Realize that this may take months, because there may be a lot of people in the organization, and your first meeting with any of them will probably not provide a complete picture of who they are and what they need to reach their individual potential as artists. Certainly, any opportunities to get to know your artists should be welcomed; the sharper your listening skills and perceptual abilities, the better. It's not too soon to start taking notes on problems, issues, and new ideas as they surface in these individual meetings, to be folded into the organizational strategic plan.

At the same time, you also need to be observing closely the interaction of people within the organization. For many structural problems, institutional weaknesses, and potential conflicts surface in the daily activities of the artists. Watching and listening will reveal a lot. You can dig even deeper by setting up meetings of small groups to discuss various topics; often, the topic itself is irrelevant. The interactions between the participants can tell you a lot about the various areas of stress within the organization.

While you are gathering information from artists, it is a good idea to find out what the upper administration or the Board has in mind for your unit. Obviously, this is information you should have gotten before agreeing to sign on for however long your contract runs. If you screwed up, you'd better dig for it now. What do the people over your head want your organization to become? Are they willing to support change? When you finally get a picture of where you think the organization should ultimately go, warn the boss. If (s)he breaks out into a cold sweat, you may have an insurmountable problem with your plan and your vision. Or perhaps both are right on target and the boss is "out to lunch." You decide. Then, either get going in pursuit of your vision or get going out the door. A tug-of-war cannot be won by the guy on the lower rung of the ladder. More about this coming up in the section on "Coping with Hostility."

Organizing a Planning Retreat

When ready, you might consider a one or two-day retreat, during which all the people in the organization are called together to work on the plan for the future of the organization. Such an approach places the right amount of importance on the process; everyone is expected to step out of his/her ordinary activities and devote a block of time to the organization. Everyone's voice is heard. Everyone has a chance to impact the future of the arts unit.

To do this, you will need a chunk of money—especially if you move the meeting off site, where a facility must be rented, food provided, perhaps even overnight lodging included. The scheduling of such a meeting must also depend upon the availability of your artists and staff. It is highly advisable to utilize regular work time. Expecting people to give up a weekend or a couple of days of their vacation will not sit well at all. Every effort should be made to poll your constituents to determine the best possible time to hold such a retreat. People need to know you are at least attempting to work with them, instead of demanding their time whenever it suits you. If there are people who are particularly important to the planning process, you may want to consult them first before opening the schedule to general debate. Effective planning retreats often include a handful of objective participants—people outside the arts unit, whose clear thinking and sharp analysis abilities might prove stimulating to the planning process.

It is vitally important to realize that the boss's opinion is never perceived to be on the same level as the employees. Whenever you are attempting to pull together a grass-roots planning effort, you, as the leader, need to keep your own views from driving the process too rigidly. You also need to make sure the people over your head are equally sensitive to the impact of their opinions, whenever voiced.

This is not to say you, as the leader, should be reluctant to lead. The whole tone of the planning retreat should be set by your vision for the organization. You need to create the image of a brighter future that lies ahead for your arts unit. The purpose of the meeting is then to develop the strategic plan for reaching that higher level. You set the destination; together, you create the road map.

Format of the Planning Retreat

The format of the planning retreat needs to be carefully prepared. Again, having input from the various groups to set both the agenda and the schedule of the individual meetings within the planning retreat is extremely helpful to the overall spirit of representation in the process. You want as many people as possible to feel they have a stake in the success of the venture. Whatever transpires at the planning retreat needs to foster a sense of team building, and of a group commitment to the new plan for the organization, whatever that ultimately becomes.

Effective use of small and/or large groups depends to a large extent upon the meeting skills of the leader(s) in drawing out the reticent and toning down the noisy ones. The goal should be to have 100% participation in the process, however you can get it. There should be a non-judgmental atmosphere throughout the process, in which everyone feels comfortable offering opinions and ideas.

Creating the Document

Most strategic plans are crafted into documents that can be studied, changed, and referred to as the organization moves ahead. Realistically, you cannot expect to come out of a planning retreat with such a document in hand. Rather, you should strive to have at least most of the data collected that will need to go into such a document. The actual drafting of the strategic planning document might be a job you take on, or one you assign to an associate or a group of associates. I confess to a personal bias against committee document-writing. (There are far too many jokes about committees writing things as a group to try to quote one or two here. Fill in your own.) Suffice it to say, if you want a document to make sense and to read well, a single writer is usually needed to pull it all together.

The ingredients of an effective strategic plan may include:

- Articulation of the overall vision for the future of the organization;
- Description of the current state of the institution—its strengths and weaknesses;
- Analysis of the place the organization needs to take in the professional world;
- Outline of specific problems that need to be addressed;
- Recommendation of solutions to be attempted;
- Description of any positive changes that need to be made in the organization;
- Overall description of shifts in emphasis that should be implemented;
- Suggestion of new initiatives that may be started, old ones phased out;
- Realistic assessment of the resources needed to implement this plan.

It is vitally important for the strategic plan, in its final form, to be realistic. For it to be feasible, the issue of available resources is key. It is not helpful to develop a "pie-in-the-sky" type of strategic plan that cannot possibly be achieved. In the planning retreat itself, the leader should try to keep people's appetites within range, utilizing resources already available or readily obtainable within the foreseeable future. A safe approach is to adopt a general philosophy that anything added needs to replace something else that is to be eliminated.

The striking exception to this rule of thumb occurs when a major fund-raising campaign needs to be launched to build a new facility or to purchase expensive, necessary equipment. When the organization's physical structure is woefully inadequate, building a better future may depend upon your ability to raise money—a lot of money. (This topic will be discussed in Chapter #4 "Handling the Finances.")

Another very important aspect of the planning process is the broader picture. That is, the group must be made continually aware that the arts unit exists within a greater environment—it exists within an overall society of which it is just a dot. Therefore, its place in the universe of arts organizations must be considered every inch of the way. The planning process must not take place in a vacuum. Changes in society must be anticipated and planned for. Future demographics should be predicted. Budgetary constraints resulting from external elements should be factored in. In other words, the people developing a strategic plan for the future of the arts unit should understand the world to which the organization belongs, how that world is changing, and what they need to do to stay on top of these changes. The final plan must help the arts unit capture its place in that future world with confidence and idealistic vision.

IMPLEMENTING THE PLAN

Far too often, strategic plans are painstakingly developed, only to lie on the shelf or get stuck in a file for future historical reference. Plans are made to be implemented, and that's your job. To move beyond the document, you need to know where you are headed, have the perceived roadblocks identified, and then get going.

It is your job to pull out that magnet and get all those arrows at least pointed in the right direction. Now, it is probably high time I admit to you that waving the magic magnet once will not do the trick. You knew this already, didn't you? You will have to keep that magnet close at hand, because as soon as you put it away or forget about it, those squiggly circles will start wheeling away in all directions again. In fact, some arrows will quit zoning in just as soon as the artists realize those metal points are the problem; the stubborn members of your organization will just remove the tips of their arrows and will then be oblivious to all your waving and tugging gestures.

Worse yet, you will probably get so busy with the day-to-day nonsense that you, too, will forget all about the vision. So, keeping that magnet, or some symbol of the vision, right on your desk or hanging on the wall where you and everyone else can see it is probably a really good idea.

Inspired leadership comes from hard work. You must be able to conjure up the picture you have envisioned and convince the artists, the staff, and perhaps the administration or Board that this image is ultimately achievable, albeit really tough. Then, roll up your sleeves and start working on those roadblocks. That is leadership.

Internal vs. External Leadership

When you set out to fix an environment, you need to know what is broken. If you happen to have been promoted from within the arts unit, you have a decided advantage, in that you have seen the problems and you have lived with them for a time. You probably don't have to look very hard to determine what needs to be changed, but you also have a few strikes against you:

- There may be a real resistance from your colleagues to accept you as their new leader, especially the older folks who knew you when. . .

- Your peers may be jealous—one or more of them may have wanted the position—and not be particularly eager to see you succeed;

- You may have a warped, one-sided view of the organization, with little knowledge of some of the other areas of specialization and how the artists in these areas view the problems;

- You may have limited experience beyond your previous position, and have difficulty envisioning a healthy environment;

- Since you came up through the ranks, this is probably your first crack at an administrative position, and you may know very little about running an organization.

OK, so those are the challenges, but let's not get too caught up in them. After all, you did get the job, so somebody thinks you can handle it; and you did accept the offer, so you must, deep down, think you can do it. This is no time for cold feet. Besides, you have the distinct advantage of knowing the institution and the people in it. You have been a part of its history. You have a solid understanding of where it has been and where it is today. This is the foundation needed to form a vision of a better tomorrow.

If, on the other hand, you were hired from the outside, you have a nearly opposite set of advantages and disadvantages:

- You probably don't have a very complete picture of the problems, but you are at least free of that internal personal stuff;

- People from within the institution don't know much about your warts just yet. Nobody has much reason to be jealous, except for the one or two who wanted the job; still, it's far easier to swallow someone else being brought in from the outside than it is to be passed over in favor of one of your own colleagues;

- You probably have a pretty even-handed approach to the overall program, having not lived in any specific area of the department;

- You have at least some picture of another place, hopefully a distinctive one, from which to form a vision of potential excellence;

- You may have come with some administrative experience under your belt. If so, you will approach this challenge with at least some confidence.

You won't, of course, have the benefit of knowing all the individuals with whom you must work. So, there will be a steeper learning curve for you, coming into the organization from the outside. Consequently, your approach to making change will have to be built upon your initial perceptions of this environment as it compares to experiences you have had in other surroundings. Astute observations and careful listening will become key ingredients in all that you do in those first few crucial months.

In either case, you, as the new leader, have to exude confidence, even if you have to fake some. People are counting on you to fix things. Your most important first task is to give them the assurance that you are capable, with their help, of doing that and much more. Your very first words to them should be full of positive energy and enthusiasm. Let them know you are eager to get started and that you are looking forward to a bright future. If you have a vision of the ideal arts environment, paint a picture of it in your first speech to the staff or in your first meeting with the artists. You don't need details; in fact, details spoken prematurely could alienate part of your audience. So, be careful. Use a broad-brush approach here, but try to accomplish two things: build confidence in your leadership and aim people's thinking toward a positive future. If you are a lousy speaker, write something down and distribute it as your welcoming words to the people in the organization.

A strong beginning is vitally important. If you have to make change happen, then you need people to trust you and have at least some hope for the future. You can't get either of these things the first day, but you can at least get started. If you get off on the wrong foot, it will be doubly hard to make a dent in the negative environment you have ventured into.

Inheriting a Good One

Every now and then, you may walk into a situation that is in pretty good shape—maybe even very good shape. After all, some leaders actually do a superb job, and you just may have stepped into some pretty big shoes. In this case, the problems you face are a whole different set.

- First, the various constituencies may not be at all happy about losing the leader they have come to trust. You may be about as welcome as a black bear in a campsite.

- Next, the immediate agenda may not be obvious. If things are running fairly well in all directions, it will be tough to know where to start your leadership thing.

- Moreover, there may be more than a little defensiveness; people will probably be concerned that "the new guy" is going to come in and mess up everything.

The fact of the matter is, your predecessor did leave, whether through another position, retirement, or (heaven forbid) death. You didn't make it happen (at least, I hope you didn't), and you can't do anything about it. So, for better or worse, here you are to pick up the pieces and move the organization forward. All the advice contained above is still applicable with just one major change: move slowly. No matter how eager you are to put your own stamp on the job, realize that, in this case, you need to be careful you don't change something that is already working very well. Remember the old adage, " If it ain't broke, don't fix it!" It will take you some time to learn enough about the ins and outs of various programs and procedures to avoid making a major blunder. So, be patient.

At the same time, you need to be working on establishing yourself within this closed environment. You are not the other guy, so don't try to be. Do a lot of listening and try to learn what people's current needs and concerns happen to be. (Don't worry, there will be a lot of these.) As you begin to get a picture of some problems, try articulating these back to the artists to see if you are hearing what they are attempting to tell you. Move with them, not against them during your first few months. There is plenty of time to make some of the changes you may have on your agenda, after you establish a rapport with the people you are attempting to serve.

In this particular setting, your first speech may be focused more on who you are than on what you are going to do. Instead of trying to get the ship moving again, you are attempting to jump onto an already

43

sailing vessel. You need the other sailors and crew to welcome you aboard as the new skipper. Don't try to change course until you figure out where the ship is currently heading. It is often said that whenever you assume a leadership position, you should hope it is under one of two conditions: the place is in such bad shape, anything you do will be an improvement; or else it is running so well, you can't possibly screw it up.

Getting Things Moving

When assuming the leadership of an organization in trouble, your greatest challenge may be to get people going again. Apathy and lethargy are tough nuts to crack. Both become prevalent as people struggle to survive within a sinking organization. Somehow, if you are to turn things around, you have to give people a reason to work harder, and these may be people who have been getting along very nicely without doing much at all. We are talking about everyone now—artists, staff, and even students, if yours is an arts educational environment.

Incentives. You need incentives. There has to be a good reason to work harder, and you are one of the possibilities. Having a new boss is one big incentive to get to work. After all, nobody knows what you will do with sleepers. Take advantage of this. Let everyone in sight know that you have great expectations of each of them, that you possess high standards of excellence, and strong hopes for the future of the institution.

You must, of course, be demonstrating this in everything you do. Your constituents will be watching. If you happen to have staff who openly duck their responsibilities, they will need to be fired. If there are any artists who don't do their jobs, they need to be disciplined, if tenured—fired, if possible.

It doesn't take much of this type of activity to demonstrate your resolve. There is also another result: Incentive #2 is now very much a part of the environment—fear. You don't really want to create any negative incentives to work harder, but if these happen to evolve in the midst of your early efforts to make positive change, they probably won't hurt your effort to turn things around. If you need to wake people up and get them motivated to work harder, fear of losing their positions in the organization may, in fact, help accomplish this goal.

At the same time, you need to be communicating like mad. Either through speeches or meetings or memos or just private conversations in the hallways, you need to demonstrate your ability to steer the ship in a new direction. You need to project a vision—your vision—of what the institution is capable of becoming. The picture needs to be idealistic, yet achievable, and you have to be able to convincingly portray your own confidence in reaching this goal. Remember, in a failing organization, people may grow accustomed to feeling lousy about the place in which they work. Your image of a strikingly successful environment just over the horizon may be met with enormous doubt, perhaps even total disbelief. People may think you are crazy. Most will find your vision far-fetched.

You cannot wait to convince everyone that your vision is doable. You need to get going without their full confidence and just scoop up the doubters somewhere along the line as you move vigorously ahead. Make changes in all directions, if needed. Get some other high-energy people on board—people who have your same kind of optimism and enthusiasm. You can't do it alone, but you are the boss, so you should have a lot of power to affect change. (Knowing what you know about this institution, you should have negotiated for a lot of elbowroom to make change as you came into this job. If you didn't, go get that mandate now, before it's too late.)

Personnel Changes

If there is a lot of hiring and firing going on, which is usually not the case in an arts organization, but may be in the instance of a troubled organization, people will fear for their jobs. When money is tight and programs begin to be cut, which does happen a lot in the arts, people panic—even those who have no reason to fear for their jobs. The possibility of losing their jobs is enough to cause great anxiety. When somebody else gets cut, or retired, or phased out, then the reality is upon them: "If it happened to him, it could happen to me!"

If the leadership takes the time and the care to communicate fully with the artists and staff, personnel changes can be made without a total meltdown. But when these changes are made suddenly, without an obvious need or a clear strategy, they may appear to be random and arbitrary. The risk to every individual deepens. If the logic is not evident, then every person on board imagines himself/herself to be the next target of the seemingly aimless shooting. Morale suffers most when such cutbacks are handled with callous disregard for the people involved.

It may be that the personnel changes described above are necessary as part of the leader's attempt to turn the institution around. When an organization is screwed up, people changes are usually needed to affect positive institutional change. Whatever the case, morale will dive to an all-time low during a period of intensive personnel shuffling. People are just plain scared! Job insecurity does not make for strong morale. Once things calm down again, and the dust settles on the organizational chart, if the changes made were smart ones, the effects of the new team will begin to be felt. Gradually, morale will be restored to its pre-upheaval level and hopefully begin to rise even further. Keep an eye on the changing morale; it can serve as a barometer of people's perceptions.

BUILDING MORALE

When people speak of building morale, it sounds as though morale is something you can put on your To-Do List—a condition that can be acted upon, like salary, facilities, recruitment, etc. It isn't. Morale is a result of everything else; it is not an area that can be focused on, targeted for improvement, and then illustrated on an overhead transparency for the Board of Directors. It cannot be measured in any objective manner; yet, it is definitely there, in the environment. You can feel it, see its effects, and know for a fact that it is high or low or mixed. Other people can identify the state of morale in an institution, as well—even strangers to the organization. Moreover, morale is a vitally important factor in the ultimate success or failure of the leader.

The reason it is important to keep an eye on the morale is that gloominess spreads like a contagious disease. Lousy morale, if left unattended, begins to feed upon itself, causing other people to feel down, until the negative attitude itself starts to block the recovery process.

So, what do you do when it is a problem? When everyone around you is down in the dumps, depressed, negative, lacking in confidence that the institution for which they work is even worth their best efforts? Change it. Not the morale, but the institution itself. You cannot work on morale; you have to work on the things that are dragging the morale down into the cellar. Morale is a symptom, not a disease; so you need to diagnose the root problem or problems and go to work on them. Little by little, the observable morale will reflect the improvements, but it may take longer than you would like.

Restoring confidence to a group of people who have been worn down by a period of frustration, disappointment, or disillusionment takes a long time. Morale doesn't sink noticeably without a lot of help. One or two little problems won't do it. It takes an overwhelming picture of negativity to sink the spirit of an entire group of workers, although once begun, this decline in mood spreads like a forest fire, engulfing everyone in sight. The restoration process is just as difficult; seeds of rejuvenation must be planted, nurtured with all the ingredients needed for healthy growth, and gradually, little by little, new life will emerge. If all the right conditions are in place, this growth will continue until the forest is once again visibly strong, morale is positive. The longer it remains so, the tougher it becomes to shake it down, but there is always the possibility of another series of destructive events weakening it once again.

The Root of the Problem

Morale is really bottom heavy. It is tougher than you can imagine to move it up; not quite so tough to send it plummeting back to earth. So, what does it take? Usually, an all-out effort to change the environment, to fix everything that is a problem. Sometimes you can determine the root causes of low morale by talking to the people in the midst of it; often, the causes they point to are, themselves, results of something else. They may articulate disgruntlement over poor salary, or a lousy office space, or too much work, or not enough vacation time; maybe they cite annoying colleagues. But beneath all of these lies the real problem: the leadership.

If you dig a little deeper, you will find the problem isn't just a low salary; it is the feeling of low self worth, that their work has not been valued, that whoever ran the place before did not appreciate the quality of their contribution; if they did, then the salary would be higher. It is that feeling of not being valued that eats at the morale; and further, not being able to do anything about it. No matter how hard they tried, they just couldn't get the positive feedback they needed to feel fully appreciated. Their salary is just a symptom of the bigger problem of self worth. Effective leadership has to support the efforts of every person in the institution.

When the artists can't get themselves over the hump of their own depression, it is just not possible to achieve a high level of excellence in their art. It is the leader's responsibility to nurture the artist's well being. So, there we are, back again in the hands of the leader of the arts unit, who may well be subject to demoralizing conditions of his/ her own. The issue of morale lives at the very top of the hierarchical structure. It also impacts every other level of the arts organization.

You could cut the stress in the air with a pair of child-proof scissors. Yet, it wasn't the stress that caught my attention; anxiety always accompanies groups of freshmen like the cloud of dust surrounding a stage coach. No, it was the suffocating presence of discouragement that lifted my attention from the roll-book. As the students ambled through the door, the classroom grew heavy with the sounds of muffled grumbling, frustration, and fatigue. Most of them were coming from a mid-term exam in history. It was clear: this group was just plain worn out.

I stopped taking attendance and viewed the scene: bleary-looking eyes, disheveled clothing, most of the guys needed a shave, the women wore yesterday's hair-do's. What a mess! We certainly weren't going to accomplish much in this class.

"OK, guys, listen up. I have one more class rule to tell you about today." As expected, they lifted their heads with difficulty. Their expressions were as close to seething mutiny as I had ever seen in this particular group. Another class rule was just what they were in the mood for, all right.

"Every semester, I look for one particular day, when the sun is out and it's not too cold, to close the books on music theory and talk about other stuff. Today is it." Expressions changed dramatically. You could have taken a pen and traced the question marks on every face in the room.

"That's right, no class today. We are going outside, we are going to sit in the park behind this building, and for the next forty-five minutes we are going to just talk about college, about your worries, about the things that are really making you mad, and maybe even some of the stuff you like about this place. You talk; I'll listen. But, the rules are: we can't discuss music theory, because that's what we usually do in this class, and you can't buzz off in some other direction. Attendance is required. Anybody have a problem with that?" They didn't. So, off we went, leaving a note on the door for latecomers to join us in the park.

Sometimes, as this example illustrates, people are just worn out. Low morale may indicate temporary burnout. Other times, there are institutional problems contributing to the low morale.

Let's examine one more possible cause of low morale: poor facilities. Is it possible that this could create a serious morale problem? Well, if the artists cannot effectively produce their art, surely that's a serious problem, but I would venture to guess that is not the cause of the low morale. Ten to one, the real problem is once again the boss's response. If the artist is given the assurance that the leader understands the importance of this situation, and further that (s)he is doing everything humanly possible to solve the problem, the artist will most likely find a way to get through the season with a positive attitude. On the other hand, if the complaint is met with no empathy whatsoever, if the artist is given the impression that nothing will be done about the problem ever, and that nobody really believes it is a problem, then you have a morale crash—and no wonder.

Sometimes the problem cuts straight through the leader of the arts unit, perhaps to the Chairman of the Board. If the arts leader is sympathetic and supportive, but demonstrates an inability to do anything about the problem, the effect is the same. The artists feel powerless to get their situation changed and they now know that their boss is also powerless to get the situation changed. The real leadership is obviously on the next level, and that person doesn't care about the problem, which also means that person doesn't value me. So, down goes the morale.

Morale is always the result of the overall working conditions and how the people feel about their relative position within that environment. If the morale is dangerously low throughout the community, that is a sign that significant changes need to be made in the overall institution. Attention must also be given to the individual's place in that environment and the signals (s)he is receiving about his/her value to the institution. A leader can succeed in turning an arts unit around and setting it on an exciting path toward a new level of excellence; but if these changes create anxiety among the existing personnel, if they don't feel secure that they are a vital part of the future of the institution, the morale will plummet to an all-time low, in spite of the improvements in the environment.

Is this a leadership issue? You bet it is! The health of the arts unit and the people in it both rest on the shoulders of the leader of that institution. The overall morale will generally reflect the state of that health. Like the tail of the dog, the morale will always be just a bit behind the momentum of the institution. When you finally see a significant change in morale, you can be sure the other changes you have put in place have begun to take effect.

Recognizing the Individual

All of this is to say it is a ludicrous waste of energy to focus on the morale of an institution and to go to work on trying to fix that morale. You can try all sorts of morale builders, but they will all come across as a mere pat on the head to the person who has serious doubts about the institution and his/her place in it. This is not to say you should ignore individual achievement. I once sent a letter of appreciation to a senior faculty who had just achieved some public recognition for his distinguished career. My letter expressed the importance of his career success to the students he taught and to the arts unit as a whole. To my surprise, upon receipt of this letter he immediately came to thank me for sending it. His exact words were, "In over thirty years of teaching at this institution, this is the first time a department head ever sent me a letter of appreciation." Sometimes, the small gestures have enormous significance.

But not when they are institutionalized. Sending a form letter out to fifty different people is at best, meaningless—at worst, insulting. This type of generic praise negates the unique value of the individual; so you may as well not send it. Competitions among employees to reward excellence also have a mixed effect: there may be one exuberant winner, but you can be sure there are numerous disgruntled losers. While the competition is saying, "You are especially important to this institution," everyone else is feeling especially unimportant. Competitions may be a positive way to focus attention and raise the standards, but it is critical to realize that they are also morale killers.

On the other hand, any step the leader can take to acknowledge the individual as a person of value to the institution is tremendously helpful, provided the gesture does not, at the same time, put down the work of others. Citing someone publicly as particularly effective in a given area or on a specific project hurts everyone else who worked in that area or on that project. Giving public recognition to anyone will, more often than not, cause others to feel unappreciated. Sometimes it needs to be done. It is probably better to express your appreciation and high regard for that individual one-on-one, either in a letter, on the phone, or in person. Knowing that the boss values your work is a reward everyone seeks. Handled privately, there is no down side.

In a large organization, even greeting someone by name can be extremely important to morale. When artists believe the head of the organization knows who they are, they feel essential to the overall operation. When they are treated in a nameless fashion, their morale goes through the cellar. A leader who takes the time to know everyone by name is sending a message loud and clear that the individual is important to the institution. Being certain of their value to the organization is at least half the battle of raising morale. The other half may be even more crucial: being certain of the value of the organization itself.

Fixing the Environment

A person may feel (s)he is valuable to the institution, but (s)he may also feel that the institution is headed straight off a cliff, or at least down the hill. When employees lose confidence in the company they serve, nothing can raise their morale except a change in the direction of that company. Serious morale problems may be the result of a stagnant institution or a changing institution or a heartless one.

When organizations stay the same for too long, they actually begin to decay. This is probably because the world is changing around them all the time. Sleepy leadership can kill a once vibrant institution, just by doing nothing. Maintaining the status quo, just getting through the day, is not leadership. An arts unit without direction loses its vitality, and gradually the people in it care less and less about achieving. It gets easier and easier to do less. By this time, the morale is abysmal; nobody feels good about the place any more. The final stage occurs when the best people start to bail out—the finest of the artists and the strongest of the staff find other positions. The mediocre stay, because they have no other options.

This transition may take years. Suddenly, people begin to wonder what happened? Nobody can put a finger on a single problem, a single mistake, a single person. It was an agonizingly slow evolutionary process—the result of weak leadership. It may be the terrible morale that is noticed first. That could be why some administrators mistakenly zero in on the low morale as a problem that needs to be fixed first. (Telling people on the Titanic to cheer up probably would not have worked.)

When morale is abysmal, leadership is clearly needed. The leader must be energetic, inspiring, and full of vision. If you happen to be this person, coming on board a sinking ship, you have to accept the possibility that the ship may keep right on sinking in spite of your best efforts to save it. It depends very much on how far down it has already gone. If you're willing to take that risk, then roll up your sleeves; you've got a lot of work to do.

GAINING SUPPORT

Understanding the Ambivalence Factor

No matter how competent you are as an administrator, the artists will probably feel ambivalent about you from the start. On the one hand, they really would prefer to be left alone to do their thing the way they think it should be done; on the other hand, they realize that somebody has to make sure the environment is conducive, the space is available, the equipment is in place, the necessary information has been transmitted to the audience, the heat is on, the lights are up, and all those other artists with their private agendas are out of the way. So, that's your job.

And, indeed it is! A major part of running an arts program involves moving out in front, getting rid of all the obstacles, acquiring the needed resources, solving problems, paving the way, so that everyone else can do their work. The less aware artists are of the work you do and the support system in place, the smoother the operation. Good management ensures that facilities are ready for optimum use 100% of the time. Day-to-day management of all the details is critical to the morale of the artists and to the effectiveness of the arts presentation.

Still, flawless management, if such a thing exists, is not enough. Getting through the day without a glitch is not even enough. That is only enough to get you through the day. There is still the question of direction: where are you taking this ship, now that you have all those arrows pointed in the same direction, all those wheels turning together, all those squiggly circles moving toward you?

Developing Credibility

Even with the strongest of vision, a leader must be able to inspire others to follow. This cannot be done unless you earn the respect and the trust of the people in your organization. Granted, some are going to be a lot tougher to win over than others, but there is a lot you can do to avoid making your own mess. I strongly advise that you refrain from any of the destructive behavior outlined below:

- Don't renege on a promise of support—ever. If you are not sure you can deliver the resources for a certain request, project, or activity, delay your decision until you check it out. Once you give the go-ahead, you just have to support that decision all the way.

- Don't leave the door open by being vague. It is always necessary to be explicit about the nature and the limitations of your support. Open-ended promises are just asking for trouble. Assume things will always cost more than anticipated; make sure it is clear just how much you can fund when you give your OK.

- Don't say you will do something, unless you will do it— absolutely, for sure. Forget the good intentions, and do articulate a time period for the action. Then, make sure you follow through. If there is any doubt about your ability to complete the action by the time it is needed, don't make the commitment. Steer the action toward someone else on your staff or just decline to step up to the plate. (It is always preferable to say "No" in the beginning, than it is to sign on and then fail to deliver.)

- Don't assume you will remember to do something. Always write it down. Whatever system you use to keep track of things should include a way to record miscellaneous loose ends, especially when the next step is yours. Even if you intend to pass the next step along to someone else, write it down until you've done that. Nobody can keep all the details of a complex managerial position in their heads.

- Don't betray a confidence. If it is impossible for you to solve a problem without taking the conversation you are having to someone else, tell the person this. Let the confider decide whether it is better to share the information further or to give up on your helping to resolve the situation. Remember, the responsibility for the problem stays in the confider's lap until you sign on to help. Make sure you actually have the elbowroom to help, that you can use the information you have just received, before agreeing to take on the problem. (The decision to reveal this information to someone else, even in the interests of resolving the problem, is not yours to make.)

- Don't make decisions—any decisions—based on what you personally would like to do. As a leader, it is your primary responsibility to make decisions for the good of the institution you serve and the people in it.

In summary, you can only gain people's trust by earning it. If you always follow through on your promises, if you always do what you say you will do, when you say you will do it, if you always keep confidential material absolutely confidential, and if you always make decisions in the best interests of the people in your organization, you will eventually be recognized as a leader who can be trusted. Even one slip-up, though, can have dire consequences. Fair or not, while it may take a long time to gain people's trust, it only takes a split second to lose that trust—forever. And often, the critical moment comes completely "out of the blue."

Two of our favorite people had helped us again. Mr. and Mrs. Major Donor had come forward to purchase a new piano for our chamber music program, and it was here. To express our appreciation, we were in the midst of a very special event: a chamber music concert just for them. To make it more intimate, we had reserved the beautiful art gallery on the main floor of our Fine Arts Building. Chairs had been set up for the small, select audience of invited guests. Engraved invitations had been sent out. Formal programs had been printed in honor of the donors. The track lighting in the gallery shone down on the beautiful new Steinway grand.

Everything was going as planned, except that the caterer had not yet arrived. We were supposed to have a formal reception all set up in the marble lobby by the time the concert ended. With no intermission, the program was moving right along, and I was growing more and more frantic. The special events coordinator had attempted to call the catering department three times, but since it was after 5:00, there was only an answering machine. We were now well into the last piece on the program.

I didn't know what to do next. I had sent one of the work-study students over to the catering office, clear across the campus, but it was closed. There was no way to contact anyone to see where they were or what had delayed their arrival. My mind raced through the elaborate menu we had ordered—the flowers—the table settings and wine—it was to have been a formal, very elegant party for Mr. and Mrs. Major Donor.

Everyone knew there was to be a reception directly following the concert. It was written on the invitations. What on earth were we going to do? I could feel the anxiety rapidly turning to panic. My heart was racing. My palms were sweating. I knew I was experiencing the classic "fight or flight" instinct of our ancient ancestors, and there was absolutely no question about it: I desperately wanted to flee!

The music stopped. The applause began. The student musicians took just about as many bows as they could. I had to do something! Smiling a smile I had to create from the memory of better times, I walked down the aisle to the front of the gallery. Raising my hands to bring the applause to a polite close, I said, "Ladies and Gentlemen, you know, whenever you have a party, you always worry about the details. Will the hors d'oeuvres be hot? Will the wine be just right? The dessert delicious? Well, tonight I am happy to report that we have absolutely nothing to worry about with our food, because there is no food."

The audience gasped. I continued. "We have no idea where the caterers are, but we do know that they are not here, where they are supposed to be." At this point, the laughter came in a burst. Then, those wonderful people applauded. I thanked them with a genuine grin and invited them to join me in the lobby for a party nobody would have to regret when they got on the scales in the morning.

The Personal Side of Leadership

So, you are who you are. But what is it you need to project? Confidence, for sure. Competence, definitely. But other qualities are also critical: Integrity. Energy. Decisiveness. Enthusiasm. Creativity. Strength. Patience. Honesty. Openness. Empathy. Fairness. Intelligence. Concern. Those are some of the big ones. There are others: Humility. Compassion. Collegiality. Humor. Resilience. Logic. Toughness. Wisdom. Understanding. Calmness. Assertiveness. Thoughtfulness. Imagination. Courage.

This is beginning to sound like a Boy Scout Handbook. Do you really need all of these qualities to run an arts program? Yes, you do, and more. Any time you fall short in one of these areas, you will know it—big time. Anyone in a leadership position is expected to be super-human. So, get out your hunk of krypton and do the best you can. You'll learn some of it as you go. One of the major benefits for you in doing this job is the personal growth you will experience. (If this job sounds a little bit like walking on fire or lying down on a bed of nails, frankly, it is.)

The Popularity Factor

How important is it to be liked? Well, that depends on you. If it bothers you a lot when somebody reacts to you in a negative way, you are going to have a tough time adjusting to this job. If you come from inside the institution, you may be shocked by the instant change in many of your professional relationships. You will no longer be viewed as just a colleague; you are now the boss. Your friendships may be strained as they attempt to adjust to this aspect of institutional inequality. You feel the same as you did yesterday, but many do not feel the same toward you. It may seem as though a wall has suddenly been built between you and everybody else. You didn't build it; it just appeared as soon as you stepped into your new office.

You may have to dress differently. Your whole appearance and demeanor must command respect; after all, you are in charge. You can no longer hang out at the Xerox machine, clucking your tongue at the administration. You are the administration, and you know that the people chatting over coffee are now critiquing you. It is a huge adjustment!

The craziest part is that suddenly everybody seems to want something from you. People appear to crawl out of the woodwork, looking for a job, for special funding, for additional resources of all sorts. People you went to college with, colleagues from other institutions, personal friends (at least, they used to be friends), everybody seems to want something. That part of the job is awful. After a few weeks of this, you may begin to wonder if even the pleasant conversations you have with people are genuine or just superficial plays for favor from the boss.

Where do you turn for personal support? Hopefully you have a life beyond the job, family and friends who don't care where you work or what you do when you get there. Then there are other people who have similar jobs. You will meet them now, if you haven't already—other heads of arts units—a whole new set of colleagues. It will take some time, but you will find your niche. Building a new network of personal support is critical to your emotional health. It's a tough job you just walked into (or fell into or were pushed into, whatever the case may be.)

Coping With Hostility

You may as well get used to the fact that some people will fight you "tooth and nail." There are always dissenters—hopefully, just one or two. Usually, it takes a while to find them, because they may be afraid to come out into the open as soon as you are hired; but sooner or later, they will surface. Try not to take this personally; every boss has at least a couple. If you're lucky, they will make themselves known early, so you can at least see what you have to deal with. Develop your patience, and above all, maintain your sense of humor.

You will definitely have some employees working under you, hopefully the majority, who appreciate what you are trying to do for the company, corporation, department, institution. Many of them will honestly like you, in spite of your job. But some, hopefully just a few, will resent you for one reason or another. Maybe they wanted your job and didn't get it. Maybe you are younger than they are, pointing up their failure to advance as quickly as you. Maybe you are a woman, or an African American, or some other category of humankind that they have long viewed as "Them," as opposed to "Us." Whatever the case, hostility just may be there; if so, you can feel it, smell it, and even, on those rare occasions when the dissenters come out of the woodwork, you can see it.

So, what do you do about it? How do you handle hostility? Now, the one thing I am not going to suggest is to ignore it, pay no attention to it, because I know that's not doable. It is going to bother you—plenty. Nobody enjoys being disliked. The last thing you want to become is an individual who is impervious to other people's unhappiness. You are, first of all, an artist yourself, or you wouldn't have gotten into this leadership position in the first place. Artists are sensitive beings, at least, the good ones are. Again, you are a good one or you wouldn't be in this mess. So, you care, all right!

Further, you really can't do your job without being aware of the positions of the various constituents in the organization. Not that you have to psychoanalyze everybody, but you do have to know where people stand in order to work with them and to get them on board ship. Sensitivity to other people is part of your job, and hostility is one of the easiest things to pick up on when you go out there sniffing the air.

The third reason you can't ignore this problem is that to ignore it often makes it worse. Really angry people do things to vent their anger, and you may have to deal with the fall-out of people's hostility. It is vitally important to know where this anger is coming from, so you can at least contain it.

Your goal should be to understand who is mad and why. If you know the "who," you might be able to find a way to ease the anger, but that depends a lot on the "why" part. It also depends a lot on your personality and how you interact with other people. I won't attempt to intercede here, but maybe I can offer a few over-arching guidelines:

- Avoid over-personalizing things. Most of the time, people's anger is directed not at you, but at what you represent— authority. They may hate anyone who tries to tell them what to do or how to do it. Or they just may disagree with the decisions you have to make. Fair enough. As leader, acknowledge their right to a different viewpoint, and try not to take it personally. It is easier to act logically when your emotions are not too deeply involved.

- Accept the fact that people also have a right to personal hostility. Don't worry if you can't turn them around. Some people just may not like you. That's OK; you probably don't like them, either.

- Deal fairly and calmly with any actions that grow out of this hostility. Do not tolerate destructive behavior toward yourself or anyone else in the arts unit. It is your responsibility to maintain a healthy working environment; make sure the angry ones know this and that they stay within the boundaries of civil behavior.

- Do not use your power to strike back.

I have a system that works pretty well: whenever I realize I do not like someone, I go at least one step further than I believe to be fair in dealing with them, just because I don't trust myself to be completely objective.

For example, when I am teaching, if a student who gets under my skin happens to wind up with a course average that falls between two letter grades, I always give him/her the higher of the two, instead of attempting to decide which one more accurately reflects the quality of the work.

When an artist whom I have come to dislike requests something—travel, expenses, time off, additional salary, whatever—if it is possible to grant the request within the current budget, I always say "yes," again, because I don't trust myself to be completely rational.

Acting in this way, you can be sure that you are not contributing to the hostile situation. When you do have to say "No," the other person may assume it is because of your hostility. But if you have objective reasons for your decision, you can stand on these, even if your judgment is questioned or appealed to a higher level.

So far, we are assuming the hostility is coming from somebody below you in the hierarchy. What if it comes from above? What if it is your boss or the chairman of the board who shows negativity toward you? Although this is happily a rare occurrence, when hostility comes down from above, it is a whole new ball game. The fundamental principle in operation here is that you cannot win a battle from a lower rung on the institutional ladder. (There are occasional exceptions to this rule, but these are so occasional, it is not worth even considering the possibility.) So, your primary goal needs to be: ease the tension.

If you become aware of a problem between you and your superior, you need to change the way you relate to that person. Step back and think about the possible causes of the problem. Have you come on too strongly on a particular issue? Are you a potential threat to this person? Have you put him/her into a difficult position in front of others? Have you accidentally or on purpose gone over his/her head to get what you wanted for your arts unit? If you can see some action on your part that has caused a problem with your superior, find a way to express your concern about this, and vow not to do it again.

However, it may not be any one thing. You may have a major personality conflict with another person, who unfortunately happens to be your boss, and you can't change your whole personality— although we can probably all use a little remodeling in this area. What to do?

- Interact in person as little as possible; lean toward written memos (carefully written not to antagonize.)

- Whenever you are face-to-face, be careful. Act professional at all times and watch out for the troublesome areas in which there may be disagreement between you. You may want to keep your mouth shut in meetings much more than is your style.

- Say "nothing to nobody" about this person. The slightest negative comment could get back to your boss, and make things even worse.

- Do the best work you are capable of accomplishing, leaving little room for criticism. If you are extremely valuable to the overall institution, you may be at least temporarily "bullet-proof."

- Pray for deliverance from this untenable position. Unless the boss is just as professional as you are about the whole thing, sooner or later, somebody is going to get hurt. And guess who? If you cannot line up another job somewhere, you need to hope the boss moves on. Good luck!

SURVIVING WITH YOUR BOARD OF ADVISORS

The importance of an advisory board to an institution cannot be overstated; for no matter what the outcome of their meetings with you, no matter what impressions they receive, advice they offer, input they give, the process itself causes you to take stock and to reassess the job you are doing. This is the case even with visiting committees sent for purposes of reaccreditation. Outside observers provide a level of objectivity you cannot bring to the organization. Yet, their effectiveness depends to a large extent on how well you handle your association with them.

The key to working with external advisors is open communication. Your instincts may tell you to hide the problems and display only the strengths of the organization, but that defeats the whole purpose of the advising process. Assuming your board contains some heavy-duty expertise, you would be crazy not to at least attempt to utilize their knowledge and experience to help solve the thorniest of problems. That is admittedly difficult to do, especially if you are a strong leader.

Understanding the Power Structure

Realistically, you will no doubt feel somewhat threatened by the presence of an external advisory board. Much depends on the balance of power in your particular situation. Some arts leaders report directly to a Board of Directors. In such cases, they serve at the discretion of their board; the board hires them, evaluates their work, and fires them when necessary. Obviously, the relationship between the arts leader and the board here is one of employee to boss. The board's central role is one of governance over the institution.

A very different set of circumstances surrounds the board whose primary function is to raise money for the organization and to expand the visibility of the institution beyond its borders. These advisory boards do not usually have the power to hire and fire the leader. Without that, the relationship to the arts leader is quite a bit less hierarchical (and far less stressful.) It is probably much easier for the leader to work in partnership with a board whose focus is expanding the resources of the organization.

Yet another type of advisory board is one set up by the head of an institution or by an external accrediting agency to help assess the workings of the individual units within the larger organization. Here, the board's primary role is one of assessment. Since the board reports its findings directly to the president or to the accrediting board, they serve primarily to advise someone else, not you. This makes a tremendous difference in your eagerness to share the good and hide the not-so-good. Even in these cases, it is possible to gain a great deal of positive support from the advising process.

There may be still other types of advisory boards not described here with a slightly different balance of responsibilities. Yet, each will deal with one or more of the following responsibilities: governance, development & public relations, and/or assessment.

Painting a Realistic Picture of the Organization

Regardless of who reports to whom, the effectiveness of your leadership will be observed and judged by the board as they work with your arts unit. Let's face it, every person on this board is going to make an independent assessment of your leadership. You should be used to this by now; after all, everybody judges the leader, even when they have very little data with which to make such a judgment. It goes with the job.

Knowing that, you may as well accept it and put it into perspective. The focus of the advising process is not on you, but since you are leading the whole mess, you will be held responsible for everything that is going on. That, too, is part of the job. So, there's nothing really new here, except that this time you actually have the freedom to provide the data. If the board gets an inaccurate picture of your arts unit or of your leadership, it is your fault. There, I've said it! Fault! Just like in tennis, if you blow the serve, somebody is bound to bark out, "Fault!" It's your serve now; so, don't blow it.

There are all sorts of ways to provide data; some techniques are discussed in Chapter #6 on "Communicating." And certainly how you do this will speak volumes about your leadership skills. I hate to say this out loud, but the greatest importance is not what data you share, but how you share it. No kidding. You really must be open about the whole place—the problems as well as the glories, the weaknesses as well as the strengths. Don't try to hide anything. Whatever it is, it will surely surface—through conversations with artist/faculty, staff, or students—through the very cracks of the walls. It is amazing how much an external group of sharp observers can actually see in a brief visit to your institution. If you have tried to hide something, your leadership will immediately come into question. The board needs to be able to trust the data you are giving them. If that trust gets fractured, the whole process is damaged.

Keep in mind that every person on your board is there to help. Nobody joins an organization with the intent to hurt it. These are good people—leaders in their field. If they don't understand your arts unit, that's your fault. (There, I've said it again. Get used to the concept.) So, your primary role is to find a way to show them where you are headed with this arts unit, the mission of the organization, its current direction, the progress already made, and the hurdles still in place. Paint an accurate picture of the place, and present this picture to your board with all the pride and confidence of the creative artist unveiling a masterpiece.

The difference is, this is a work in progress, not a finished masterpiece. Sure, there are flaws. But, that's why you're here. You have the leadership skills to meet any challenge that comes down the road. They can see that from the way you handled past challenges. The ones you happen to be wallowing in at the moment are no tougher than the ones you have already solved. It's just difficult to let other people poke their noses into the process.

Preparing for the Process

One of the biggest frustrations of this advising process is trying to make time to do it right. With so much to communicate and so little time, preparation has to be extensive. You need to step back and decide what information can best be provided through written documentation, what you can describe most effectively through an oral presentation, perhaps using slides to illustrate data, and what should be left to be discovered through conversations with artist/ faculty, staff, and students. Making sure all facets of the operation are covered through some media, you then set out to produce the materials and plan the agendas.

You will want to prepare slides or overhead transparencies of everything from financial data to admissions statistics, personnel descriptions to curricular listings. Planning documents should be shared, history recounted. Whatever documents you can assemble that will illustrate the direction of your arts organization and the path it has been following for the past five to ten years, should be pulled together. It takes a ton of work to prepare for a meeting with a board of advisors, especially if these meetings are scheduled infrequently.

But, the work will pay off. The more knowledge of your organization you can impart, the better your board will be able to grasp its strengths and weaknesses, and find ways to help. A well-informed board, making objective observations about your arts unit, can be a tremendous asset to its future development.

Written materials need to be succinct yet thorough. Carefully organize the topics for clarity and make certain unnecessary details are pruned. You don't want to hide the forest by focusing on all those trees, or worse yet, on the leaves of the trees. Specific data belongs in appendixes or in backup files, which can certainly be made available to the board without having to be crammed into the exposition of your document. Make sure the stuff they are expected to read can be absorbed by a stranger to your program with complete understanding; and try to keep the documentation to a couple of hours of total reading time.

Your oral presentations require just as much preparation as the written materials. Whether you speak from notes or a full script, you need to plan your speeches with extreme care, making sure you can cover the ground in the time allotted. It is far too easy to speak extensively on a single area, and run short of time for others of equal or greater importance. If someone else is speaking, or if there are multiple sessions, there is the added problem of one session overlapping another, thus cutting something short. Agendas need to be planned with some elastic built in to avoid this problem.

Board of Trustee Meetings

A meeting with members of your board of advisors is normally a highly structured, formal occasion, but keep your sense of humor at the ready. Even with the most careful planning, unexpected problems may arise.

> *The Advisory Board was here—an impressive bunch of people, to be sure. The schedule was packed tighter than a Volkswagen with a family of six. Meetings ran straight through breakfast, lunch, dinner, and in between. No time to waste.*

> *Somehow, I needed to host this luncheon while steering the conversation toward a fruitful discussion of our space problems. Speaking of fruit, the elegant china was covered with a luscious fruit salad—not the fruit cocktail type of salad from a can—but real fruit, arranged beautifully on the delicately sculptured porcelain. This was not your typical committee meeting on campus. (You could tell the President's office was picking up the tab.)*

I began to speak, lifting my fork from the linen tablecloth to signal our guests to begin eating. Carefully choosing my words, I inched toward the desired topic, hoping to sound somewhat casual, yet making the points that needed to be communicated. Taking a breath between sentences, I reached for my knife to slice the peach that served as the centerpiece of the decorative salad arrangement before me. As I began to speak again, I cut into it. 1/3 of the peach remained in place. The other 2/3 shot like a wet walrus right off the plate, landing with a sickening plop in the middle of my lap.

Hosting the On-site Visit

During an on-site visit, the members of your board will become guests to your institution, and, yes, they will need to be wined and dined accordingly. If your board is from out-of-town, a lot of care must also be given to travel arrangements, lodging, and transportation to and from the meetings. The schedule of meetings will need to be pretty tight, since these are busy people, but some elbowroom is desirable. Allow for a bit of time in between sessions and a significant block of time at the end, so they can meet together and discuss their findings and observations. After all, they are supposed to function as a body; so they will need some time to compare notes and to get their act together.

Unless the process in your institution is far less formal than the one described here, your advisory board will be expected to provide a summary of its observations at the conclusion of the visit. This is ordinarily done in writing, soon after the visit. Sometimes, a preliminary discussion is also held with the leadership before the board departs. This can be extremely valuable, while everyone is still focused on the exchange of information. In such a meeting, the arts leader may be able to clarify questions or correct misperceptions before the board moves forward with its official recommendations.

In any event, once the board actually presents its observations, you have a tremendous opportunity to reassess what you are doing and how you are doing it. Even if you believe they are wrong in some aspects of their analysis, you will still learn a great deal about the perception you and your associates have created of the institution. You may need to work on communicating more effectively; or you may have some real issues to resolve. Usually, the issues that surface come as no surprise; but occasionally the board makes recommendations you feel are dead wrong for the arts unit you serve. Hopefully, there is a forum for further discussion of these matters.

Dealing with Criticism

The purpose of an advisory board is obviously to give advice. But far too often, advice sounds and feels like criticism. Brace up. Nothing is perfect, and even the strongest leadership can stand some help from time to time. If the observations of your board lead to recommendations for positive change, listen carefully and respect their ability to see the organization from a fresh perspective. Dismissing their opinion out-of-hand negates the whole advising process. It's far better to roll up your sleeves and find a way to incorporate their views into the operation of the arts unit just as soon as it is feasible to do so. Above all, don't take it personally, unless of course their main advice is to tar and feather the leader. Then, you just might want to consider a quick exit.

CHAPTER #3   TAKING CHARGE

As I look back, the scope of my first leadership position was the most surprising aspect of taking charge. There was simply no way to anticipate some of the things I would be called upon to do and the vast array of skills that would be required of me. Some abilities were already there, just waiting to be tapped; others had to be acquired on the spot, quite often under intense scrutiny and enormous pressure to succeed.

The door of the cab slammed shut. I was alone, in the back seat of a vehicle headed for wherever Sheila had sent us. Silently, in the dark of night, I prayed that the Chinese conversation back there had worked. (Sometimes Sheila didn't understand the local dialect, even though she was a native of Taiwan and spoke fluent Chinese.) What would I do if this driver took me somewhere other than the Hotel Hilton? Together, we had too much luggage for a single cab; so we had to split up. My third trip to Asia, but the first time I wound up alone, without a translator.

All I could say in Chinese was "Thank You," and that was touch and go. Usually, I would get the inflection wrong and the recipient would look puzzled, and then burst out laughing. Very disconcerting. Even a good "Thank You" wasn't going to help me get to my hotel, if this guy thought I wanted to go to the zoo or a museum or something. "OK," I told myself, "ease up. He's probably headed in the right direction. Where else would I be going at this time of night, when I just got off an airplane?"

Even this late, motorbikes were everywhere. I counted the lanes of traffic on both sides of the cab—there were eight—all going twice as fast as conditions would warrant. There was an entire family on one bike—the Mom in front of the Dad, a baby in each lap, and another one on the young father's back, in a book-bag type of carrier. What on earth were they doing out here at this hour?

I reached for my purse to get organized for the paying of the cab fare. The last time I was in this country, I tried to pay a driver the amount on the dashboard, which had turned out to be the clock. Sheila had really loved that. Well, this time, I knew the ropes, and already had a bunch of Taiwanese money ready to go. (Doesn't look real—just like monopoly money.)

Hallelujah! The word "Hilton" up ahead. We stopped. The driver hadn't uttered a sound, but why would he? Obviously, we couldn't communicate with each other. He looked pretty grumpy. I read the numbers up front and carefully selected several bills from my wallet. As I got out of the car, I handed the driver his fare and attempted my best Chinese "Thank you," complete with a small bow. His face lit up like a man who suddenly recognized his best friend. I was amazed at the effect of my routine expression of gratitude. He bowed, dozens of times, as he extracted each of my bags, that magnificent grin still electrifying his face. I returned the smile and another bow before hurrying inside to check in. He held the door for me, still bowing and grinning.

Once safely tucked into my new home for the week, I plopped down on the foot of the bed to reorganize my credit cards and money from the recent string of transactions. I stopped. Where was that other bill? It was then that I realized why the cab driver was still grinning. I had tipped him the equivalent of fifty dollars—American.

It may be difficult to imagine yourself alone in a taxicab late at night in a foreign country. I certainly did not expect such experiences when I stepped into the headship of the Carnegie Mellon University School of Music.

DISCOVERING THE SCOPE OF THE POSITION

Leadership positions are like that. When you are in charge, you have to handle whatever comes along, and the range of "whatever's" can be staggering. Picture yourself in each of these circumstances:

- Officiating at a memorial service for a beloved member of your organization—someone who had once been your teacher and mentor;

- Convincing an airline steward in Hong Kong to hold an airplane on the ground, while your colleagues feverishly worked their way through customs;

- Delivering an introductory tribute to a candidate for an honorary doctorate in front of several thousand people at a graduation ceremony;

- Flying to Spain for a weekend to attend the premiere of a colleague's opera, commissioned by the King and Queen of Spain;

- Going on national television to talk about the life of a renowned artist, who had recently passed away;

- Signing a contract in front of 600 people, requiring you to raise over half a million dollars in five years from people with little or no history of giving;

- Negotiating a complex contract in an airport coffee shop with an Italian producer and a Russian conductor;

- Working to bring two gifted musicians, husband and wife, to America from a war-torn Sarajevo at the peak of their country's conflict;

- Fighting through bureaucracy to get one of your artist's visa cleared, so he could return to the USA from Chile.

None of these are normal responsibilities of a job like yours; yet, any one of them could happen tomorrow, and you would be the person called upon to act. The skills required to give a major public address are very different from those called upon to counsel a troubled artist.

Still, you may have to do both, and within minutes of each other. It's all in a day's work.

When You Don't Know What You're Doing

How often have you been in a situation in which you said to yourself, "I don't have the faintest idea what I'm doing?" How far are you able to move into experiences about which you know very little or nothing at all? Do you push forward? Or take a step back? Can you grit your teeth and meet the challenges head on? Are you able to convince others to follow you, when you are not at all sure of the outcome?

If the answer is yes, you are a born leader. If the answer is no, you may still be able to become a leader. How? Simply by finding yourself in a number of situations in which your leadership is essential to the very survival of the organization you run. If your vision is strong and your decision-making sharp, you will recognize those opportunities to move your arts unit forward wherever and whenever they present themselves, and they do seem to appear out of nowhere.

Much of the time, you do not have to grab onto them; mediocre institutions have long histories of opportunities missed. But if you really want to move your organization ahead, help make it significantly better than it is today, you are going to have to seize any opportunity you can find to leap-frog forward. Major growth requires major change and major risk taking. (Later in this chapter, we will be discussing both of these topics.) If you know how to make change and can develop a tolerance for taking risks (and this can be developed,) then you would be able to move into any of the experiences described above with energy and confidence—yes, even when you haven't the vaguest idea how to do it.

Any leadership position requires a vast range of skills. Since the arts are such a public media, it is unlikely that you, as an arts administrator, can escape the glare of the footlights for very long. Sooner or later, you are going to be called upon to represent your organization in all sorts of public situations; you will also be expected to serve as advocate for the arts in general, whenever they come under the gun. You must have that fire in your belly. You must really believe in your arts unit and in the importance of art itself.

This passion for excellence, when it is there, helps ignite the desire to make things happen. Suddenly, your lack of experience in a certain area appears to diminish in importance. The gritty determination to see things through to completion and to find a solution, no matter what—this determination is the core of the dynamic leader. The specifics of a given situation matter very little; the skills needed to meet any challenge are all contained within the vision, fueled by passion and determination. You can learn whatever you have to learn as you need to learn it. Jump off a cliff, and you will soon find your feet.

Dealing in the Unknown

OK, so maybe that's a bit drastic, but the point is, you will, as a leader, get into situations about which you know very little. You may find yourself negotiating a union contract, or dealing with immigrations people, or talking with architects about the construction of a new performing arts building—whatever the circumstances, you know you are in way over your head. How do you handle this?

First, know that it isn't always necessary to be fully up to speed in a given area in order to deal effectively with people who are. After all, they probably don't know as much about the arts as you do, yet they are dealing with you. Leadership is all about stepping back to view the big picture, considering the available options, and making sharp decisions in the best interests of your organization. That's what you will need to do. You may not know a whit about unions or immigration or architecture, but you certainly do know how to make good decisions—this, you do all the time.

So, take it one step at a time. Don't let the sea of stuff you know nothing about wash over you. Collect the specific information you need to act on behalf of your institution, consult with whomever can give you good advice on this, then move ahead—inch by inch. As you go, you will undoubtedly need to know specific things about this other field in which you find yourself. Just ask. People are aware that you come from another area of specialization, and they don't expect you to know a lot about their area. Never feel you have to pretend to be an expert in their field, too. You aren't. Acknowledge this and request backup information as you need it.

On the other hand, it is not advisable to be too open with your lack of knowledge. You need always to deal from a position of strength, your feet firmly planted on the ground. If others perceive you are not up to the task at hand, you will have no credibility or respect, and they will simply walk all over you and the organization you represent. (At this point, you will have no choice but to send someone else into the situation to take your place.) So, portraying confidence and strength of purpose is essential. Stay focused on the objective, and keep the long-term interests of your arts unit in front of you like a compass, guiding your path through unknown territory.

Be observant. It is amazing how much you can learn just by sitting quietly and observing others, whenever possible. Who are these people with whom you must deal? What is their relative position in this situation? How can they help or hinder you in achieving your goals? Really listen to what they have to say and to how they say it. If you are in their work culture, not your own, you will have to find an effective way of communicating without alienating anyone important.

Observe their approach to the task at hand. How much bureaucracy is involved here? How quickly are these people accustomed to moving? Remember, if you are dealing in their territory, you will have to play by their rules. You are not going to change their way of doing business. Better to observe these things and find a way to fit in, so there is some hope of being accepted as a respected colleague (or a formidable opponent, whatever the case may be.)

This calls to mind a situation we encountered while engaged in a recording project with our student orchestra and RAI, Italian television network.

We had a guest conductor from Russia, who spoke little English, but fluent Italian. Our translator was a television producer from Italy. We had extensive rehearsals scheduled four days a week for three weeks. Each of these days (Monday, Tuesday, Thursday, and Friday,) there was to be a three-hour morning rehearsal with another three-hour rehearsal in the afternoon.

I had it written into the contract that Wednesdays were to be off as well as all Saturdays and Sundays. Yet, ever since he had arrived, the conductor had been ranting and raving about needing more rehearsal time. We had already moved some mountains to clear the hours we had agreed to schedule, and I was determined to protect the students from any further demands on their time for this special project.

Each day was the same. As soon as the afternoon rehearsal ended at 5:00, the conductor and the producer were in my office. The conductor needed to talk to me about Wednesday. He had to have rehearsals that day. There was no way to do this project with the amount of rehearsal time we had allotted. The conductor gave long, impassioned speeches in Italian, complete with banging on the table, shouting to the ceiling, alternately clutching his head then his chest to emphasize the enormous impact this project was having on him, and just how much he was giving of himself to make it a success.

It was difficult to avoid laughing. The histrionics were excessive—melodramatic, even. The steady drone of the producer's interpretation after each emotional outburst was hilarious. It was all from some other planet. By the end of each day, I was completely worn out from the continual flow of emergencies this project was generating day after grueling day. Nevertheless, my assistant and I sat there, listening with respect, nodding our heads in all the right places, attempting to look as deeply concerned about the situation as our guest conductor obviously was.

At the end of each of his orations, I always did the same thing: calmly and rationally repeated all the reasons why we could not schedule the student musicians beyond the agreed-upon times. I pointed to our signed contract, steadfastly shook my head "No" to all his requests for extending the schedule, and then sat back and waited for my answer to be translated.

Inevitably, another tirade was then unleashed, this time even more emotional, complete with threats of his quitting, calling off the project, going somewhere else to do the recording, etc. It was really stressful, because we weren't at all sure he would not quit. These sessions had been going on since Friday, when they arrived. By Tuesday, they had really heated up to a fever pitch, since Wednesday was the day scheduled to be free. If he was to get that extra rehearsal, he had to get it that night.

I was losing my mind and my patience, so I decided to try something else. This time, after his introductory speech (twenty minutes or so,) I responded differently. Picking up on his statement that he cared deeply about this project and obviously I didn't, I leaned forward and began to shake my fist at him and pound the table, just as he had done every night since he arrived. I acted personally insulted that he had accused me of not caring about the project, and did my best to blow up, mimicking his own particular style of elocution.

This time, I threatened to cancel the project. His eyes widened as he watched. The producer began to translate, the conductor shaking his head to acknowledge his understanding of the message. Much to my amazement, the maestro then rose from the table, shrugged, and said, "Well, then, I guess we must wait until Thursday." With that, they left, giving cordial good-byes as they walked out the door.

It is not always necessary to go quite this far in order to speak the same language as the people with whom you must deal. When push comes to shove, while in unknown territory, you can usually get further by adopting the culture of the people who work there. Observe carefully how business gets done, and be prepared to adjust your style accordingly.

Understanding Your Role

One of the keys to survival in unfamiliar situations is to be absolutely clear about who you are and what you are doing here. Nine times out of ten, your role is to represent your arts unit. You can do this anywhere. You know your organization inside and out. You know its strengths, its weaknesses, its needs, and its ambitions, because you were instrumental in setting its mission and in designing its strategic plan for the future. You also know the operating rules. You know how far you are able to go on behalf of your arts unit without seeking the counsel and advice of the people under whom you serve. So, whatever new situation confronts you, consider what it is you seek to accomplish on behalf of your institution, and how you can best achieve this goal.

At the same time, recognize when you are not the right person for the job. There will be times when the right answer to a request for your involvement is "Nope." If you know that someone else would be better able to handle this particular task, recommend that person. If it's really important for your arts organization to be represented, you will want to make certain that other person says, "Yes," so you may choose to contact him/her yourself. If, however, it fits neatly into someone else's job description, no special requests are needed; just steer the task to the appropriate office.

The stickier issues are those which you feel are important, but you just know you would not be very skillful in handling, and neither would anyone else in your institution. Consider carefully the ramifications of saying, "No," to these requests. If it wouldn't hurt your organization and if you feel you would not be passing up some opportunity for new growth for your arts unit, then politely refuse.

You can't do everything. It is even necessary to say "No" when you are the right person for the job, but you are just too busy to take on another commitment. Do so with a clear conscience. Take on only those tasks that are important in advancing the arts organization you lead—tasks you are capable of completing for the greater good of your institution.

Then, once you are committed, keep your role clearly in focus. You are there because you are the leader of your arts unit. Your objective is to further the cause of your organization; everyone knows this. In the process, you may even grow some new wings yourself, and perhaps find some personal strengths you didn't know you had. Then, the next time one of these situations comes along, you will be even better able to deal with it. You will actually know what you are doing.

Managing Your Time

Heading an arts program is such a chaotic job, with so many demands on your time from so many different people, you will need to find some way to strike a balance between the continual crises and people-oriented problems and the goals you have set out to accomplish.

Whatever it takes to help you find time to do the work you feel is a priority—that is a step worth taking. If, by some really bad luck of the draw, you have wound up in an arts administrative position without an assistant, run, don't walk, to whomever is in charge and demand some help. Having done this type of job for a year and a half with an ineffective assistant, I can assure you, nothing is more important than having skilled help to keep some of the interruptions out of your face.

A high level of accessibility to people, an open-door policy, for example, is really difficult to maintain when there are a great many people needing your attention. If your artist personnel is larger than, say, fifteen or twenty, as many arts units are, then you will need a traffic cop of some sort to keep your day from turning into a free-for-all. Artists are extremely demanding, and as stated many times in this book, they all need to believe they are at the head of your list whenever they want something. If you permit people to interrupt your meetings, nobody feels well served, certainly not the person who was interrupted in the middle of a discussion with you.

Of greatest importance is developing a system that shows you respect each individual's time and self worth. The artists may be really irate that they are not permitted to barge in any time they wish to see you; but, on the other hand, they will eventually realize that nobody else is allowed to barge in on their time with you, either. They may have to schedule a time to see you, but so does everybody else. If you really respect your colleagues, you will do everything in your power to stay on schedule, so that people are not kept waiting for their appointments with you.

No matter how well you run your office, you will still have people who demand to see you right now. These people do not care what you are doing or who you are talking to, their problems are obviously more important and should be tended to at once. After all, it is an emergency! In time, you will discover, and so will your assistant, that everything is an emergency with this person. Knowing that, makes it a little easier to deal with Artist Unreasonable.

Even if you are super human, and willing to work around the clock, you will still find there are not enough hours in the day to satisfy all those artistic temperaments and egos. If you permit yourself to get chewed up by the day-to-day minutia, you will not have the time or creative energy to exercise your leadership abilities. The best you can hope to achieve is a record of good management. Moving the arts unit forward requires time to think, to reflect, and to take actions that will lead to that vision of a better artistic environment. In short, leadership takes time. Make sure you protect some of yours for the greater good of the institution you serve.

Dealing with Emergencies

Webster's College Dictionary defines an emergency as "a sudden, urgent, usually unexpected occurrence requiring immediate action." Now, let's compare that definition to a couple of real-life situations:

> **SITUATION #1:**
> *A member of the voice faculty "has to see me immediately! It's an emergency!" I fell for this one, and canceled another appointment to meet with him. Topic: he disagreed with the casting (three days ago) of two of his students in next season's opera (six months from now.)*

Now, how does this situation fit into the definition? The aspect of suddenness is certainly missing. The level of urgency is somewhere in the middle on a scale of 1 - 10. Unexpected? Nope. Totally predictable. It happens every year. And the most important part: is this something that requires immediate action? Not in my book, but that's just the problem. This assessment is from the perspective of my overall job and the number of hours in my day.

Taken from the faculty's viewpoint, however, it is sudden. Student "X" just had a lesson, and was too upset about her role in the opera to sing. So, the problem just hit the studio teacher. The level of urgency is a 10 for the faculty, since he's the one who just spent the better part of an hour with a sobbing soprano. The unexpected part is also a factor from the standpoint of the faculty, since this is his first year as a full-time faculty member.

Does this situation require immediate action? Here's where the definition of emergency falls completely apart, even from the side of the faculty. When asked point blank just what he expected the department head to do about this problem, the faculty admitted there was nothing that could be done this year. He felt the auditioning process was flawed; that next year, it should be done differently. Fair enough. So, why was he demanding my attention now? Because he's an artist. And he's upset. And he wants the boss to listen. Because he is, after all, #1. This problem is the most important thing in the world to him at the moment, and he can't imagine anything being more important to anyone else.

Does he really think it is an emergency? You bet, he does. Do you think it's an emergency? Well, now, that's the real problem, isn't it? Who gets to define the word "emergency?" The leader of the arts unit? Or the person trying to get a chunk of the director's time?

> ***SITUATION #2:***
>
> *The director of advising calls down. She has to speak to me right away. It's an emergency! I take this call immediately. Janet never interrupts me unless it really is an emergency. Topic: "Freshman Class-Cutter" hasn't been seen in the department for several weeks. "Student Concerned" just stopped in to report that "Class-Cutter" is her roommate, and that she won't leave the dorm any more. She just cries all day long and can't sleep. "Student Concerned" is scared— thinks her friend is having a total breakdown.*

Now, this is what I call an emergency, and the truth is, if the voice faculty from Situation #1 had to choose between the two problems, he, too, would jump to the "Class-Cutter" problem in the blink of an eye. He has no way of knowing the kind of complex agenda the boss is dealing with day after day after day. He sees only his own part of the world, and he needs you to see it, too. When his emergency bell goes off, you'd better be able to hear it.

Now, multiply this by 60 or 80 or 100, however many people you have in your organization; throw in a handful of staff; make room for external folks, and you have the total picture It isn't pretty.

Coping with Simultaneous Activities

To gain an appreciation for the complexity of activities in an arts organization, it is useful to envision trying to run an arts company with a full season of productions or exhibits. In addition to the regular artists and staff employed, there are probably guest artists to be hired, contracts to negotiate, travel arrangements to be made, lodging to be reserved, and a myriad of acts of hospitality to be taken care of on behalf of these out-of-town artists.

If it is a performing arts organization, there may be instruments to be moved, sets to be built, copyright issues to be resolved. In the visual arts, there are the issues of installing works of art, shipping and handling them safely, archiving the work. Add publicity, ticket sales, posters, radio announcements, newspaper coverage, season subscription sales materials, and a round-the-clock information line. Then, add programs, recordings, ushers, lights, piano tuning, props, etc. and you have some idea of the scope of the performance side of an arts unit.

Perhaps, nothing can better illustrate the extent of the managerial nightmare presented by a typical arts company than to describe the process of presenting just one opera. It is often said that the best way to judge a music school is by observing whether or not it is able to produce opera. It is, truly, an organizational challenge of the highest degree, especially when it must coexist with a bunch of other educational and performing activities. Opera is like a black hole that scoops in money and people and time and whatever is left of your sanity; but what an educational triumph, when it works!

When we first set out to restore fully-staged opera productions in our program, I refused to believe you actually needed all those people: a producer, a stage director, a music director, a set designer, a costume designer, a lighting designer, a production coordinator, a stage director, a prop manager, a makeup artist, as well as the cast, the chorus, the orchestra, the stage crew, the costume crew, the run crew, the lighting crew, the recording team, the vocal coach, the piano accompanist, the acting teacher, and of course the voice teacher. You know what? You do. Trust me on this one. Having attempted to do opera without each of the above, I regrettably admit that even this list is optimistic. Over time, we have had to add assistants for just about everyone listed above. This is not even touching the public relations, programs, ushers, box office personnel, and other typical support staff that all performances require.

Then there is the problem of how to manage intensive rehearsals to prepare the thing and especially how to free everybody under the sun for what is known as "Tech Week," when the set is installed, costumes and lighting added, the orchestra moves in, and the cast gears up for opening night. When everyone involved is a student, perhaps you can envision at least some of the conflicts this creates. Oh well, when the curtain goes up, even you will be amazed at the level of achievement this whole ordeal has fostered. That, after all, is what it is all about. I know of no better way to accelerate young performers' artistic growth than to put them "on the line" in a high-profile professional performance venue like opera. Besides, it makes the rest of your job seem relatively easy.

Learning to Prioritize

On the issue of time management, we have to learn to prioritize. A lot of us are perfectionists, who are used to doing things very well; but we cannot let ourselves get chewed up by the little stuff, and it is the little stuff that hits day after day after day. We are all artists; emotions run high; every problem is a crisis. Somehow, we need to balance our days in such a way that there is time for the big stuff.

One rule of thumb is to make sure you spend at least part of every day working on issues requiring strong leadership; don't let the administrative details of the job completely consume you. This may mean some of the tasks do not get done, or are forced to wait until tomorrow. This will not hurt your institution nearly as much as a lack of leadership. Setting clear priorities for your arts unit, going after the funds for a new building—these are far more important in the long run than settling a dispute between two members of your staff. Yet, you know very well which problem is going to make the biggest noise, demanding your attention now.

There are lots of books out there on time management. I want to add just two suggestions of my own: you may want to try working at home one day a week. I did this for eight years, and this practice alone made it possible for me to concentrate on the leadership side of my job. After a while, everyone will adjust to the fact that you will not be in the office on, say, Wednesdays. This is the day set aside for uninterrupted work: to write important reports, speeches, papers, and strategic plans; to place high priority phone calls that would most likely take some time; to plan large-scale meetings, read long documents or catch up on stacks of correspondence. One day a week, where you can work as long as you want without losing your train of thought, may make it possible to tilt the rest of the week more heavily toward meeting the needs of all those other people with whom you must deal.

My second suggestion is to start each week with a short list of priorities—the important stuff—but no more than three or four. Write them on an index card in big letters and prop the card up on your desk facing you. Make sure they are long-term goals, requiring strong leadership. By keeping these right out in front of you, there is a much better chance you will find the time to address one or two of them during the course of that week. If you find, week after week, that you are not getting to any of your long-range priorities, you need to step back and assess the things that are eating up all of your time. Either delegate some of these or fire the guy that's causing all the trouble. (I'm only partially kidding.)

I know there are a lot of systems for keeping track of the paper in your life. Some expects advocate handling every piece of paper that comes your way only once. Now, in attempting to follow this advice, I developed a filing system that almost worked some of the time. It consists of a series of folders labeled: TO DO, TO READ, TO FILE, and TO KEEP HANDY. And of course, the wastebasket was always there to receive the rest, but it wasn't until I added one more folder, that my system began to function as it was intended. This became my favorite file; it was entitled: CHAOS.

MINIMIZING BUREAUCRACY

Nobody enjoys bureaucracy. You, as the leader of an arts unit, are in a position to maximize or minimize the impact of bureaucracy on the people working in your environment. For goodness sake, do everything in your power to make it invisible.

Granted, there are some aspects of the artistic world that just have to be structured: performances and exhibits must be presented as scheduled, and advertised well in advance. These types of activities require a certain amount of organization and consistency in the processes that make them happen. However, it is very easy to go too far in setting up these procedures.

For example, we developed a process for monitoring the external performances of our vocal performance majors. The reason for this was that voice majors were accepting too many roles in community and professional theater companies; this outside work was interfering with their vocal training and was creating serious scheduling conflicts within the voice program. Some of the opportunities to perform were on a very high level; such openings into the professional world were obviously important to the students' future careers. They would certainly be approved by the faculty. Others, were simply temptations to get on the stage; many of these were under the direction of people who lacked sensitivity to the development of young singers. These experiences could be vocally harmful and a tremendous drain on the students' energy and ability to function 100% in their educational program.

The process was simple. The voice major who had an opportunity to perform off campus was to pick up a form in the Director of Student Service's office, fill it out, and have it signed by all of the teachers involved in his/her professional training: the private voice teacher, the opera music director, the acting teacher, dance instructor, and finally the department head. The form itself required that the student describe the opportunity, state briefly why (s)he wanted to accept it, and list all the times and dates of the rehearsals and the performances, indicating any that would conflict directly with a class or performance activity at school.

After we stumbled through a few months of typical implementation snafus, the process began to work quite well. Students were now less likely to take on commitments they knew the faculty would veto, and the important opportunities were better supported through official excused absences from classes that conflicted.

It worked well, that is, until one day when a distraught tenor showed up on my doorstep. He had done everything he was supposed to do: he had picked up the appropriate form, filled it out, and had gone to each of his teachers for signatures. The problem was, his voice teacher didn't want to sign it until the opera director had approved, the opera director refused to authorize it unless the studio teacher said it was OK, and all the rest of the faculty were waiting for somebody else to say "yes" before any of them would sign. After two weeks of running from teacher to teacher, the poor student had gotten nothing accomplished, and he had to either accept the part or turn it down. Now, that's bureaucracy at its worst.

Any time a person winds up making a full circle without accomplishing a goal, you have a problem with bureaucracy. Either that, or somebody is ducking his/her responsibility to take action. It only takes one cog in the wheel to get stuck and your process falls apart. That, I believe, is the real Achilles heel in complex organizations: the more structured the procedure, the more sensitive it is to individuals performing perfectly. Let's face it: they don't!

Consider, for just a moment, any personal experience you have had recently with bureaucracy. I'll bet somebody screwed up. When everyone does his/her job, we are not even aware of the bureaucratic structure supporting the process. We slide through organized procedures all day long without giving them a second thought, unless we get stuck somewhere in the process. That's when we become aware of the bureaucratic nature of the activity. Nine times out of ten, the glitch was caused by somebody not doing the job. In the other case, the process itself was probably flawed. Regardless of the cause, it is usually the procedures that need to be changed, because the people will just keep on screwing up—guaranteed. The more people involved, the more likely it is that something will go wrong, or that the entire process will take so much time, the person trying to stumble through it will cry, "Uncle!"

Tightening Up the Process

So, what's the solution? Tighten up the process. Either eliminate a step or remove a person from the loop. This can often be accomplished by authorizing stronger decision making at a lower level. Consider the simple example of returning some merchandise to a store. It used to be the case that you would have to go to the department in which you made the purchase, tell your tale of woe to the sales clerk, and then wait while (s)he ran off to get the manager's approval. Usually, you then had to take this written approval to another part of the store (often, the basement, way back in the corner) to actually get your money back. You probably had to wait in line at the cashier's counter, as a final irritant.

Now, contrast this with the newer procedure: you walk into the store with your merchandise, and the service desk is right there by the door, staffed with multiple people, each of whom has the authority to approve your return and refund your money. That's how to satisfy the customer. It doesn't bother you a bit that the Service Desk person stamps your receipt or asks for your signature. All of that is bureaucracy, too, but, you only notice the procedures that make you jump through multiple hoops. So, look for these, and eliminate whatever hoops you can, empowering the staff to make some of those decisions on the spot. (More about helping others make decisions in Chapter #5.)

Understanding the Birth of Bureaucracy

Now, how did you get into this mess to begin with? You personally hate bureaucracy. You would never, in a million years, create a cumbersome process on purpose. No, but the cells of future bureaucracy live in the desks of every person in the organization. They may be in the drawer, or under the blotter, but you can be sure they're there. The more structured the person, the more apt (s)he is to create a system to handle some specific process that (s)he is responsible for managing. It may be inconvenient or cumbersome for everyone else, but it makes life much better for the person who created the system.

As the leader of the arts unit, you need to be on the lookout for signs of bureaucracy springing up here and there. Sometimes the new procedure is needed to solve a problem or to streamline a process. If the system makes things ultimately better for the people who have to use it, fine; if it is solely for the purpose of the person in charge, it's not so fine. After all, the person in charge is being paid to be in charge, not to make everybody else miserable.

Sharing the Burden

We are, after all, social beings. We know we have to do things in a way that ensures the health and productivity of the group, not just ourselves. Most of us are willing to adopt yet another process if we believe it is necessary for the successful outcome of the larger constituency and its mission. We are also happy to adjust to new procedures when they will clearly improve things; but needless bureaucracy cannot be justified. The more we move away from personalized care toward faceless procedures, the more we resent the environment in which we work.

This is one of those leadership issues. It is the responsibility of the person at the top to ensure that the work environment is a positive one for everyone in the organization. So, get out your Geiger counter and look for those seeds of bureaucracy, before they sprout into a labyrinth of infinite loops, choking the morale of everyone in the place.

"Is Inspector Rentacop there, please? Yes, I'll wait. No, it's not an emergency, thank you."

I was calling campus security for help. The guy who had been living in the arts building had struck again; this time, he took the trail mix out of a staff's desk. No, he didn't touch the computer, the typewriter, the answering machine, the small stereo. Just ate the trail mix and left. He even locked the desk drawer when he was done, and used his key to set the dead bolt on the door. (We like neatness in our thieves.)

But, he must be at least a little bit strange. That's what worries me. We have students in those practice rooms on the mezzanine at all hours of the night. This guy must have a master key. He has been seen coming out of classrooms, offices, and practice rooms at night and in the morning. Not a safe situation.

"Yes, Inspector, I'm calling about the thief your men apprehended on the mezzanine two nights ago. I understand they released him?"

"What? You have to warn him before you arrest him? Now that's bizarre. Tell me, did the officer take our keys back before he let him go?"

"What do you mean the keys were to another university? He is still breaking into things. Last night, he let himself into a staff office and stole some trail mix out of the locked desk drawer."

"No, he didn't take anything else. Obviously he has keys to our facilities, and I'm worried about the students who practice in the building late at night. His master key will also open their practice rooms. He must be some kind of kook, stealing candy and trail mix and gum. Yeah, he does sound

hungry. We need to have someone patrol the mezzanine until this guy is apprehended."

"What? You have to charge my departmental budget for extra security? When your guys let him go? OK, Officer, thank you very much. Yes, one guard should be fine. And, oh, Officer Rentacop? Please tell the guard to bring chocolate. This guy really likes Hershey bars. Yeah, just put 'em on our bill."

Keeping the Vision Clear

Bureaucracy doesn't have to cost money to be annoying. In fact, it is usually created by well-meaning staff, just attempting to do his/her job. Staff, whose job it is to implement large areas of activity like, for example, ticket sales have a broad spectrum of responsibilities. Therefore, they have to have procedures to handle routine tasks; otherwise, their jobs become undoable. While you can't eliminate all of these processes without making a real mess, you can, at least, monitor the situation from the user's perspective. Every now and then, step back and try to envision the steps a person must take to get something accomplished. If it feels too cumbersome, try to tighten up the process. Even though you want to enable staff to do their jobs as they wish, you may have to step in, on occasion, to encourage a change in procedures, which are annoying other people.

Enabling the Artist

All of this is not to imply that the entire organization must stand on its collective nose just to make people happy. In fact, people are never totally happy, so that cannot be the goal. You just want to be sensitive to the needs of the folks inside and outside your organization.

The needs of the artist must be balanced, as well. Artists are likely to rebel against anything that stands between them and their artistic goals. You won't have to look for these things; the artists will be happy to point them out to you, in no uncertain terms. Hopefully, this will happen before they quit. Yes, bureaucracy is that important. (See the section on Why Artists Quit in Chapter #1.)

Even if they don't quit, you won't want a bunch of miserable people on your hands. So, whatever you can do to make them feel free of unnecessary restraints is worth the effort. Even if they are masters in the art of creating bureaucracy themselves, they will still resent anything that makes them feel like one of the sheep. The feeling that you are just one of a hoard of people is demoralizing for all of us. An artist's need to be #1 transcends any understanding of your need to organize something. No, they don't understand. So, you may as well not even try to explain it to them.

Your best bet is to reduce the obvious bureaucracy affecting the artists as far as you possibly can. If you can't get rid of it, try to make it invisible. The magic word is flexibility. Rigid staff, who just won't bend their own rules, can be a tremendous problem. On the other hand, artists who refuse to fit into the structure can be equally troublesome. Only you can ease the tension here, and cajole everyone into an agreeable compromise.

Supporting Your Staff

There are definitely staff who over-organize everything. They are probably the same people you can't imagine living without. These are the people to watch most closely for those cells of bureaucracy in the drawer. As soon as you see another system developing, stick your nose in to make sure it will make things better for the artists and others in the organization, rather than just for the staff in charge. Remember, the staff person who earns the title "Wizard" is the one who somehow gets everything done without people even being aware of the process. You might want to encourage some wizardry from everyone on your staff. If they know that invisible bureaucracy is a valued goal of yours, it will become a focus for each of them, as well.

The bottom line is to achieve a healthy balance between efficiency and service. You expect your staff to accomplish a great deal. So, you have to let them structure their jobs in ways that make it possible to achieve results. Yet, at the same time, you need to ensure that the environment is conducive to effective art making. This requires a lot of elbowroom for everyone in the place, including your staff.

A lot of times, the procedures staff invent to organize aspects of their jobs can work like a charm if they just keep a few important points in mind:

- A lot of lead time is needed in setting deadlines for artists. Since artists travel a great deal, they may not even have read their mail or their e-mail by the time a deadline arrives. So, if a staff member needs a response quickly, it is best to contact individuals by phone, even in this age of high-tech communication.

- Flexibility is necessary when artists are expected to do something on site. With extremely busy professional lives, it may not be possible for everyone to be in the office or studio by the desired date.

- New procedures should improve things for everyone, not make additional busy work. Everyone in the arts has a great many demands on their time; they will not welcome any new ones.

Serving Others

Staff need to focus on the people they serve. They should all be encouraged to adopt a "People Before Paper" attitude. They may prefer to focus on the task side of their jobs, ignoring the people. Certainly, everyone can get a lot accomplished each day if they don't have to deal with other people. But, as stated many times in this book, artists demand attention. So, it is absolutely essential that everyone on the administrative staff realize their key role in maintaining a productive working environment; and productive means supportive of the work everyone is attempting to accomplish.

At the same time, you also have to make sure the whole operation is humming along like a well-greased machine. Balancing the needs of the people in the arts unit with the goals of the organization is a central responsibility of the arts leader.

IMPLEMENTING CHANGE

Nobody is going to hand you power in one of these jobs. You really have to empower yourself. Much of this book is focused on taking the helm and steering the institution toward a higher level of excellence. You actually have a lot of potential power to make change and to lead the organization forward, if you just know how to use it. Understanding the people with whom you are working is the key. Call this political skill, if you wish, but when channeled toward the greater good of the arts unit, it is leadership of the highest order.

Change doesn't have to be traumatic. Sometimes you just have to understand people's needs and be willing to meet those needs in the process of making the changes you view to be essential. You can't expect everyone in the organization to embrace your desire for change. Maybe they like things just the way they are.

Anticipating Change

You can give your organization no greater gift than to instill in it a readiness for change. Position your arts unit to meet the challenges of today and of tomorrow. Don't allow it to get stuck in yesterday's patterns. Use the experiences of the past to inform and inspire your vision for the future.

As a leader, you need to develop a highly sensitive antenna for change; you need to be able to see it coming, to smell it, hear it, taste it, and feel it. You also need to be able to embrace the concept of change, to relish it, savor it, thrive on it. Some times you will have to adapt to change; other times you will shape it; then, there will be opportunities to actually reach out and create it.

It is a central part of the business of leadership to sniff out change— long before it actually hits the organization. The reasons are obvious: changes affecting your arts unit will also affect other arts organizations. If you see them coming and prepare your institution for these changes, you will have a great opportunity to move out in front of the pack. If you don't, you and your colleagues just may have to swallow some serious dust as you watch the innovative leaders move on by with their arts units in tow.

How do you spot impending change? Well, first, you have to look for it. You can't afford to just go about your day-to-day management tasks with your head buried in the sand—or in that mountain of papers on your desk. Somehow, you have to find the time to get out of your office, get out of your building, and find out what's going on in the world. Your vision for your arts unit needs to be shaped by the real world, and just about everything out there will have an effect.

Take the recruitment of students, for example. The quality and the quantity of applicants to your school will be directly affected by the economic picture. If your tuition is high, and tough times hit, well, you can expect to have a drop in the number of applicants, all other factors remaining constant. If most of your students come from a certain region of the country, the economic well being of that particular area is going to be vitally important.

The arts are also affected by the political scene. If there is new leadership in the oval office, there may be a huge shift in the available funding for the arts. Government grants and loan programs may become more generous or they may shrink, making the financing of artistic activity a whole new ball game. This will have a direct impact on your arts organization.

Looking at an even broader picture, as barriers between nations disappear, new opportunities to recruit international artists and/or students open up. As various economic positions in the world market improve or decline, attitudes toward the arts change accordingly. Countries developing rapidly in the world economy may begin to steer their children toward business and technology, rather than the arts. As sweeping changes in the fabric of our own society take place (like the current shift from an industrial society to a technological one), the relative position of the arts changes, as well.

All of this has and will continue to have an impact on the job we are doing in the arts. A time when people are tightening their belts is not the time to launch a major fund-raising campaign. As our society grows more and more litigious, we need to anticipate more lawsuits, and tighten up our mode of operation. As the fear of violence increases, the safety of our artistic activity becomes more and more important.

These are all things you can see happening, if you just look for them and realize their potential impact on the arts unit you lead. So grab your binoculars and look out there in all directions. You cannot possibly be too well informed!

Adapting to Change

It's one thing to see them coming; it's quite another, to actually do something about the changes that are headed your way. Let's consider how we can successfully adapt to change. Staying with the recruitment example, let's say you anticipate a serious drop in applications, due to some societal change you can see developing. What do you do?

First, dig for data to try to determine just how bad it's going to be. With some help, you should be able to tap into such information as: the total number of students coming out of high schools over the next five years. Is that number decreasing or is it increasing, helping to balance the other factors contributing to a likely decline in your applications? If there is a big enough pool of potential students out there, you may be able to absorb some of the negative factors tugging them away from your school.

Look for additional data. How will other schools in your market be affected by the negative changes? Will you stand to be hit harder for some reason (due, perhaps, to your higher tuition rate) or will your competitors face the same kind of problem you see coming? Maybe your unit will be less seriously affected (perhaps the problem will be toughest for the public institutions, and you are a privately funded one.) Analyzing this situation from all directions will help shape your perspective on the pending situation. The potential problem may be less serious than you once surmised—or it may be even worse.

Once you have a better sense of the likely impact of the changes you see coming, you can position your organization to meet these new challenges. Perhaps you should increase your recruitment effort, to expand your pool of applicants? If there are more students in the pool, you can afford to lose more in the process, and still wind up with a solid class. Or maybe you need to increase your scholarship support? If money will be the problem, find a way to offset this problem. If parents are growing more reluctant to see their children move toward the arts, perhaps you need to focus your institution's attention more directly on the problem of job opportunities? Developing more aggressive placement help may be the key to attracting tomorrow's applicants.

Any of these efforts will take time. That is why you need to be standing out there on the bow of the ship, scanning the horizon for hints of change. You're going to need some time to get your vessel and the people on it ready for these changes. Keep in mind, it is the unexpected hits from behind or those that broad-side you that threaten to sink your ship. Nor can you afford to let yourself run full speed ahead into something you should have been able to see coming.

Reacting to Change

When you do get hit with change you didn't anticipate, your leadership skills need to be particularly strong. For once change is upon you, there's no choice but to deal with it—fast. This is not the time to beat up on yourself, because you didn't see it coming. You've got a lot of people on board, and you need to stay sea-worthy. So, as quickly as you can, assess the impact of the unexpected change, and figure out your options.

Usually, these will include:

- Attempting to reverse the change, if it is particularly negative to your organization;
- Trying to delay the impact of the change on your arts unit, until you have the organization positioned to handle it;
- Adapting to the change, making whatever adjustments are necessary to contain the problems resulting from it;
- Embracing the change, turning it into an asset or strategic advantage for your arts unit.

It is often the case that you will run through this whole list. First, you'll try to reverse the change. When that doesn't work, you'll try to delay its impact, all the while racing to get your organization in position to adjust to the change. Once there, you may be able to turn the whole thing into a bonanza. Naturally, your real goal will be the last one on the list—turning the unexpected change into a strategic advantage for your unit. So what if you didn't plan it that way? If opportunity comes along, grab it! Serendipity is often a central factor in an outstanding leader's success.

Naturally, you can't do any of this alone. All the people who will be impacted by the change, which is usually everyone in the organization, will need to be involved in the adjustment process. How you do this depends on your individual situation. But, several things should be kept in mind:

- the faster the change, the more anxiety you will find;
- the bigger the change, the more resistance you will meet;
- the greater the personal impact is perceived to be, the more deeply each person will react to the risks;
- the more involved people are in the change, the more apt they will be to accept it.

Change usually involves taking risks, and a lot of people have trouble with that. Taking risks takes courage, because we never can predict exactly what lies ahead. There is safety behind the walls of a fort or a castle. Opening the gate and charging forth to meet the unknown enemy is a huge risk. Why else would the people who did that sort of thing wear armor and carry spears?

TAKING RISKS

The arts call upon you to jump off cliffs almost daily. You are always putting your talent on the line. Most of the time, you have to depend on other people to help you produce an artistic product. Your entire personality is engaged in communicating the musical score or the script or the sculpture to an audience, whether you are a performer, actor, painter, composer, playwright, or conductor. That is really tough to do; it is also one of the most exhilarating, the most satisfying experiences of life itself.

Understanding the Fear of Taking Risks

As an arts leader, the ability to take risks is a tremendous asset, because it is usually essential to take some risks in order to drive an institution forward. Still, even the most courageous of leaders will probably have to work through some fear. Whether it feels exciting, like adrenaline fueling the process, or sheer panic threatening to hold you back, fear generally accompanies risk-taking. Let's take a closer look at this issue of fear.

What we fear most may be the fear of failing. Yet, failure doesn't exist unless you yourself create it. As long as you are trying, you are in the process of succeeding. Even if you hit a dead end, you can always change directions. You can't possibly fail unless you stop completely and give up. You are the only person who can declare yourself a failure. Personally, I don't believe in the word. I wish everyone would take a bottle of whiteout, and remove the word failure from their dictionaries. Try it. When you're finished, tell yourself, "Failure doesn't exist," and live the rest of your life as though you believe it.

Now to be consistent, the same has to hold true for success. Irving Berlin was quoted in Theatre Arts as saying, "The toughest thing about success is that you've got to keep on being a success." Life is a process, a wonderful maddening process that never sits still long enough to let you catch up. So, I guess I don't believe in the word success, either. But, let's not get carried away; it won't hurt us a bit to keep that word in our dictionaries.

You know, some people are actually afraid of success. A lot of books have been written about the fear of success; one of the best I have encountered is a book called The Impostor Phenomenon: Overcoming the Fear that Haunts your Success, by Dr. Pauline Rose Clance, published in 1985 by Peachtree Publishers, LTD, 494 Armour Circle, N.E., Atlanta, Georgia, 30324.

> *In this book, the "Impostor Phenomenon" is identified as an anxiety, which can be anywhere from mild to very acute, usually found in winners—people who are high achievers, who accomplish their goals and then feel somehow unworthy of their own success. These people commonly believe their success was based on good luck—that sooner or later, "they," whoever "they" are, will surely find out that the success was without merit.*

> *Persons with this type of anxiety fear that, sooner or later, other people will discover they are a fake. To the external world, these folks are extremely successful and competent; yet, the anxiety builds with each achievement. The higher the success, the more there is to lose when the whole thing collapses. The self-esteem, that should grow with accomplishment, somehow diminishes for these people.*

Now, you may be sitting here right now saying to yourself, "Oh dear, that's me!" We arts leaders are prime candidates for the "Impostor Phenomenon," because most of us, if not all of us, are high achievers. When we succeed, more is usually expected of us. This is an intense source of pressure. If, on top of that, you lack the self-confidence you need to carry off your own success, you probably see yourself very differently from the way others see you.

If you can conquer your fear of failure and your fear of success, there is nothing left to fear when you set out to make changes that involve some risk-taking.

They were on their way from Italy—fourteen technicians with a truckload of television equipment. What were we getting into? Three weeks of around-the-clock rehearsals. All on camera. A Russian conductor who spoke Italian, no English. A producer who spoke both, but couldn't be trusted any farther than you could throw him.

Ever since the phone call came, telling us our student orchestra had been selected for this prime-time Italian television series, the problems had been endless. The series of six one-hour shows would be on the six symphonies of Tchaikovsky. Our students had to be fully rehearsed to play Tchaikovsky's third and fifth symphonies; conservatory orchestras from Moscow and Milan would perform the other four.

Preparations for the filming process had been monumental. The rehearsal hall had to be rewired with a generator brought in to handle the production lighting. The fixed stage had to be cut in half and partially removed to make enough space for the orchestra plus the camera crew. Arrangements had to be made to have the stage restored after the project was complete. Students' schedules had to be cleared completely for the three-week filming.

Additional players had to be found to make the student orchestra the exact same size as those in Milan and Moscow. Contracts were drawn up. Budgets were set with "guessing times two" as the primary tool for estimating costs. Finally, parking had to be found for the truck from Italy. That was the toughest of all. The truck would take up ten parking places for three weeks in a lot that was in huge demand. Hazel, the director of parking, was famous for her inflexibility. Nobody talked Hazel into anything. Period. Getting her to agree to move a truck into the Fine Arts Parking Lot was a sheer miracle—only one of many accomplished by assistant head, Stanley Metcalf, in making this happen.

Hazel finally agreed that we could move the truck in on Saturday, provided we personally roped off the area needed Friday night after hours, when the lot would be empty. Stan agreed to do the roping. He would have agreed to just about anything at this point. The television project had already hit the newspapers, and we were committed to making this thing work, no matter what.

Then it happened. The office door opened and Karen announced, "They're here." As I turned to Stan in desperation, I heard the producer say, "Hey, guys, they brought two trucks. How do they get into the lot?" All I could think to say was, "Omigod, it's not even Saturday!"

You know, the bigger the risk, the more likely you are to succeed, because huge risks have such enormous consequences, you can't afford to fail. So you put everything you've got into the process of making it work, and you just don't give up. The moral of this story is: don't bother taking little tiny risks; take huge ones.

Helping Others Cope with Change and Risk

Now that you are ready for the challenges of risk taking and change, you need to get all those other artists on board, too. You may want to consider some of our previous discussion on "Gaining Support." You know there will be some artists who won't cooperate, no matter what. It is also important to know that just because individual artists take personal, creative risks in their own work, doesn't mean they are comfortable with other types of risk-taking—especially those over which they have no control. So, if you feel the need to make change, you can expect a lot of anxiety and resistance from the artists in your midst.

The best way to help people through the anxiety of change is to win their trust. If people have confidence in your ability to lead the arts unit, they will be able to cope with the changes they fear by trusting that you will pull them through it. I know this sounds like a real abdication of responsibility on their part, but there is no question, if you are in charge, it is your responsibility to make it work. They can help (or hinder, unfortunately,) but you are the one out front leading the charge. You will obviously get shot first; and there really is some comfort in that for all the people who work under your leadership and are stuck with your decisions and your judgments.

In short, when you take a risk, you'd better make it work. When you decide to make a change, you better know how to implement that change. You can also maximize the help of the others in the organization. The secret is to keep them well informed. Nobody is going to sign on for a change they don't understand, or don't believe is right, or don't really think will work. So, you need to communicate like mad. Half the battle is selling your colleagues on the need for change, and it is really important to project confidence and strength of purpose. Don't try to hedge your bets. People will pick up on your ambivalence faster than you can open your mouth to deny it. If you need to make a change, go for it. Be committed to it, and be able to convince the world it is going to work. Who knows? With a little bit of luck and a lot of gritty determination, it just might.

MANAGING THE CHAOS

One of the biggest adjustments in this job is learning to live with chaos. Take a walk through the halls of an arts school; the intensity of the work is right there for you to experience: a cacophony of sound spills out of the music practice rooms, Stravinsky mixed with Bach, trumpets, pianos, violins all seeming to contribute to one massive demonic symphony. Walk through a large art studio full of art students, with easels and drafting tables covering every inch of space; colors, and textures, and visual structures emerge from every scrap of material available. Actors walk the corridors, mumbling lines; dancers move intently to some internal music or artistic sonar system; set designers saw away in a shop that sounds and smells like a witch's haunt.

Artists learn primarily by doing; but they also learn by watching. So, role models are vitally important, and the most effective arts teacher is often the person who is also practicing his/her art. Now, if all those teachers are busy making music or theater or visual art, some of their work is bound to spill over into the educational environment. The result is artistic chaos.

Artists' work is noisy, messy, and wonderful. It is the nature of the beast called the arts school to be chaotic. The temptation for the highly organized manager may be to try to keep things under control—to not take on anything more until you get this stuff done. Unfortunately, you can't run an arts program that way. Well, I guess you could, but if you do, it won't amount to much.

Creating More Chaos

As if you don't have enough to do already, I'm now going to advise you to create even more activity. It is hard to imagine why anyone would take on extra work, when you are up to your nose just with the regular stuff—running the arts programs and overseeing all the public events that come with the job. Yet, you probably need some special projects, as well. Why?

To answer that question, let's take a closer look at the presentation aspect of our art. We know that teaching is the primary activity of any arts school; we also know that everyone in the place is also performing and creating new art, all the time. Well, the faculty's work often generates special projects that involve the whole place. Faculty composers and playwrights are constantly creating new works, which the arts school may choose to premiere—perhaps even record. Visual artists are producing works the arts school may want to feature in exhibition. These are definitely important opportunities for the institution, because they undoubtedly lead to high-profile events, linking the distinguished faculty to the school, increasing the visibility and enhancing the reputation of the entire organization.

The best part of this picture, though, is that the students become deeply involved in the creative work of their teachers—an enormous contribution to their education. Performing new art is always a technical challenge, especially for young performers. They also learn up close what it takes to be a professional, working hand-in-hand with their mentors, contributing to the creative work of the people who are in the process of guiding them into the profession. This is the master/apprentice style of teaching at its best. So, we certainly don't want to say "No" when an opportunity comes along to feature our faculty—an extremely desirable part of the overall educational climate. Besides, productive faculty are only one factor in our ever expanding calendar of special projects.

All sorts of collaborative activities evolve naturally out of the art institution's position in the community. Groups of faculty and students are invited to work with other arts organizations in presenting special events. Neighboring educational institutions link up with the arts school for special collaborative educational projects. Other colleges form consortiums with the arts school to present special concert series, theater series, art exhibits. Local radio and television networks create partnerships with schools of art. International projects evolve as the arts school becomes broadly known and respected.

Opportunities come along that the imaginative leader of an arts unit just can't pass up, usually because of one of several potential large-scale gains:

- expanding national and international visibility for the arts unit;
- connecting artists to the community;
- disseminating new art to the public;
- enriching the educational environment for the students;
- raising community awareness of the arts unit for development purposes;
- increasing the reputation of the arts organization for recruitment purposes.

All of these goals are a central part of the mission of the arts institution. When a chance to make significant progress in any of these areas comes along, the already worn-out arts leader generally reaches out with one hand to grab the opportunity, while reaching for a bottle of TUMS with the other. Crazy? Probably. But necessary, nonetheless.

Managing the Mess You Have Made

OK, now what? There are a zillion things going on at once in your organization. How do you keep all of this activity moving along without losing your mind? Well, clearly you can't do it alone. Delegation is a primary survival skill for arts leaders. To delegate effectively, you have to develop a sixth sense for how much or how little of your attention is needed to support each activity. This will depend a lot on the capabilities of the people to whom you are delegating.

Every activity in your organization needs a leader, someone in charge of the nitty-gritty details of the operation, and this person should not be you. To run a complex organization effectively, you need to be out of the details, back where you can see the whole picture clearly—how your arts unit relates to the outside world, how it is functioning, and how each of its parts is contributing to the whole. You need to be free to move in as closely as necessary to analyze specific activities that are sliding out of focus, and to make essential adjustments in these areas. You also need to be unbiased in your approach to balancing the organization. Your personal presence in a single area will, while you are so engaged, tip the scale of power and support toward that activity—if not actually, certainly in the perceptions of the people who work in the organization. So, you need to be as even-handed as possible in your involvement within the arts unit.

That being said, if it is the first time your arts unit has implemented a certain type of project or program, you may have to stay right beside the person in charge of that activity every step of the way. The ultimate goal is always going to be to help that person stand alone, absorbing the difficulties as they emerge, and handling most, if not all, of the decision-making and problem-solving as the needs arise. If you have done your job well, the next time this type of project comes along, your leadership will be needed only from a distance.

Learning to delegate is not all that easy, especially for a person with extremely high standards. You can always say to yourself, "That person is not doing that task as well as I did it, or as well as I could do it." Even if this is true, so what? There is a definite limit to the amount of detail you can personally oversee. As the base of activities broadens, you must struggle to move further back, so you can see all of it. This inevitably means someone else has to become directly involved in those details you may have been handling before. So, difficult though it may be, you will be forced to delegate whenever the number of activities exceeds your ability to handle things at your current level of detail.

Initially, when you first delegate a task, it will be necessary to oversee it pretty closely. Don't worry, you are still saving time. Instead of doing all the details yourself, you are periodically reviewing the work, making suggestions, perhaps corrections, and encouraging the manager of the project to keep going. Gradually, you will review less, and encourage more, until ultimately your role might become more inspirational than supervisory.

The further back you move, the more important it will be to keep at least one finger on each of these delegated areas. (If you run out of fingers, there are always your toes, your ears, and your eyes.) To do this, you need to develop techniques for keeping in touch with your managers, without stifling their ability to run their operations. Whether it is through routine meetings, or direct phone lines to your office when they have questions or problems, managers need to have access to their supervisor. When you have questions or see problems emerging, you need to have access to your managers. The frequency of this two-way communication will be based on the type of activity, and the people involved.

Delegation does not mean letting go of an area and forgetting all about it. Each time you entrust an activity to someone else, you need to stay tuned—at least, until you are absolutely certain the person in charge is handling the new responsibilities well. Even then, you will want to have occasional reports, just to stay informed and to keep your managers aware of your interest and your support for their work. Training others to handle more and more responsibility is part of the role of the effective leader.

The Temptation to Control the Chaos

There are times, however, when the temptation to cut back on the activity level can be nearly overwhelming. It is really tough to keep so many irons in the fire day after day after day; there is no question, it takes a special kind of leader to do so. It is enough to have to deal with all the complexities of an intense arts organization; add to that, a diversity of public concerts, shows, or exhibits in various stages of preparation and presentation, and you really do have a sea of artistic chaos. If all the complications and problems come your way, who can blame you for wanting to decrease the level of activity in your environment?

That is exactly the wrong direction to move, if you are a dynamic leader who cares deeply about the future of the organization. Artists must make art. That's your business. You want everyone in the institution to be striving for excellence, pushing themselves past their previous limitations toward a new level of artistic expression. You need the artist faculty to be productive on the highest possible level, so that their students have visible models for their own ever-increasing achievements. Artistic chaos is an absolute necessity.

When it feels overwhelming, you may just need a day or two out of the office. Or perhaps you are attempting to hold onto too many of the details; try delegating a bit more. A lack of sufficient space can add a great deal of tension to the environment; so can insufficient funding. Take a step back and consider the situation. Nine times out of ten, you will determine there is really nothing that should be eliminated; just a bit more tolerance for chaos may be needed.

Dig deeper and rise to the occasion. However, every now and then, something does need to be changed.

Knowing When You've Gone Too Far

Increased activity requires staff support, budgetary support, people support, space support, and leadership support. You know you've gone too far when you don't have enough of any of the above to sustain the level of artistic activity you have helped to create. You may not notice the problem until it actually hits you right between the eyes. When you have delegated everything there is to delegate, and you still can't keep up with the job, you know there is a problem.

When you have a great project on the horizon, but nobody has time to do it, a bell should go off, telling you to ease up a bit. You just may be reaching for more activity than your organization can handle at the moment. When you set out to do something new, but have no place to put it, you know you have a space problem. If juggling the schedule around doesn't create a solution, you have an intractable space problem. Either get more space, or don't do it. The same holds true with your budget. If you think some new venture is really important to your organization, but you don't have the funding to implement it, either find the funding or don't do it.

These are obvious statements, but this is a book about leadership, and effective leadership typically reaches beyond the boundaries of the institution to make things happen. The strong leader will always opt to expand the boundaries, rather than trying to squeeze the organization into its existing frame. So, the issue of how much is too much needs to be addressed.

An organization on the move has excitement in the air. You can feel it, smell it, and see it. You can almost reach out and touch it. Morale is noticeably up. Everyone is working just about as hard as they can, and each new success feeds the overall atmosphere of ever increasing optimism. Temporary upsets are absorbed in this climate with relative ease, making hardly a bump in the forward momentum. Anxieties brought on by rapid change are becoming less and less evident, as people gain confidence in the process. The nay-sayers no longer disturb the rest. Nobody really doubts that the institution is on the rise.

This is how it's supposed to feel. When, instead of this, you begin to see harried, worn-out faces, good people working harder and harder but still not quite able to fulfill their jobs as they feel they should, deadlines bumping into deadlines, some folks needing to be in two places at the same time, others beginning to jettison vacation time to "catch up"—you've probably pushed too hard, too far, or too fast. Remember, increased activity requires staff support, budgetary support, people support, space support, and leadership support. As the leader of the arts unit, you need to make sure you are keeping all these areas of support moving ahead of the growth in activity. Maintaining a healthy balance between these two aspects—activity and support—is crucial. Going too far without adequate support, will cause the rubber band holding the whole organization together to snap under the strain. Maintaining a healthy working environment is one of the most important functions of the effective leader of an arts organization. So, while you are out there on the bow of the ship, scanning the horizon for exciting new destinations, don't forget to periodically check on your crew and your passengers. Make sure they are getting enough food, enough exercise, enough money, and enough moral support. And, oh by the way, don't forget to check your fuel. You just may not have enough gas to get where you want to go.

CHAPTER #4   HANDLING THE FINANCES

Financial Management is one of the key skills needed by the leader of any arts organization; it is also one of the areas most often cited by arts managers when asked about gaps in their preparation and/or training for their jobs. Nearly all the people who land in their first arts administrative position find the financial management aspect to be a huge challenge, and it is one of the biggest stress factors in the job itself.

BALANCING THE BUDGET

OK, so nobody ever has enough money, and arts programs are often considered black holes that swallow money as fast as you can dump it in. Why is the budgetary process in an arts unit so tough? Why is it so difficult to estimate costs and maintain a balanced budget?

Well, for starters, the personnel picture is just a whole lot messier than in other disciplines. Lets first consider arts education. In music, for example, part-time faculty are needed in large numbers to teach private studio lessons. After all, it takes an expert euphonium teacher to guide the progress of the serious euphonium student; a violin teacher just won't be that flexible. Nor will the harp teacher, or the piano teacher, or the professor of clarinet. These teachers only earn money when they actually have students—so, the more students, the higher the salary. Therein lies the main budgetary problem. Predicting just how many of each instrumental area you will have next year is a job for the finest state-of-the-art crystal ball; most of us don't have one of those, so, we guess.

Now in the best of all worlds, everybody makes the same hourly salary, so it doesn't make a whit of difference who teaches what. In reality, people wind up with different hourly rates, because some have been in the school longer than others, some are more experienced, more renowned than others, some may actually be full-time faculty who also teach private studio lessons. The typical arts program has a wide enough range of individual agreements that winding up with more clarinets than trombones, for example, could create a budgetary crunch. If the enrollment spikes up, and the school succeeds in attracting more students than predicted, the overall cost of private instruction can soar beyond expectations.

That's only one aspect of the problem. The cost of running even one large ensemble is tough to predict. Day to day costs depend upon:

- repertoire—whether the music selected for each concert is already on the shelf of the music library, or whether it must be rented or purchased;

- instrumentation—whether large works can be performed with existing players and instruments, or whether specific instruments must be rented or players hired to fill in the gaps;

- soloists—whether student soloists are appropriate, or whether guest artists, faculty soloists, or alumni artists are used to enrich the performance experience;

- venue—whether all concerts can be performed at home, or whether special performances are to be held out of town, out of state, or out of the country;

- There are a myriad of other occasional costs—usually unexpected—that permeate the performance programs: departmental instrument needs to be repaired—fast; grand piano has to be moved, with the piano tuner following close behind, waving his/her bill; price for printing programs suddenly takes a leap; it may just be the cost of paper, but multiply that by thousands and thousands of pages over the course of a year;

- Xerox machine collapses under the sheer volume of in-house production; somebody gets sick and a professional is needed to step in and play the part.

I remember one situation, in particular, that created a unique budgetary crisis.

"You need what?" OK, so the Varese "Ameriques" is not exactly a standard work; but it is a twentieth-century masterpiece. Who am I to tell the conductor he can't do the piece? So, we'll find a siren; how hard can it be?

Well, the truth is, it will be approximately twelve times as hard as it seems at the outset. Why? Because you are not dealing with any ordinary fire here. This is art, and the siren you need is an artistic siren—one that can be started and stopped with a conductor's baton; one that can crescendo, diminuendo, accelerando, and ritard. You need a siren that can be played like a musical instrument, one with expressive capability and absolute control.

Does such a siren exist? No, but if you have hired all the right kind of people on your staff, you will have someone who knows how to build one, or buy one, or borrow one, or rent one, or modify one. You can bet it's going to cost plenty, and you can also bet it's not in your budget.

The list goes on. With each individual ensemble moving forward with gusto under the direction of a dynamic, high-intensity conductor (and is there any other kind?) these parallel paths of continual music-making produce an overall environment of chaos—wonderful chaos, it is true, but chaos nonetheless. Try budgeting in advance for all of that. Better still, try telling your dynamic, high-intensity conductor he can't program the Mahler, because it isn't in the library; or try telling her she can't do the Beethoven Piano Concerto, because it costs too much to move the piano. You tell them. I, for one, would rather do whatever it takes. After all, the show must go on, and that concept is probably the number one culprit in demolishing an arts organization's budget.

Preparing for This Part of the Job

It doesn't seem to matter whether the leader has had specific training in an arts management program, or has come up through the ranks of the profession itself, very few new administrators feel prepared for the complexities and the pressures of the money side of the job. Perhaps this is due to the size of the budget itself. Suddenly, you are worrying about hundreds of thousands of dollars—perhaps millions. This is a far cry from managing your own income, planning your family's budget, balancing your checkbook in dollars and cents. Now, you are projecting expenditures of hundreds of dollars, sometimes thousands of dollars at a time, with an income base that may fluctuate wildly. This is especially true when a large portion of each year's budget must be raised through ticket sales and/or fund-raising. Unexpected costs can absolutely balloon into major budgetary catastrophes, and everyone is asking you what to do about it.

You are attempting to raise the quality of your arts organization, yet quality costs money. You are continually put into the position of deciding just how far to go in support of your artists and their work, while keeping a sharp eye on the financial ramifications of this support. It's not a question of whether or not you had higher math or accounting in college, although if you didn't, you will probably feel even more anxious about all of this. It's more a question of having the courage, the skill, and the confidence to deal with big chunks of money, all the time; having the ability to take risks, since you may have to spend money before you make it; having the strength and the wisdom to say "No" to people with great ideas that cost too much; and having the overall vision to set artistic and educational priorities that will maximize the use of whatever funds you do have.

Setting the Budget

Every skill you own is called upon here. Your ability to make long-range plans and to anticipate potential problems is key, because the financial management of your arts unit probably has an annual budget set and implemented over an entire fiscal year. If you are fundamentally the person who sets this budget, your initial decisions about the allocation of available resources speak mountains about your vision for the arts unit. Unless you are starting a brand new arts organization from scratch, there will be a history of spending patterns to be studied. You will be able to see what worked and what didn't.

How was the money allocated last year, and the year before that? What areas stayed within the budget, and which ones spilled over? What will be different next year? Is there anything that happened last year that probably won't happen again? Is it possible to bring in more money next year? Will any funding sources be drying up? All of this goes into the process of setting an annual budget.

In addition, you may have to deal with a sizable deficit left over from a previous year or from a number of years. You may be called upon to reduce this deficit, to cut costs somehow. You will definitely have to project potential changes in the spending patterns of the organization, brought on by internal as well as external factors. Any changes in the organization you anticipate making will have budgetary implications. Some of these may be hidden at the outset.

Anticipating Unexpected Costs

For example, say you have just hired a highly acclaimed artist. You have the money in the budget from a couple of retirements, so no problem, right? Well, you can bet that person will come with a lot of "baggage," over and above whatever salary and expenses you have agreed to pay. Maybe your Super Star has allergies—needs a humidifier or a dehumidifier or an air cleaner. Maybe (s)he has to have a work space with a window. Maybe the window has to open, and yours don't. Maybe you agreed to cover expenses, and (s)he eats caviar three times a day. (Don't laugh; it has happened.)

Beyond these personal needs, there are also the expectations of a certain level of quality. Super Stars only work for the best. All of a sudden you learn what being the best actually means. Your typical publicity efforts may be puny compared to what the best arts organizations arrange. Forget about the free radio and television appearances; what about ads—paid ads—to make people aware of Super Star's performances and/or exhibitions? What? You don't do public receptions to welcome Super Stars to your arts community? Well, you can't expect Super Star to use that desk, or that chair, and where's the locked storage space for Super Star's professional equipment? On and on and on! Some of this stuff, most of it, costs money—money you didn't anticipate spending.

So, why not just say, "No?" How hard can that be? It all depends upon how important it is to your arts organization to be known far and wide as a mediocre operation. Hmmm. That changes things, doesn't it? Since Super Stars are known all over the world, do you really want them running around telling everyone yours is a second-rate arts institution? If you care enough about quality to hire Super Stars in the first place, you no doubt want them to be artistically productive in your environment. You also want them to enhance your reputation in the field, not demolish it.

If your new Super Star is to be a long-term member of the organization, you also have to realize the impact this will have on the rest of the personnel. They will probably ratchet up their demands to meet those of the competition. Remember, everyone needs to be #1! As soon as Super Star gets a room with a view, everyone else needs one, too. On the more positive side, other members of the arts unit will, no doubt, increase their productivity in the presence of the Super Star. This increase in productivity over time makes new demands on the environment. You may not be able to put your finger on exactly where or when it happened, but even subtle increases in artistic and/or educational activity can stress the available resources. Multiply this by however many people you have reacting to the new competition, and you could have a significant increase in expenditures throughout the organization, just because you hired one new person.

Making Decisions

Probably the most challenging aspect of financial management is the day-to-day decision-making. Virtually every decision you make, no matter how big or how small, has budgetary implications. Keeping track of where you are financially in the grand scheme of things as you make all these decisions, is extremely difficult, especially since your mind is focused on the problem at hand, and the potential solutions available. Just about every problem you face, with the possible exception of employee relations, every request that comes to you, has a monetary side to it.

Since you probably don't want to project that money is the only thing that matters to you, most of the mental calculations of "How much will this cost?" and "How will we cover this if I say 'Yes' to this person?" will be happening in your head while you are discussing the request. The cash register has to be working in the background of everything you say and do in this job. That's a tough skill to learn, and it's probably impossible to prepare for the pressure it will add to your administrative position.

Dealing on a Daily Basis

It is, of course, possible to always check the books before giving an answer. In reality, though, this will double the number of meetings or conversations you will have with people. If you always have to get back to someone before giving approval or denying that approval, you will quickly find yourself in an impossible position. First, you won't have time to analyze the long-range budgetary effect of every little expenditure. Second, you won't have time to discuss the same thing twice. If the answer is "yes," the conversation will be admittedly brief; but if the answer is "no," you will probably need to listen to the rationale for approving the request all over again. Who has time for that? Detailed monitoring of the budget every step of the way is probably not feasible.

Alternatively, a lot of leaders find themselves making most of their decisions on the spot, especially the small ticket items. Then, you have to develop your ability to assess all the ramifications of your decision right there while you're talking to that person. If you have a financial advisor or manager working with you, you may want to drag him/her into the meeting as soon as you see dollar signs. The point is, you will probably spend the money on all the small stuff day to day, and then look over your own shoulder on a monthly or quarterly basis to see how you're doing. One university vice president for finance joked that on a daily basis he would go in to see the President at 5:00 and say, "OK, how much did today cost me?"

He knew that whatever appointments the leader had had that day would mean promises and permissions that would cost "X" amount of bucks; this financial manager tried to keep up with the damages on a day-to-day basis. But that was his job.

You probably won't be that lucky—to have a person dedicated to the task of money management. Most arts organizations have tight enough budgets that the chief executive is the person who manages the finances. This is actually a blessing in disguise, because whoever controls the money, is really the person who controls the decision-making. Hopefully, you will have someone to actually do the payroll, handle purchasing, and generate all the paper work for tracking the income and expenditures, but you are the guy who makes the decisions. You are the person who says "yes" or "no." You are the one who oversees the whole operation, sets the priorities, implements the vision. So, you are the one spending the money, the one actually responsible for the fiscal health of the organization. The ultimate responsibility for delivering a balanced budget is yours.

Monitoring the Budget

Throughout this process, you need to be monitoring the books. This may happen quarterly or monthly or even weekly, but you need to see how things are going, in order to make corrections, before it's too late. If you are spending more money in a given area than you have budgeted, you have only a few options: pull money away from some other area that is under budget to cover this need; slow down the spending in this problem area, so you will wind up on target by the end of the year; or find a way to bring in more money to augment your allocation. It is unthinkable to go through the year without some routine monitoring system. Not knowing where things stand is like playing Russian Roulette. Assuming that your over spending in one category will be covered by under spending somewhere else is wishful thinking, bordering on fantasy. In a tightly budgeted operation, which most arts organizations are, there is never enough elbowroom to cover a significant overage. When you see one shaping up, look for a means to cover it now. Whatever book-keeping method your organization uses, even if it is a computerized budgeting system that looks rather intimidating, the bottom line is pretty simple: you need to know how much is budgeted in each area, how much you have already spent (or committed to spend), and how much is left for the rest of the year. Whether or not you want to review every line item is up to you. If you have an experienced financial person keeping the books, you won't need to do this. If you are breaking in a new employee, or if you are developing a new budgeting system, you may need to make certain (s)he is not making costly errors, or entering things into the wrong categories—skewing the picture you are reviewing. Of utmost importance, you have to be able to count on the data being correct. Once you are sure that it is, you need only look at the summaries, and then make decisions to adjust your spending patterns.

Limiting the Number of People Who Can Authorize Expenditures

Perhaps yours is a highly complex operation in which a lot of people are making decisions. Beware! Every time you delegate decision-making, you have to find a way to deal with the financial fall-out. For any time a person is able to make a decision without having to worry about what it costs, you have trouble. Ideally, everyone making decisions should have to be responsible for that portion of the budget. The problem with this approach is that you then lose the ability to take up the slack—that is, if a certain area costs less than anticipated, the person in charge of that portion of the budget will probably find a way to spend the entire allocation any way. After all, it's his/her money. As soon as you say, "Don't spend more than 'X', you have committed 'X' amount of big ones to the cause. Forget about collecting any change. You won't.

Another problem is that not everyone is good at managing money. You may have a theater director who is fantastic in putting together a wonderful production, but who lacks the skill of tracking the costs. Well, somebody has to do it, or you will have magnificent shows that sink your ship. If you don't have time to meet with him/her every time a decision is made to buy or rent or make such-and-so for the set, then somebody has to be put in charge of managing the operating budget for the theater program. The same holds true for the orchestral program, the playwrighting option, the multi-media art studio, etc.

If you are unsure of the financial abilities of the people running these programs, don't give them the whole budget for their activities. Hold some back for emergencies or for screw-ups. If you have allocated $25,000 for opera, tell the person managing the money that (s)he has $20,000. Hold onto the extra $5,000. If you have budgeted carefully, they'll need that additional $5,000. With you holding it, the director will have to come to you for the optional stuff, and you get to decide whether or not the soprano really needs a crown of jewels to make the production a success. Remember, the power to make decisions goes hand in hand with the control of the finances. (If you have somebody in charge who doesn't have a clue when (s)he's over or under the budget, and if you have too many other things to worry about, you will be forced to get rid of this person or put some other watch dog over the whole mess.)

Holding on to a contingency amount is also a good solution to the problem of over-allocating funds in any one area. When the budgeting is designed to be just a little less than is probably needed in a given spot, the person making the spending decisions will have to ask you for permission to do anything that is out of the ordinary or optional. This way, you maintain a portion of financial control over all the operations, without having to deal with the nit-picking details of each one; but you have to decide if you really want to squeeze people that tightly. Having absolutely no financial elbowroom can be demoralizing, and may make the whole business of managing that area too stressful. Once you know your people, you will be able to decide how much financial responsibility each of them can effectively handle. Obviously, anyone with a history of mismanaging funds needs to be reined in and kept on a short leash until there is evidence (s)he can handle some additional slack.

Supporting Artistic Activity

All of this discussion falls flat on its face when we begin to consider artistic license. That is, how can you possibly provide for artistic exploration when you have to put a price tag on every aspect of the process? This is the central problem in financial management for the leader of the arts unit. If the painter has to worry about the cost of choosing red instead of yellow, where does that leave the creative process? If the conductor has to select repertoire according to the cost of renting or buying the parts, where does that put the needs of the players or the aesthetics of the ensemble? As the leader of this arts organization, you cannot let it all come down to a battle between aesthetics and money. If you don't have the basic funding needed to produce the quality of artistic product to which your organization is committed, then you are ostensibly out of business. Whether your mission is an educational one or a public presentational one, your primary budgetary allocations need to be focused on the support of your primary mission. This is where the corners cannot be cut.

It may be nice to have a computerized database of your mailing list, but when push comes to shove, that is less important than the quality of the artistic work you are producing. So, decisions have to be made, priorities have to be set, and you may have some people who you deliberately don't want worrying about money. Whoever runs your choral program should not have to worry about what the music costs when choosing repertoire; however, it is certainly necessary to talk money when (s)he decides to take the choir to Europe. Wherever aesthetics enter into the picture, it is your job to make sure the quality of the art is supported first and foremost. Beyond that, you can pinch pennies (or hundred dollar bills) wherever you are able.

Now, some decisions will impact the bottom line so dramatically, that you do have to step in. You have to deal with the reality that some forms of art may be beyond the scope of your mission. For example, you may not be able to troop a bunch of live elephants into your tiny theater; if opera "X" requires live elephants, it is probably not a good choice for your next season. Everyone in the arts organization does need to keep their artistic appetites within the overall scope of the arts organization, and it's your job to see that that is done.

Bottom-Line Budgeting

Most budgeting processes permit a lot of flexibility. If, by the end of the fiscal year, your bottom line has been preserved, and your total expenses have stayed within the allocated budget, then it may not matter how you had to juggle the funds to make it work. Ideally, you will have the power and the flexibility to move money not needed in one area to another, where spending ran higher than expected. But, this is not always the case.

If you have no flexibility to shift money allocated from one place to another, then you are going to need some discretionary money to cover unexpected expenses. Sometimes, this can come from ticket sales for public concerts, shows, and exhibitions. Other times, it can be brought in through targeted fund raising. Perhaps, the sale of concert tapes or artwork created "in house" can provide some extra resources. Occasionally, a major gift will be donated that pumps a significant amount of money into the arts program, helping to balance the budget for many years to come. Whatever the source, money that can be used in a discretionary way, wherever it is needed, is just about essential in an arts unit, where unpredictable costs cannot be avoided.

In an academic environment, financial management is particularly tough. Here, you do not usually have the option of rolling over extra funds you may have saved from a good year. This money is typically used to cover problems in other units by the central administration. However, it is not uncommon for an individual program to be forced to carry its deficits over to the following fiscal year. Obviously, the flexibility then is only working in one direction. If, in addition, the development activities are centralized, and an individual unit like yours is not permitted to raise funds solely for its own use, then you are really in a jam.

The only way to ensure staying within your budget is to have more money than you actually need—good luck on that one. This dilemma requires great creativity on the part of the leader. If that person happens to be you, find a way to build yourself a discretionary fund.

You must. Otherwise, you will have no elbowroom. Without a good chunk of flexibility in your financial management process, you will have no real space to make decisions or to implement change. In this powerless situation, you will be reduced to merely a manager, not a leader.

Summarizing:

So, in summary, financial management is going to include:

- setting a realistic budget, allocating portions of this overall budget to individual areas according to the mission of your institution and your vision for its future direction;

- monitoring expenditures on a regular basis, using real data to show where you actually are today in each budget area, as compared to where you need to be by the end of the fiscal year;

- keeping a sharp eye on others in the organization with financial management responsibilities, making sure they are competent and their operations are financially solvent;

- making all decisions within the framework of the organization's total financial resources, setting priorities according to what is possible, not just what is desirable on an individual basis;

- finding creative solutions to inescapable budgetary problems. If all you do is wring your hands and pull your hair when you start running out of money, you will soon run out of hands and hair. Don't just sit there, do something.

The phone rang. It was Rodney from the Development Office. "Marilyn, I have some good news and some bad news." (Don't you hate people who say things like that?) "OK, Rodney, give me the bad news first." "Well, we just received word that Mrs. Anonymous, an 82-year-old alumna of our university, was murdered last night in her nursing home." "Omigod, that's horrible! What's the good news?" "She left her entire estate to the Music Department." The only thing I could think of to say was, "Rodney, I didn't do it!"

DEALING WITH LIMITED RESOURCES

No, I do not recommend violence. Occasionally a major bequest comes in that can make a tremendous difference in your arts organization and its limited resources. I know of at least one arts leader who jokingly claims they need a few deaths every year just to keep their organization solvent. Imagine what that does to your head. The point is, such events cannot be predicted, and you certainly can't count on them to happen. When they do, you should be prepared to target the money toward areas of greatest concern. A major bequest can really make a difference.

Sometimes, the best use of such funds is to increase the endowment that supports your arts organization, if you have one. The advantage of this decision is that it makes the interest from the investment available for the operation of your arts unit in perpetuity. The greater the endowment supporting your institution, the more secure it will be to weather the tough times ahead; but there may be another more compelling need for immediate financial help. Perhaps, the organization has a long-standing deficit that could be eliminated. A deficit hanging overhead can be a debilitating problem, constraining every new initiative that is proposed, even those that could make a considerable difference in the future of the organization. Retiring this debt might be your top priority. Or, perhaps there is a building project on the drawing board that could make a huge difference in the day-to-day operation of your arts unit. A sudden burst of funding might get this project off the ground. Determining the greatest current needs for the long-range health of your arts organization should be the core of your strategic planning process. With these institutional priorities set, you are ready for those unexpected gifts, whenever and wherever they happen.

Implementing New Initiatives

When you don't have what you need to move ahead with a new initiative, you have only two choices: to give up until you can get the resources, or to find a way to do it without the resources. The problem with the first approach is that you will have enormous difficulty getting the resources from anyone before you demonstrate that you really can't live without them. It is the easiest thing in the world to say "No" to a new initiative. If your arts unit has lived this long without doing "X," then why do you suddenly have to do it now?

On the other hand, if this new initiative is that important to your organization, and if you believe strongly enough that it is part of your mission to move forward on this project, then figure out how to get started without the resources. For example, let's say you have determined that your vocal performance majors have to do one or two operas a year in order to gain the practical experience needed to prepare them for successful careers, but you have no theater suitable for the production of an opera. There is no way you will ever convince the administration they should build an opera house. Would you build an opera house for a department that has been surviving without doing fully-staged operas for the past zillion years? Of course you wouldn't. Neither will anyone else.

But you are convinced it is vitally important to your arts unit to do one or two operas a year. Well, start with the goal and work backwards. The real goal is to give the students the needed educational experience; so, do it. Forget the fancy costumes; forget the expensive sets; forget the special lighting; forget the orchestra. Start with a piano and a stage and some very creative teachers. Add the talented students, and voila! You have an opera. (Of course, it's not that easy, but you get the point.) If you do small operas in small spaces with minimal props and costumes, the students will still learn the roles. Having done this, you can build up to the point where the excellence of the program demands more support. Try doing your operas in a neighborhood school or church or theater. You can probably sell enough tickets to rent the space. Eventually, you just may be able to make a case for the resources needed to support your own opera space. If not, well, it may be even better for everyone involved to take opera out into the community.

Diverting Other Funds

When the priorities in your organization have shifted, and new needs have arisen, it is time to restructure the spending patterns of the organization. Your first step should be backwards. Step back and assess the overall picture. Where are the available funds presently being allocated? What can you afford to prune or eliminate altogether? Are there ineffective artists who could be retired or phased out? Are there any programs that have outlived their usefulness? Are there activities that have become merely a habit? Is there some overlap in staff responsibilities? Can positions be combined or eliminated? Could some activities be offered every two years instead of annually? Does anyone have an assistant who can be shared with someone else?

While tightening the institution's belt may not be the most attractive option available, it may be the most sensible. Organizations have a tendency to expand over time; without occasional housekeeping, these tentacles of growth can become inconsistent and illogical. It's always tough to take something back. For example, maybe a faculty member goes on a semester's sabbatical. You hire a part-time person to cover some of her teaching responsibilities, while colleagues cover the rest. When the regular faculty returns, she makes a convincing plea to keep the part-time person, just until the new creative project begun on sabbatical is completed. Professor Part-Time becomes a valued member of the team, and no further thought is given to this "temporary" arrangement. Professor Sabbatical has long since happily adjusted to her lighter teaching load.

Another example: Professor Perfection is responsible for a certain aspect of the program. He finds the students are entering the program with vastly different levels of preparation. He divides the group into two sub-groups, so he can more effectively meet their needs. You certainly support this move; after all, Professor Perfection is on a full-time salary, so the only cost is in his own time. But gradually, he divides the classes into smaller and smaller groups—always with the best of intentions—to teach them more effectively. Eventually, there are not enough hours in the day to teach all these mini groups, and Professor Perfection comes to you with a plea for an assistant. You happen to have a graduate student who needs an assignment and who has some skill in this area. Two years later, when that graduate student is about to don cap and gown, Professor Perfection pleads the case that he can't live without his assistant. Since this part of the program is showing excellent results, you find a way to pay the graduating student a small stipend to stay on—"temporarily," of course.

Professor Sick has open-heart surgery. You hire somebody to "temporarily" take her place. When she returns, she needs to take it a bit easier, so you keep the somebody you hired until Professor Sick is on her feet again. She never seems to be quite well enough to ratchet her teaching load back up to where it had been before the operation. The Temporary Somebody stays on. Temporary solutions tend to become permanent solutions. Why? Because you never have quite enough time to fix the things that do not appear to be broken. And because it's just too hard to take something away, something that may be important to another person in the organization. Besides, who in their right mind would create problems that currently don't exist? Especially when there are so many other problems on the plate already.

When resources are insufficient to fulfill the ever-evolving mission of the institution, there is a real incentive to look for these types of optional costs. If the need is compelling enough, it may be time to prune back a bit and reallocate the dollars saved to the area(s) in need of additional funding.

Addressing the Problem

Let's say you have tried all the available approaches to "making do" with what you have, and you simply need more money. How do you expand the given resources of your arts unit? Barring an unexpected windfall from one of your elder donors, all new sources of income probably require your leadership, fund-raising skill, and determination to solve the problem.

The menu of options is not that extensive:

- Lobby for more support internally. If your arts unit is part of a larger educational institution, try to make a case for an increase in your allocation.

- Apply for any funds that may exist for special projects, new initiatives, whatever.

- Attempt to raise more money through ongoing artistic activities. If you aren't already charging admission to public events, you may have to do this. If you are selling tickets, try raising the prices slightly or increase your efforts to sell pre-season subscriptions.

- Seek help from your board.

- Approach a major donor for funding to meet a specific need.

- Draft a proposal to a foundation, corporation, or government supported arts council.

- Launch a major fund-raising campaign.

Increasing Your Internal Allocation

Let's look at the internal picture first. If you are running a totally independent arts organization, you may want to skip this discussion. For better or for worse, you probably have no internal allocation of funds to operate your arts unit. If you have an established endowment that covers even part of your annual expenses, then this topic may be pertinent. There just might be some elbowroom in changing the percentage of the interest on this endowment that you can draw each year for your operating costs.

Arts programs in higher education are typically part of a larger college, university, or school. If you lead one of these programs, most, if not all, of your operating costs are covered by funds allocated to your unit annually. Somebody is in charge of this process, just as somebody makes the decision as to how much can be drawn annually from an endowment. Whoever this person is, be it the President of your institution, the Provost, the Vice President for Finances, the Chairman of the Board, this is the person who has to understand the needs of your arts unit. Even in systems that appear to be locked in bureaucracy, there is a human being who decides how money should be allocated to the various programs. There may be iron-clad policies on budgetary allocations; but policies are set by people, and these same policies are changed or modified by people. Moreover, there is always room for interpretation in any policy. The bottom line: somebody makes the ultimate decision as to who gets what.

If this person truly believes that your arts program is vitally important to the overall health, visibility, and stature of the institution as a whole, then the Financial Decision Maker will do whatever possible to channel the necessary resources toward that program. If the arts are viewed as fluff, or mere icing on the cake, there will be no compelling need to support them. One of the most important roles of the arts leader is to serve as chief advocate for the arts, and much of this advocacy work should be focused internally. (A more complete discussion of Advocating for the Arts appears in the last section of this book.) Suffice it to say here that there may be a significant amount of arts advocacy work needed at home, in your own back yard.

There could be several major impediments in your path toward gaining additional resources.

- First, everyone else in the institution may need more, too. If so, the entire place will be stretched tighter than a well-tuned timpani. When there is no more, there is no more. Granted, there could be more for your unit if somebody else got less. Here we are again, talking about priorities. Somebody up there is deciding who should get what. Stopping just short of advising you to take revolver in hand, you may still be able to get a bigger slice of the pie. By making the value of your arts unit known to all the right people, it is always possible that there are some discretionary funds somewhere that can be used to help your program with legitimate and urgent funding needs—without taking food from the mouths of your colleagues.

- Second, your immediate boss may sit between you and the Financial Decision Maker. If so, you will need to be highly sensitive to issues of hierarchy. If your boss is not the aggressive type, and you are, the problem becomes even more acute. You cannot go over the head of a supervisor without creating havoc. Unless your boss is willing to take up the mantle with you or for you, or unless this person gives you permission to move on up the ladder in your quest for additional support, you are stuck. Although you are not free to go ask for resources, you are free to bring your arts unit to everyone's attention through just plain quality. The arts are among the most visible units in the educational environment. Make sure the people at the top of the institution see and hear the excellence of your program. This will pave the way for your boss to help you get the resources you need to maintain that quality and to raise it even higher.

- Third, your institution may have a long tradition of focusing on other areas. It is incredibly difficult, maybe even impossible (although I don't personally believe in that word) to change the balance of power in an organization. If the leaders are inclined to support the status quo, you just may have an intractable problem.

Educational leaders need to know that the arts are relatively expensive units to house. Any institution that operates with a false sense of equity, that is, with the belief that all units need to be treated equally, will fail to recognize the uniqueness of the performing and exhibition aspects of the arts programs. As you well know, the arts have the ability to enhance the institution both internally and well beyond, but international visibility can only be achieved through international activities—and these cost money—big time.

Your ability to obtain needed resources from within your own institution will prove to be one of the key ingredients in your success as an arts leader. This is not the only place to derive support for your arts area, but it is certainly one you cannot afford to ignore. All of your dealings with colleagues and with administrative leaders in your organization should be handled carefully, with this over-arching principle in mind. In the meantime, let's go look for some more money elsewhere.

RAISING MONEY

Identifying your Donors

The crux of the problem with fund raising for an arts program in academia is that the alumni are seldom rich. Now, that isn't the only problem, but it's a big one. When one considers the possible sources of financial support for arts programs in an educational environment, the list is really quite short: alumni, friends, foundations, corporations, government, and God. (That last one is on the list to cover gifts that only occur after a person dies, the timing of which is usually an act of God, not a matter of personal choice.)

As already stated, arts alumni are not usually the wealthiest group in the world. Happy? Yes. Fulfilled? Probably. But rich? Not likely. Now, there are notable exceptions to this rule of thumb: people who marry well, people who move out of the arts as a profession, but still love it and support it, and people who actually do make good money in this most unlikely of livelihoods. After all, it is possible to make big money in movies and television—even occasionally as a visual artist or performing musician, but the numbers are few and far between. So, any fund-raising campaign targeted to arts alumni better be modest in its expectations or compelling in its appeal to the masses.

As for the second category, friends, those who are well endowed and most likely to support the arts, are a wonderful group of individuals who are unfortunately known by every arts organization in the community—make that the state, or perhaps the universe.

Arts benefactors are scooped up by symphony orchestras, opera companies, ballet companies, theaters, museums, you name it, faster than it takes to say "Gimme." And these organizations usually have the focus and the staff and the glitter to stage public events that bring glamour and recognition to their major donors. People can actually get a lot of positive feedback for their support of the arts in the community. As a result, major donors to arts organizations usually read like a "Who's Who" of the city of "Whatever."

Where do arts educational units fit in? Far too often, they don't. The impression people have of colleges and universities is that it is their responsibility to support their own arts programs, whereas the community symphony and opera and ballet companies are totally dependent upon public and private support for their very existence. Even when you have the names of the arts lovers in your city, they are most likely tapped out through giving to the independent arts organizations in the community. If you happen to be leading one of these independent arts groups, meeting all the "right" people is one of your most important activities.

Then there are the foundations. Here, with the right level of research, money can be found. But seldom does the arts unit have its own staff to do the research or the proposal writing or the personal follow-up needed to get the big bucks. (Most foundations, which support the arts, do not, by the way, give big bucks.) In most institutions, the Development Office is centralized for the entire organization, and probably has its sights set on larger capacity sources. This makes it difficult for the arts unit to become a fund-raising priority.

Corporate giving is complex, but nonetheless unlikely to bail out an arts unit in financial trouble. Corporate support for educational institutions usually comes in the form of large research grants, putting it in the same category as the government. The corporation or the government agency sponsors the research, but they jolly well better get something back for their efforts. I don't know about you, but I find it difficult to envision the Department of Defense needing an art department to research anything worthy of a few million big ones. Likewise with the chemical company, the aluminum industry, or a score of other potential partners in education.

Now, we are pretty well getting down to the level of the Salvation Army. Yes, there is the National Endowment for the Arts, but that and state-supported arts foundations are primarily designed to help the individual artist. Larger support can be gained for special projects, though, and with a lot of initiative and the right set of goals, it is possible to tap into government-supported agencies to some advantage. One note of caution here: beware the opportunity to raise money for projects you don't want to do. There may be a lot of money in researching zithers, for example, but your music school just may not have a gut-level passion for the zither repertoire.

The primary problem is that the needs of the arts program are often too specialized to fit into a general university or college fund-raising campaign, yet we really don't have a good target toward which we can shoot for our own resources. The picture for the independent school of music or school of art or drama may be quite a bit brighter, since they may have a staff dedicated to fund-raising solely for their own purposes, and they can often make a stronger case for needing the public support to survive; but it still isn't easy.

So, where does that leave the rest of us? Probably feeling like a poor stepchild of the institution to which we belong. There are solutions, which we need to explore. First, let's take a closer look at the process. Unless you've raised money before, even the thought of asking someone for a donation can cause your hair to stand on end. No need. It isn't all that difficult; you just need to have some courage and a little confidence, even if you feel you know nothing at all about fund-raising.

Knowing How to do It

Now, you do know something about development. Development is just selling, and you know more about the product you are selling than any one else in the world—including the professional fund-raisers. You are going to attempt to sell your arts program to people with discretionary money and an interest in supporting the arts. It's just a matter of matching the right project to the right donor.

You are absolutely the ideal person to do the selling, because, as the arts executive, you know first hand what your arts unit really needs; you know the strengths of your program and the people in it; and above all, you care deeply about the future of your arts institution. Therefore, you have the passion to convince people that this is the perfect place for their support. I know, it takes courage to dive into fund raising, and it is hard to ask people for money; but it isn't all that hard to talk about what your arts unit needs to move forward into the twenty-first century. Spend some time thinking about this. What are your roadblocks to success? What is it that prevents your arts program from being twice as excellent as it is now? What would it take to remove these roadblocks?

Sit down and make a wish list. Shoot high. Assume money is no object. Then, take your list and divide it into the following categories: programming needs, buildings and equipment, and people. The reason you need to sort these things on your wish list is because different people like to give money for specific purposes. Some lean towards making a long-term commitment that would endow a major component of the arts organization. Others prefer to give a one-time gift with no guarantees of future support. Many people like to be able to see what they bought; specific equipment like computers, or pianos, or easels, or even a part of a building are just the right projects for these folks. Whatever the preference, you probably have a need that matches every style of giving. Identify these needs, so that you are ready when opportunity knocks.

Whatever role you are asked to play in the fund-raising business, there are some things you will need from the people who specialize in this work:

- you will need somebody to research the donor base, so you are not wasting your time and energy approaching people with insufficient funds or with insufficient interest in the field of the arts;

- you will need somebody to tell you what the things on your wish list cost;

- and you will need somebody to explain your institution's guidelines on fund-raising. Who are you permitted to approach for support? How much money does someone have to donate to set up an endowment for your program to receive, say, $1,000 a year? Things like that. There aren't many of these. Then, you are ready. You have the product; you have the passion to sell that product; and you have the prospective buyer. Go for it!

Making the Ask

Even if you have done all your homework, and you are absolutely certain the person you are about to ask for support has the means to give it to you and the desire to support your arts area, even then, it is tough to actually do it—to go ask for the money. But go you must. Don't try to duck by writing them a letter or calling them on the phone. It is a whole lot easier to say "No" on the phone, and incredibly easy just to pitch a written request into the nearest trashcan. So, like it or not, you need to summon up the courage to look them in the eye and ask for the gift. After all, the worst that can happen is they say, "No."

Investing your Time in the Process

There have to be some real payoffs to justify the time it takes to pursue fund-raising. This is a full-time job, and you already have one of those. Whatever role you choose to play in this activity, your time has to be optimized. Let's assume you are called upon to personally sell your arts organization to a potential donor. This is probably the most effective use of your leadership position. But, as stated above, somebody needs to invest the time in researching potential donors, laying the groundwork, and following through with the management of the gift. If you don't have somebody whose job it is to do all of this, you have a major obstacle in your fund-raising path, because you will not have enough time to do it right.

You can help a lot in keeping donors happy after they have signed on to support your program. This, too, takes time, but there are a lot of ways to incorporate this attention into your regular business activities. Personal invitations to visit your arts unit can center around a show, exhibition, or concert you are already presenting to the public. Choice seats, dinner beforehand, public recognition at the event—all of these gestures of appreciation will help make the donors feel good about their gifts. A private tour of facilities, which they helped build or improve, can be handled rather easily by you or a member of your staff. Casual introductions to your key artists can be achieved just while walking through the building. Special events in their honor can be events you would do anyway. The extra time spent on these particular guests will be modest compared to the time it would take to go visit them. The bonus is that the donors gain a sense of belonging to the institution, which is very effective in holding on to their support.

Other gestures of friendship can be incorporated with even less time and effort: free season passes to all your artistic events can be mailed to major donors at the start of the year; a newsletter can be sent to contributors, just to keep them informed; complimentary recordings or posters from upcoming exhibits might be sent as gifts for the holidays or in the middle of the year, whenever they are produced. Major announcements of new programs or exciting guest artists or even new personnel can be mailed to donors as well as to the media—anything to keep them feeling they are a part of the arts organization they support. It doesn't take a lot of time to do any of these things, and the results will greatly reward your effort.

If someone supports a special scholarship in your program, whenever possible, make sure that donor knows something about the person who received it. At a minimum, send a letter of thanks with a brief description of the student(s) who are being helped by their contribution. A personal letter of thanks from the recipient is an even better way to express appreciation. Or, if the donor can come to visit, it is ideal to arrange a personal meeting with the student(s) and/or artist(s) who are benefiting from his/her generosity. Encourage recipients to invite their donors to special performances and/or exhibits of their work. Even if the person is out of town, the invitation and perhaps a recording or a poster of the event will be deeply appreciated and will definitely help connect the individual to the arts institution.

This process is not without its risks, especially when dealing with young people.

> *I once set up a luncheon for a major donor to meet the student who was receiving scholarship support from his generous gift. The donor had to drive a couple of hours to get to campus, but was happy to do so to meet "his" student. Well, the student never showed up. Major donor and I had a delightful lunch, thank heavens, and he took the snafu in stride; but he was clearly disappointed not to meet Jerry. (Follow-up: "Gee, I'm really sorry, Dr. Thomas, but something came up and I just couldn't get there.")*

> *On a happier note, Rosalie had received some much-needed financial assistance from a major donor. Once again, a lunch was planned to meet the gentleman and his wife. Only this time, Rosalie was there with a spectacular bouquet of flowers for Mrs. Major Donor. The student was so gracious and appreciative, the couple absolutely fell in love with her, and are still thanking me for giving them the opportunity to help this young lady. Yes, they thanked me for enabling them to donate $1,000. Now, that's more like it!*

People who contribute to a program usually have a specific interest in that particular type of activity. They want to know that their support is making a difference. Find ways to tell them and to show them that it is.

Developing a Written Proposal

When your funding source is a foundation or a corporation or arts council, there is an equally strong need to follow through. In this case, the mechanism for doing so is ordinarily built right into the process of gaining the support. Here, the funding process is a much more formalized one, and following all the procedures to the letter is vitally important. First, the proposal.

No matter where you are going in your attempt to raise money, if a written proposal is suggested, there will probably be guidelines for submitting this proposal. If you don't have these, you need to contact somebody in the organization to get the necessary information. Preliminary research entails finding out exactly what type of projects or activities this organization is interested in funding. Don't even consider sending them a proposal that lies outside their realm of interest. If you have a good fit, then you need to know who in the organization receives such proposals and in what format. Do they prefer an introductory letter and a brief description of the project first? Or do they accept full-blown proposals at the outset? Remember, if you approach them from the wrong direction, your request won't even make it into the pile.

A typical proposal for funding includes a compelling description of the project with a carefully worded explanation of the need for this activity, who will benefit from it, what long-term (and short-term) impact it will have; a detailed projected budget indicating the portion of the expenses you will be able to handle internally, plus any additional sources of support already promised or likely to be received; and finally, some supportive materials illustrating your institution's ability to carry out this project effectively.

Clarity and concise descriptions are essential. The person to whom you are sending your proposal will probably be wading through a mountain of these requests. You want yours to be compelling; you also want it to be read in its entirety. Make it as brief as you can without losing any necessary information. Above all, follow their instructions. If they say they want a one-page summary, don't send them three pages. Use small margins. Shrink the type, if you have to. (Aren't computers great?)

Make sure your expenses are clearly displayed and easy to read. Don't try to hide the bottom line; that's the first thing they will look for. Make it absolutely clear how much support you are requesting from them, and what percentage of the total cost you are hoping to receive from them. Nearly everyone wants to know that the project they are about to support also has significant funding "in house." Try to put a number on the internal costs, even if these are being absorbed in your regular day-to-day budget. People who will work on this project have salaries; calculate the portion of their time that will be devoted to this activity. This is a real cost to your arts unit. Secretarial support, telephones, postage, even office support (lights, heating, desks, chairs) all have costs. Do your best to figure this out, or get some help from a proposal-writing expert.

Which leads me to one final bit of advice: if this is the first time you've been involved in writing a proposal, get some help from someone who has done it before and has actually succeeded in getting funded. It's not that hard, but doing it right is essential. Proposals have been rejected for even tiny diversions from a funding agency's specified format.

Following Up on Your Proposal

Sometimes you are asked to make a face-to-face presentation of your proposal to the granting agency, as well as the written version. This is a great opportunity to "sell" your project.

Pittsburgh's Allegheny Regional Asset District (ARAD) is a government-sponsored agency that allocates money to parks, libraries, museums, and independent arts organizations from a 1% tax collected by the city. In addition to a complex written proposal, organizations applying for ARAD support must make a three-minute public presentation of their proposal.

River City Brass Band was in desperate need of a computerized box office system. This professional brass band presents a series of concerts each year in seven different venues, selling season subscriptions for each site, as well as individual tickets to single concerts, which can be purchased clear up to the time of the event, at the door.

Craig, the band's Box Office Manager, kept track of all of the seats in the seven halls by hand, with a complex color-coded system applied to graphic pictures of the seating charts of each hall. Keeping track of seats available in each venue was a nightmare of detailed record keeping. All of this could now be handled automatically by the slick new computerized box office systems on the market, but they were very expensive— way out of reach of this independent arts organization.

So, a proposal to ARAD was assembled and submitted. The evening of the public presentations, as Executive Director of the RCBB, I had to make the three-minute plea for support, along with the band's Artistic Director, Denis Colwell. Waiting our turn, we heard representatives of group after group drone on about their organizations' needs—every three minutes, a new pitch. It was gruesome, and this was the third evening the members of the ARAD Board had to sit through these presentations.

When our turn came, we were prepared. With just a few words of introduction, identifying our need for an automated box office system, Denis and I produced our graphic. We had taped together all of Craig's hand written charts, fastidiously colored in various hues to depict which seats were filled in each hall with what type of ticket-holder. As Denis and I separated to reveal our banner of charts, they spread clear across the entire room. Everyone on the Board dissolved in laughter. So did the rest of the representatives in the room, awaiting their turn to present their projects. River City Brass Band got its new box office system.

Waiting for the final decision on a grant proposal can be really stressful. With a little work, you will probably be able to find out when a decision on your proposal can be expected. Submission deadlines are ordinarily published with the materials describing the funding opportunity, and with this usually comes an indication of how long it will take for decisions to be reached. If this information is not provided, there is usually a phone number to call with questions.

It is perfectly acceptable to phone and ask when a decision will be made on your submission. It is also reasonable to make a follow-up call a month or so beyond this date, if you have not yet heard. You may want to ask at this time if any additional materials are needed to facilitate the process. (That's a polite way to say, "What's the hold-up?")

When you finally receive word of the decision, if it is positive, dash off a brief letter of appreciation, acknowledging the receipt of their letter and/or check. Do read carefully any requirements for follow-up procedures. There are often progress reports that need to be filed or final reports, providing information about the results of the project. Whatever is needed must be done promptly and well, that is, if you ever wish to submit another proposal to this agency.

If, on the other hand, your proposal is rejected, it is sometimes possible to get some feedback on the reasons. Provided you haven't already overdone it on the phone calls, you might try contacting the agency to request help for future submissions to their agency. Be particularly polite and understanding of their inability to fund everything that comes down the road, and express your appreciation for the time spent on your proposal. It never hurts to send the agency a follow-up letter of thanks for their consideration. Don't give up! Fund-raising, like nearly everything else, is a learning process. There may be some major support just around the corner waiting for your next proposal.

Planning a Major Campaign

When you need big money, you may have to go to a lot of places to get it. Now, you are talking about a major fund-raising campaign; you are also talking about major organization, major staff, major creativity, major fund-raising talent, and major time. If you don't have all of the above, forget it. If you do, read on.

"The President's Office–on line 72." As I picked up the phone, I braced for the worst. "Dr. Thomas, the legal office feels your contract with Steinway should be signed by the

*Department, not the University. Go ahead and put it through
with your signature and probably the head of the local piano
dealership. The President will be glad to attend the ceremony
kicking off the fund-raising campaign tomorrow night, and
would be happy to meet the President of Steinway."*

*As I muttered my appreciation, the realization slowly spread
that I was literally on my own. I was about to go in front of
a couple thousand people and announce our plan to replace
all sixty of our piano inventory with new Steinway pianos.
We were setting out to raise over $600,000 from an alumni
base that historically donated less than $35,000 a year. I was
about to make a public fool of myself.*

*I contemplated the insanity of this venture, which a week ago
had seemed like the only possible solution to the massive
problem of so many worn-out instruments. I heard the phone
ring again. My secretary stepped into the office and said with
eyes wider than usual, "KDKA television is on line 73; they
want to come to campus to do some footage of the practice
rooms for the 6:00 news. Apparently, Steinway called them
and told them their deal with us is the biggest institutional
acquisition in the history of Steinway." My head hit the desk
for just a minute before reaching for the phone.*

It is important to state at the outset, that when you are heading an arts
program which is part of a larger educational structure—a college,
university, arts institute, etc.—you may be limited in your freedom
to launch a fund-raising campaign specifically for the benefit of your
part of the institution. Generally, development efforts are centralized,
so that people within the organization do not compete against one
another for the same dollars. An institution can usually maximize its
effectiveness in raising large donations by consolidating its efforts
into a single well-planned campaign.

However, on occasion there are specific needs in a single department
that lend themselves to targeted fund-raising; perhaps the alumni
of a given arts program are more likely to support the institution

through a carefully focused project that will have a direct impact on the educational unit that prepared them for the profession. When a subset of the overall donor pool is relatively untapped—that is, not yet participating in annual giving programs for the institution—a specific campaign may be just the trigger that is needed to get them involved.

In such a case, it is possible to break all the rules of fund-raising by targeting a lot of people to give a modest amount, instead of the tried and true method of courting a few people to give a ton. In the Piano Project, cited above, music alumni were given the option of buying an entire instrument, with a choice of an upright for a practice room, a small grand piano for one of the teaching studios, a larger one for a classroom, or the granddaddy of them all—the concert grand for one of the recital halls. In order to encourage the not-so-wealthy donor, to make certain everyone realized a gift of any size was needed and appreciated, a person could buy a bench, a chord, an octave, or even a single key. With each piano having eighty-eight keys, and sixty new pianos needed, it was easy to see that everyone needed to contribute something!

A big fund-raising effort can be a lot of fun. When it succeeds, the satisfaction of achieving a huge goal is absolutely worth the effort involved, and the effort is enormous. Everything stated above about researching, soliciting, and nurturing major donors has to be multiplied by however many of those wonderful souls you manage to dig up. In addition, you will need to cast out the nets to large numbers of potential donors, at all levels of giving, and this, too, requires a lot of skillful planning and implementation.

But, we're getting ahead of ourselves. First, let's worry about the purpose of the campaign. After all, people are not going to be interested in writing a check for just anything you happen to decide your arts unit needs. The need has to be compelling. The persons being approached have to understand its importance to your arts organization. They have to care enough about you or your institution to want to help. Above all, they have to know their contribution will make a difference and that somebody will appreciate it. That's the stuff you have to tell them in your very first attempt to solicit their contribution.

The campaign needs a clear focus; and a title that captures the essence of that focus can be very helpful. After all, a major fund-raising campaign takes time. You will be writing about it, talking about it, and worrying about it for many months to come. You may as well have something to call it—the "catchier" the better. People in this television age are used to slick marketing. If you have access to media specialists, use them. You are into advertising here, whether you like it or not. An eye-catching flyer or brochure describing the campaign can make the whole effort appear more legitimate, and that's another concern. People have to know this is a serious project, that you have invested some significant time and effort into organizing it; otherwise, their money may be wasted. Do whatever you can to launch your fund-raising project in a professional manner.

Kicking Off the Campaign

Sometimes there is a silent phase of a fund-raising campaign before it is actually announced to the public. The purpose of this initial stage is to get some of the key supporters on board and to make certain there is a strong possibility that the fund-raising project will be supported. In other words, you may want to test the waters before you go public with this campaign, and it is always good to make sure you have a few key people committed to the cause. These early supporters should be major ones, so you can use their donations as leadership gifts—to inspire others to jump onto the bandwagon. Once the campaign has an overall plan, private visits to a few key donors can be extremely helpful in fine-tuning the project.

A steering committee is also a really helpful ingredient of a large fund-raising effort. This might be the board of directors for your arts unit or it could be an entirely new group of people, selected for their particular interest in the project and/or their stature in the field. Since the steering committee may be viewed as leaders of the campaign, it is desirable to have people who are highly visible and generally respected. They don't have to be famous, but if they are, it certainly won't hurt your project. Ideally, the steering committee will represent the various constituencies you expect to contact for support. The chair of this steering committee could be a huge help in coordinating and managing the campaign or might be just an honorary chair who adds stature to the cause by virtue of his/her name alone. If you opt to use a steering committee, their names should be listed on all correspondence and all written materials representing the campaign. After all, that's one of the reasons you have a steering committee; so, let them steer.

Which brings us to the announcement. The more dramatic, the better. Find an opportunity—an arts event, or a social occasion, anything that gathers a bunch of people together—to kick off your campaign with as much pizzazz as you can muster. If the goal is big enough, and if your organization has enough visibility, get the press there. This is another level of exposure to potential donors you won't want to pass up, if you can get it.

This is not the time to worry about whether or not you will succeed in raising the money you are setting out to raise. Go for it! You have to roll the dice and set the goal—high enough to be exciting, low enough to be achievable, big enough to actually serve the purpose for which you have started all of this in the first place. Publicly announcing the campaign, its purpose, the goal, and the length of time you will be working on the project is all necessary to get the message out to the people who may contribute. Granted, this is not an activity for the meek or timid. But, you know that already, don't you? If you have fireworks, light them. If you have a band, raise the baton. You have officially launched a public campaign to raise money; there's no turning back now.

Sending out the Mail Solicitation

Let's talk about the general mail solicitation effort. A letter is generally not enough to capture the attention of everyone you want to send you money. Try to come up with a glitzy-looking brochure that will reach out and grab their eyes and their wallets. I know, you probably don't have the talent to do that yourself; but talent can be hired, and it takes money to make money. (By the way, be prepared to spend at least some of the money you bring in to cover the expenses of this project; there will be expenses. You already spent some on the band and the fire works.)

The very first piece of mail someone receives needs to be the most complete. Once they know about the campaign, other letters can go out begging, cajoling, and seducing them into joining all those other people who have already contributed, preferably their friends and neighbors; better yet, their enemies and competitors. Hey, this is serious business we're in now. That first mailing should provide an easy way to respond. You may want to have a tear off section for their name, address, and phone number; you will need this information for the database you will be developing of your donor list. Including a self-addressed envelope for donations makes giving even easier.

If you have created various titles for different levels of giving, this, too, needs to be specified in this first mailing. Hopefully, there are some benefits to the donors for moving up the ladder of contributions. Make sure they know about these "perks," as well. In the Piano Project, we put engraved plaques on pianos recognizing the name(s) of the donors(s) of each instrument. We also put plaques on benches and posted lists of major donors (over $1,000) on the walls of the practice room wings. This, along with the publication of all donors' names in each of the concert and recital programs throughout the season, as well as a major cover story on the campaign in the annual alumni newsletter, kept the project visible and the donors well recognized—an important ingredient of any successful fund-raising venture.

Handling the Correspondence and the Money

It's going to take some work to identify the people to whom your solicitations will be mailed. Identifying prospects can be difficult, especially if you are a part of a larger educational institution; there may be restrictions on the people you are permitted to contact for your campaign. It is vitally important that you have a clear understanding of your donor base before beginning any major fund-raising drive.

Once you have selected the groups to be targeted, you can usually obtain mailing lists for these various constituencies. From the outset, you need to set up a separate database specifically for the purposes of this fund-raising campaign—for communicating with potential and with active donors.

Now that you have enticed them and convinced them to join your effort, you need to be ready to receive the money, acknowledge the gifts, and record the donations. This, too, takes a lot of time. A single staff person can probably handle this part of the process, provided (s)he is computer literate and has a chunk of release time from other responsibilities to do it. Wherever you went to gather mailing lists for your first solicitation, these lists need to be kept in your database for future record-keeping purposes. Anyone present at the special event, where the official announcement of the fund-raising campaign was made public, should also be included as a potential donor in your database. It should be clear from your records just who has received what mailing and any contributions they have made in response. Extreme care must be given to this process, so that donors can be acknowledged promptly and appropriately.

It is impossible to over stress the importance of keeping in touch with your donors. The viability of your fund-raising project depends upon establishing credibility and good faith in the overall operation. Timely correspondence with everyone involved in the campaign will keep people feeling good about the process and the cause to which they have chosen to contribute.

Utilizing Telemarketing

Whether or not you choose to enhance your campaign with telemarketing will depend to a large extent on the institution within which you are working. The primary disadvantage of this particular approach is that it can really make people mad. How many times have you been interrupted during dinner or while in the midst of an important activity by the telephone, only to find it was somebody asking for money? If you are the person doing the calling, how do you know when a phone call will be especially irritating to someone?

If you do hit them at the wrong time, you just may get an ear full of words you know are not in the dictionary.

So, why risk it? Because telemarketing works. That's why so many people use it. As stated before in this book, it really is harder to say "No" to someone in person, even on the phone, than it is to ignore a letter. People who have all good intentions of responding to your mail solicitation may forget to do so. A cheerful phone call may just be the tap on the shoulder they needed to move them toward their checkbook. Under the assumption you will gain more donors than you will lose in the process, let's take a closer look at the management of telemarketing.

Once again, good organization and careful preparation are the keys to success. It takes a lot of volunteers to make hundreds, perhaps thousands of phone calls in a timely manner. These volunteers need to be thoroughly trained. All callers need a clear understanding of the purpose of the campaign, pertinent background information on your arts unit, and the list of rewards for pledging at various levels. The callers also need enough understanding of the process to be able to field very specific questions about the campaign. They need to be trained to stay cool if the person they call blows up at them for some reason. Each caller must be an effective representative of your arts unit, as well as a skillful talker and a sympathetic listener.

Above all, it is essential to keep the big picture in mind. There are all sorts of people out there. If one or two react negatively to the calls, that does not necessarily mean the telemarketing effort should be scrapped. You will have some unpleasant conversations. A lot of people will say "No," but you will also raise some money. You need to step back out of the process and keep an eye on the overall effort, to determine if/when the calling should be wrapped up. No one should be called more than once, unless they specifically request a call back. It's an imperfect system designed merely to enhance your other efforts to raise money, so don't over do it.

Wrapping Up the Campaign

Speaking of overdoing it, every fund-raising campaign has a shelf life. People eventually just get sick of hearing about it. After all, there are a lot of fund-raisers out there, going after the same people for the same money. You are just one of them. Appreciate the environment in which you are operating and gauge carefully when your campaign begins to lose its steam. Wrap it up before it fizzles.

If possible, close it with a bang. If you launched the campaign with an event of some sort, you should close it with a celebration. This doesn't have to be expensive. In fact, people will resent any obvious waste of money, and may even fear that their contribution went to pay for the party instead of helping with the advertised need. It is important to find a way to declare success and thank all the people involved in the fund-raising effort.

Above all, you want your fund-raising project to actually be a success, and success means more than raising money. Yes, it will be great if you meet your goal, but, even if you don't, you need to make your donors feel good about their support. Hopefully, your arts unit is a whole lot better off than it was before you started the campaign. (If it isn't, I'll bet you at least learned a whole lot about fund-raising in the process.) Don't get greedy. As soon as you have achieved what appears to be the maximum benefit from the effort, bring it to a gracious close.

There may be some folks still in the hopper—people who made a pledge that remains outstanding. You should make at least one final attempt to bring in these pledges as you wrap up the campaign. Announcing the successful conclusion of a fund-raising project before people send in their money just could signal to them that their money is not needed. You don't want that, now do you? Consider sending a letter reminding people that the campaign is about to be brought to a close and that you are counting on their contribution to help reach the goal. It is legitimate to count your outstanding pledges in the final tabulation, and to let people know these outstanding pledges are being counted as you close the project. That will introduce an added incentive for them to follow through on their promises.

As you sweep up loose ends, don't forget to make a plan for the continued nurturing of your donors. Make sure your database is brought completely up-to-date. It can serve as an important source of information for future campaigns. Those who contributed to this project should be considered "friends" of your arts unit. Keep in touch with them. They are your best prospects for continued financial support. Make sure you leave them feeling good about the institution and the contribution they made to its cause. By the way, make sure you feel good about the enormous challenge you have just met. Running a major fund-raising campaign is a huge job. If you somehow found a way to do this while leading an arts organization, you are an impressive leader!

CHAPTER #5   MAKING DECISIONS & IMPLEMENTING THEM

We were in the midst of a major fund-raising campaign to replace our inventory of worn-out pianos. Small donations were pouring in, sizable contributions appearing from time to time, seemingly out of nowhere; we were making great headway. We had already replaced all the practice room pianos on the one mezzanine, and had bought a few of the larger instruments. Each time there was sufficient funding to purchase one of the larger grands, we hit a serious snag: somebody had to decide which instrument we should buy.

"Andrew, I have some great news! Mrs. Major Donor has just sent us a check for $40,000; we're ready to buy that new concert grand for Alumni Concert Hall. I need you and the other piano faculty to go down to Trombino's and pick out the one you want. They have three Model D's in the show room. We'll buy whichever one you like best."

It was mid-November. I made four of those calls that day— one to each of the piano faculty. It took a long time, because each of them had a lot of reasons for not doing this. Nobody wanted to take the heat. I assured them there would be four people, not just one, making the decision, and that I would wait until they had all been down to the show room before making the purchase. "No, I will not pick the instrument; this needs to be a faculty decision."

(Yes, I realize I am a pianist; I'm also the boss. If I had picked the thing, everybody would have been unhappy. It would absolutely have been the wrong instrument, and no one would have wanted to play it—ever. Oh, no, I was not falling into that trap.) I was now a veteran in purchasing pianos, and this time, it was going to work. There were only three pianos from which to choose, and four faculty members. Two of them had to agree. This time, we would not be wallowing

*around in endless debate. I was gleeful in the knowledge that
I had at last devised a process guaranteed to net a decision
by the group of faculty who needed to be involved in making
that decision.*

Now, for the results:

- *Professor A called with a strong vote for Piano #1; I had
  to listen to all the reasons and all the things wrong with the
  other two instruments, but that was OK—he had made a
  commitment.*

- *Several days later, Professor B came into the office with her
  vote: it had to be Piano #2. She condemned the other two
  pianos, naturally.*

- *Professor C came on board soon after. Yep, Piano #3 was the
  only one worth considering.*

*Aha! Just as I had predicted. Now for the decisive vote. Days
went by, and finally the call came from Professor #4. I picked
up the phone with a huge grin on my face. The moment had
come when my administrative wisdom would be rewarded.*

*"None of them are suitable!" exclaimed Professor #4.
"Somebody needs to fly to New York and pick a different
one!"*

Choosing an Instrument

Selecting the "right" piano is an intensely personal decision-making
process. Each instrument has its own unique tone quality, touch,
responsiveness—not to the man-on-the-street, perhaps, but certainly
to the expert. Unfortunately, we were only dealing with experts here.
Even more unfortunately, we quickly discovered that no two experts
could agree on this vitally important topic. Trombino's Piano Gallery
always had available more than one exquisite Steinway of the desired
size; typically, there would be three or more in the showroom from
which to choose.

Whichever instrument was purchased was loved by somebody and hated by somebody else—usually by everybody but the one who had picked it. Pianos were accused of being "too brittle," "too dark," "too thin," "too harsh." It was beginning to sound like a building full of wine experts.

Here we were, spending thousands of dollars on the best instruments in the world and everybody was bitching. The piano technician was going absolutely crazy trying to keep up with the demands of revoicing this instrument, and tightening that, and brightening this other one; then, someone else would scream because (s)he preferred a different voicing, a looser action, or a darker sound.

To illustrate just how serious this problem had become, there were two concert grands on the stage of Alumni Concert Hall. We attempted to keep one of them tuned for student recitals and the other pushed into one of the huge boxes on the side of the stage for use when two pianos were needed. Nobody could agree on which piano was the better of the two. One was brand new—a perfectly gorgeous instrument; but at least two of the faculty claimed they liked the old one better. Depending on whose student had to play that evening, the faculty were pulling and pushing pianos in and out of boxes as though they were changing a pair of shoes. These were the same people who absolutely refused to move a few music stands that might have been left in their studio without calling for help.

At one particularly grim faculty meeting, everyone was complaining about the piano technician not doing his job. As evidence, the voice faculty cited Soprano X, who had just given her recital, and "the piano was in deplorable condition." It was so out of tune, even someone in the audience had apparently commented on it after the recital. After some poking around for more information, it was discovered that the piano accompanist had pulled "the other" piano out of the box prior to the recital, because she "liked that one better." Naturally, the one on the stage had

155

> *been thoroughly tuned and prepared for the recital by the poor embattled piano technician, just before being shoved unceremoniously into the box to sit out the performance in well-tuned silence.*

Here is a prime example of the wrong decision just waiting to be made. Had I acted on the complaints against the piano technician, without looking into these complaints a bit deeper, the wrong person would have suffered some undeserved criticism. The goal is to make the best decisions you can, based on as much solid input as you can find; then, to implement these decisions with as little negative fall-out as possible. Given that you are working with a large number of artists, each with a vested interest in strengthening his/her own area of specialization and becoming or remaining #1, this is no small task. Everybody cannot win all the time, and successful artists are people who are used to winning. When key artists have opposing needs, your decision-making better be based on something other than their input, no matter how convincing it happens to be.

Determining the Right Thing

Decisions need to be made in the best interests of the institution as a whole. If you always attempt to determine the "right" thing for the arts unit, and then do it, no matter how tough, or complicated, or unpopular this decision might be, you will be standing on firm ground when your decision is challenged—and it will be challenged 99% of the time. That other 1% represents decisions that everyone can happily support. (I would provide examples, but I can't think of any.)

It is vitally important that you keep your personal feelings and desires out of the decision-making process. The "right" thing to do is nearly always directly opposed to what you want to do, because you know when taking a certain step will crunch somebody's toes. You know how miserable Artist Difficult gets when his/her toes are even bumped, let alone smashed flat. So, why in the world would you even consider doing "that?" Well, maybe "that" is going to be the direct result of "doing the right thing" for the institution.

Former President Lyndon Johnson liked to say, "Doing the right thing is easy. It's determining the right thing to do that is so tough." How do you figure out the right thing to do? The first major consideration is whether or not you are in emergency mode. If you come to work some Monday morning and find a portion of the ceiling has fallen in on one of your major rehearsal spaces, it is clear that:

- you need to get the people out of the space and keep them out;

- you need to move all the scheduled rehearsals and classes to some other place;

- you need to get facilities management over there right away to fix the roof;

- and you need to find somebody to pay for the problem, because it is going to cost plenty, and that kind of money certainly isn't in your budget.

OK, so you are busier than you wanted to be this cold, wintry Monday morning, but the decision-making is clear-cut and obvious. You may be terrific in such situations or you may have an associate that is even better at implementing emergency actions; in any case, the series of steps that need to be taken are spelled out by the nature of the problem. Emergencies are often like that.

What about the broader issue of decision-making when the problems are complex, the stakes high, and the ramifications of any decision will reach out into just about every aspect of your organization? How do you determine the right thing to do in these cases? You can, of course, opt to do nothing. Lots of people in management positions take this approach—when in doubt, do nothing. Some even go further; they do nothing most of the time. If they are not absolutely forced to act, they don't. Make no mistake, you can head an arts organization by just getting through the day, reacting to whatever crises come along. There will be enough of these to keep you plenty busy. But this is not leadership. The effective leader finds time to get above the problems, to look past them toward that vision we spoke of in Chapter #2, and to make decisions that will advance the arts unit toward an exciting future. Ducking decisions is not part of the profile of the dynamic leader.

When to Do Nothing

However, doing nothing does work from time to time, because some problems do take care of themselves. A highly regarded music executive from Wilmette, Illinois, Dr. Frederick Miller, advises: "What appears today to be a crisis may be only a concern by tomorrow and a memory the day after. So, it may be worth 'doing nothing' for a time, to see if the problem will subside or disappear. Unless the situation truly is a crisis, and this is a vastly overused term, I think, it will probably keep or at least get no worse."

But sometimes a problem only seems to take care of itself. In reality, maybe somebody did something about it, and if it wasn't you, then somebody else is doing a piece of your job. Great! In general, it is probably safe to let the little things go for others to solve, just as long as you are dealing aggressively with the real problems.

On the other hand, there are a lot of problems that should not even become the business of the arts leader, because they belong inherently to the artists themselves. Sometimes the artists have even created these problems—problems they then try to dump in the lap of the head of the program. I can think of one shining example:

> *Two faculty members were serving on a jury at the end of the semester. One wrote a comment on his jury sheet about the student's performance; the private studio teacher of that particular student saw the comment and went ballistic. As the student left the stage, and another came on to warm up for her jury, Professor Irate made some hostile comments to Professor Critique in a tone of voice that would have reached both of their ancestors. Obviously, the bemused students heard the attack, loud and clear, and could barely contain their glee as the juries proceeded.*

Minutes after the juries concluded that day, both Professor Irate and Professor Critique landed in my office, each demanding that the other be fired. This was one of the few instances I opted to do nothing. Well, I did do something; I told each of them it was their battle, not mine. If they were so incensed, they should deal directly with one another—out of range of the students and, for that matter, away from the work place. (I believe I suggested a dark alley.) The startled expressions on each of those dignified faces told me further action was most unlikely. I also made it clear to both of them that I was not going to start arbitrating personal disputes between the faculty.

In the arts environment, emotions run high. People do go at each other over all sorts of issues. These two members of the faculty were the same sex and the same faculty rank, so there was no good reason to protect either of them from the other. I was not about to get sucked into the role of playing judge, knowing that at the least little sign of my favoring one person's position over the other, there would be a real problem well into the future with Professor Loser, who would no longer believe he was #1. Oh, no! There are more important uses of my time—perhaps not as entertaining, but definitely more directly related to the leadership position I had agreed to fulfill.

Instances in which doing nothing makes sense are those that definitely fall within the range of responsibilities of the artists involved. When artists have problems with students or colleagues, they need to be nudged back out the door to go solve these problems themselves. Maybe that's a bit harsh. You may want to offer some advice first, since Artist Oops just may not have a clue as to how to handle the situation. If (s)he screws things up any further, you know the problem will move up the scale into the crisis category, and you will then have to clean up a much messier situation.

Here's one of those cases:

Professor Oops has a set-to with a student in her arts history class. The student says something she interprets as disrespectful. So, she throws her out of class—not for the day, mind you, but for the entire semester. The problem is, this arts history course is part of the required core of professional courses needed for graduation. In addition, the first two years of professional courses are used to determine each student's suitability for the arts major; so, these professional courses are not allowed to be dropped.

What to do? Yes, Professor Oops had created the problem by announcing to Student Belligerent, in front of 52 student witnesses, "Get out! And don't come back!" What was done was done. After reminding Professor Oops of our course requirements, we moved onto the fact that we cannot very well require students to do something and then refuse to let them do it. That is, in effect, dropping them from the program without due process. (Something told me the parents of this young woman might find this whole situation mind-boggling; I know, I did.)

Now, what to do? Reversing the position Professor Oops had taken in front of the entire freshman class was obviously not a viable choice. This would cause irreparable damage to the faculty's position of authority in the classroom. Somehow, I had to find a way to support the student's dismissal from the course.

I called the student in, made it clear that she was dropped from the class, and that she now had to make up this course during the fall semester of her Sophomore Year, because it was a required course which she needed for graduation. Since the same professor would be teaching the course at that time, I further advised the student to find an opportunity to apologize to Professor Oops in the not too distant future. As for Professor Oops, before our meeting ended, she knew I would support her action, and she also knew that I would not take kindly to being backed into any more untenable corners.

There is a fine line here: getting involved in every little problem anyone has is a straight path to insanity and to the loss of effectiveness as a leader. You can so easily get swallowed up into a morass of trivia. So, every situation that hits your desk needs to be first considered in terms of who should be dealing with this? If it falls into the venue of a member of the administrative staff, pass it back out the door. If it should be handled by the person who brought it to you, give it back. You may wish to offer a few tidbits of advice along with the jettisoned problem, since the thing would not have come to you in the first place if somebody else had known what to do with it. Under no circumstances, should you start doing other people's jobs. Yours is already plenty big enough.

CONSULTATION IN DECISION-MAKING

What about the problems that are yours? How do you make those major decisions that you know are vital to the future of your organization? Consult, consult, consult. You need data from any place you can get it. Most academic institutions have built-in hierarchies—the Board of Trustees, the administration, tenured full professors, other tenured faculty, non-tenured faculty, part-time faculty, visiting faculty, staff, and students. Freestanding arts organizations also have a Board of Directors, often an Artistic Director as well as an Executive Director, various specialists in Development, Marketing, Operations, etc. Within an arts unit, you, as the leader, probably need to consult with just about all of these constituencies at some time or other, and that may not be all. There may also be alumni, parents, public audiences, major donors, the legal department, and a myriad of other areas that sometimes affect a decision.

Most decisions have an impact on the arts unit itself, but many also have an impact on the larger institution. Just about every decision has a budgetary implication. Nearly all decisions have complex effects on the people involved—primarily the artists. The organization you run is highly complex; tweaking the smallest piece of it sets up reverberations throughout the entire system. It is probably impossible to overestimate the need for consultation as you make any major decision.

Even the tiniest decision is major to somebody, but you obviously cannot consult everybody all of the time. The most important steps in effective decision-making are to:

- Seek input from anyone who can actually help you determine the "right thing" to do in a given situation, preferably those who have very different perspectives from your own. (This may be a single person who has become your chief advisor, it may be one or more of your senior professors, it may be a confidante outside your arts unit, it may be a cross-section of people. Whoever helps you think through a problem and anticipate various outcomes should be consulted.)

- Consult with anyone who even partially determines your ability to move forward with this decision. (This may be your immediate boss, it may be somebody from one of the other administrative units, it may even be someone who works for you—like the person in charge of managing your budget. You may face some structural restrictions that will limit your options.)

- Consult with any group with whom you are supposed to consult. (Perhaps your institution has a tradition of strong faculty leadership; or maybe one or two artists are key to the future of the organization. If so, you need to honor this structure, even if it isn't the most helpful way to gain your own perspective.)

- Consult with at least a representative of any group that will be immediately or ultimately affected by your decision.

The quicker the decision needs to be made, the fewer people you can involve in the decision-making process. When time permits, it is highly advisable to follow all of the steps outlined above, and consulting means actively listening to the input. Making a final decision before listening to other views is usually a mistake.

MUSIC DEPARTMENT MEMO

TO:	VOICE FACULTY
FROM:	DEPARTMENT HEAD
SUBJECT:	GRADUATION
DATE:	APRIL 19, 1995

We need to recommend a single student to sing the National Anthem for graduation. Since you know all the voice majors' ranges far better than I do, would you please send me the name of the graduating senior best suited to perform this piece? I need to send our selection over to the President's Office by the end of this week.

Thank you very much. mtt

RESULTS:

Four voice faculty received this memo.

Each one sent me two or three names, not one.

Each faculty sent only names from his/her own private studio.

All names submitted were different—eleven in all, which just happened to cover all nine of the graduating senior voice majors, plus. . .

One of the voice faculty, who did not have any graduating seniors in his studio, sent the names of two of his students— who were not graduating.

I then called the Director of Choral Studies, who gave me his opinion of the graduating senior who could best sing the

> *National Anthem. I sent that name over to the President's Office and promptly decided next year I would sing it myself.*

In most cases, you will hear conflicting points of view. If you do not, you are probably not consulting widely enough or you may be listening only to what you want to hear. Weighing the pros and cons on a given issue typically involves anticipating all possible outcomes. This is where you may get blinded by the fear of a single person's likely reaction. No matter how beastly Artist Difficult may be, (s)he is only one person. You have a whole organization to run. Hopefully, you have a vision of what this arts unit can become. Try to make every decision with this vision in mind, considering carefully whether or not this is the "right thing" to do for the future of the arts unit.

Problems with the Consulting Process

Having consulted everyone in sight, you now have to weigh very carefully the input you have received; and here it is vitally important to keep in mind that advice is sometimes given for all the wrong reasons. Most people will be primarily concerned with their own area of work and how this decision might affect them. Artists find it very difficult, if not impossible, to step out of their personal zones of artistic work to see the bigger picture. The snapshot of "Who should sing for graduation?" at the beginning of this section is an example of this problem. You have to sift whatever advice you are given and use your own best judgment. When all is said and done, it is your decision.

Throughout this process, there will always be some people who think they should be consulted more than they are. These folks want their view known on just about everything, and they get highly indignant when their opinion fails to prevail. Others hate to be asked to take a stand, and are quite contented to let somebody else—anybody else—make decisions on their behalf. The best solution is probably to offer an open invitation to the entire organization to give input on as many issues as possible. This is not as time consuming as it might appear to be; most people are very poor in responding to requests for input. Now, there is no dearth of complaining after the fact, but that doesn't mean they want to be responsible for helping to make the decision.

Another problem in consulting is that you can't always provide the person with whom you are consulting the most important information that is needed to make a given decision. There may, for example, be a specific budgetary impact, which you are not free to share with other people. Issues of confidentiality must always be maintained; this limits the number of people with whom you can talk. Certainly, not all people maintain confidentiality. Those who inappropriately convey information to others should not be consulted again; this is the only way I know to minimize destructive behavior.

For all these reasons, personnel can only help with part of the decision-making process; so, trust is needed. The bottom line is that decisions often involve conflicting needs. Somebody has to weigh the pros and cons in terms of the overall picture. That's your job. The goal is to make the right decisions for the long-term health and development of the arts unit. In the final analysis, your leadership will be judged by your effectiveness in making these decisions and your skill in implementing them.

Weighing the Pros and Cons

How do you make the right decision, when you have decidedly different points of view coming in from those whom you have consulted? We often speak of weighing the pros and cons, but how is this done? There are really only two sets of issues to be weighed:

- the relative risks of doing X versus Y;
- the potential gains of each possible action.

Here is where you really need a clear vision. The long-term health of your arts unit is always the central issue, so you want to focus on the long-term risks and the long-term potential gains in making your decision. Is your action more likely to help or hurt your institution well into the future? If the potential gains of implementing a given decision could move your organization significantly forward toward its desired destination, then it is probably worth the risks involved. If the risks could potentially knock the arts unit backwards, away from your vision of its distinguished future, then you will not want to take those risks.

Finding a balance between long-term risks and long-term gains is certainly not an easy task. If you make a habit of thinking long-term first when making important decisions, there is often a clarity to the problem that gets muddied by considering it from a short-term perspective. Nevertheless, most people think first of the immediate ramifications of an action. When thinking short-term, the risks can usually be seen more clearly than the potential gains, because the immediate reactions of people opposed to your decision can be easily imagined. If there are enough problems foreseen in this near-sighted picture, it is difficult to even get past them to envision the possible gains. As a result, many, if not most, arts administrators get swallowed up by the little stuff and never get to the bigger picture. They base all of their decisions on the avoidance of immediate problems, which absolutely ensures a lack of direction and momentum for the organization as a whole. Remember: an arts unit that is sitting still is decaying.

Major decisions are those that have the greatest long-term effects. These are the decisions that should occupy the majority of your time, but seldom do. It is actually the day-to-day little stuff that devours your energy. Hopefully, you can develop some skill in quickly assessing the pros and cons of the short-term problems that crop up with annoying frequency, and learn to handle them on the spot. Even these need to be made with long-term precedent setting in mind, because there can be enormous fall-out from the smallest decision, if it is a bad one.

On-going Listening

In general, when leading an arts organization, you cannot afford to be insular. Because artists are so emotionally involved in their work, it is vitally important to consult with them continuously in an ongoing, fluid style. Even casual conversations in the halls with individual artists can put you in sync with a wide range of people and can provide you with essential information about these persons' needs and attitudes. While this is certainly a nontraditional style of collecting input, it has the advantage of crossing boundaries of titles, tenure, status, etc. and helping everyone feel involved in the program. In a large organization with a wide diversity of specializations, keeping in touch with each person is tough, but necessary.

Whenever external consultation is needed with people from the Board, the Development Office, Legal Affairs, etc. it is important to have ready access to seek this advice. Establishing a good working relationship with people in all supportive areas is crucial to the success of your leadership and the health of your decision-making.

It is also important to stay in touch with the artists and staff in all areas of your arts unit. When decisions are being made in a specific area, you must get all the participants in this area actively involved in the process. If you cannot consult with them prior to making a decision, which is highly recommended, then at least make sure you work to get them on board before you try to implement the decision. Above all, these folks should not be the last to learn of a decision affecting them. Reading about a cut in a given program in the newspaper, for example, before hearing about it from the leader of the arts unit, is a deadly sin, and it happens all the time.

You can learn a lot that will come in handy later, when decisions need to be made, just by listening carefully in meetings with artists and staff. Routine meetings are an excellent source of information regarding artists' needs and biases. These venues are also ideal for gaining support and building consensus in matters of change, and nothing can be more critical than another set of ears. If at all possible, develop a consultant relationship with a trusted assistant or associate. Thinking out loud and testing some new ideas on a safe partner may be just what you need before running off and doing something really dumb.

The Big Picture

No matter how immediate the problem, your decision will have far-reaching effects. Every decision you implement sets a precedent. One of the biggest mistakes you can make is taking a pragmatic approach to decision-making without looking deeper into the ramifications of your action or without looking further into the future, to anticipate what precedents you may be setting. Can you live with this decision if ten other people come to you with similar problems, looking for the same solution? Will doing "this" now create a bigger problem down the road?

Leadership is all about decision-making, setting the direction, and keeping everyone on track. Once you determine the "right" thing to do in a given situation, don't look back. Focus on making it work. Shoot for those potential gains and diligently work to avoid the risks you identified as you made your decision. If you arrived at the wrong decision, you can probably make it work anyway, just by skillfully directing the implementation process. Conversely, even the best decision in the world can go up in smoke if the implementation is seriously flawed.

Dealing with Artist Difficult

Getting Artist Difficult on board is central to accomplishing your goal—especially since not getting Artist Difficult on board may cause the whole thing to blow up in your face. You know for a fact that the Artist Difficults will be your biggest problem. So, you need to figure out how best to handle these persons, before the decision is actually implemented. You have the following options:

Prepare them before announcing your decision. Let them know that you do care about their needs and that you do realize this will be a difficult decision for them to support, but that it is necessary for the good of the arts unit. Provide as much specific data as you can to show the logic of your decision, and to demonstrate that it is not being made frivolously.

If you do this well, the Artist Difficults will feel as though they are still #1; after all, you acknowledged their importance by asking for their support before proceeding. This is almost as good as doing what they wanted, and by being magnanimous "losers," they can demonstrate further their power as your #1 confidante. Trust me on this: being valued is the issue with artists—all the time.

If, on the other hand, you blow it, and the Artist Difficults refuse to buy into the decision, perhaps storming out of the meeting in a huff, you can expect some serious repercussions, because the Artist Difficults of the world never go quietly into the night. So, you may as well get busy working on your new problem; (it is now a whole lot bigger than the one you thought you were dealing with a minute ago.) If you have an assistant or associate who works closely with you, this is an ideal time to call in the reinforcements. Send him/her to talk to Artist Difficult—ASAP—and attempt to diffuse the upset before it takes on a life of its own.

The second option is to plan to meet with your Artist Difficults right after announcing your decision. This is risky, especially if the format in which you announce your decision is a public one. Artist Difficults will feel they have been "blind-sided," and may blow up. After reacting negatively in front of anybody at all, they will be obliged to remain publicly opposed to this decision to their dying day. After all, somebody saw that they had not been consulted on this matter; they were obviously surprised by it. Therefore, they are clearly no longer #1.

Now, you have committed two crimes: you have made a decision that steps on the hallowed toes of the Artist Difficults, and you have done this without even consulting them. Clearly, you have deliberately taken a personal shot at them, they believe. (I know this is a leap of logic, but we are no longer dealing with logic here.) This is all about emotion, and make no mistake, it is now also about war.

On the other hand, if you cannot cue them in before the decision is announced, at least schedule a private time to talk with them about the decision just as soon after the announcement as humanly possible.

169

It will help to tell them beforehand that the meeting is related to an announcement you have to make prior to your discussion with them, and that you are unfortunately not able to talk with them before the announcement. Even this much of a warning will prevent them from being taken totally by surprise; they will know you care enough about their reaction to schedule time with them, and maybe, just maybe, they will be willing to wait until your conversation takes place before trashing your decision in public.

Your third option is to say, "The Hell with Artist Difficult!" and go ahead with your decision. If this is your choice, please warn me, so I can be sure to be in some other place when it happens.

Let me just say unequivocally that this is never the best route; but on some rare occasions, you have to take it. Here are the circumstances:

a. Artist Difficult absolutely detests you;

b. No matter what you do, it is always "wrong;"

c. Even if your decision was exactly what (s)he wanted, it would still be resented and criticized;

d (S)he is diabolical enough to turn any conversation with you into misquotes and damaging misperceptions. (To be blunt, (s)he lies.)

If these are the circumstances, then you may as well proceed. By now, everybody else probably knows of this person's hatred of the boss, so there may not even be that much damage control required.

Widespread Dissension

What if there are a lot of Artist Difficults? Well, your options are still the same: consult with them privately or as a group prior to announcing your decision, meet with them directly after the decision is announced to attempt to get them on board, or just stonewall and move ahead in spite of their opposition. What if there are too many dissenters to follow any but the third option? Then, you have moved too fast. Or you have not succeeded in getting enough people on board. If most of your artists or staff disagree with your decision, it cannot be successfully implemented. Either it is the wrong decision for the arts unit at this time, or you need to do a whole lot more work building a consensus before moving forward.

Your job during the decision-making process is to anticipate the problems that will arise from a given action; this includes any potential opposition to your decision from the Artist Difficults. As the leader of your arts unit, you need to have a deep understanding of the people with whom you are working. Hopefully, you know where your employees stand on various issues; further, whatever decision you are making will probably have the deepest impact on a subset of the arts organization, so these are the folks that will require your closest attention.

Sounds logical? Now, this is in the ideal world. Remember, we don't work there. In our profession, virtually everybody takes everything personally. That means that decisions you believe will only affect the people in one area of your arts unit will also be a threat to the rest of the people. More often than not, the people who will react most strongly to your decision will be those you did not anticipate, and even the folks you thought agreed with you may fall apart at the seams when the going gets tough. There will always be surprises, and you can expect to spend quite a lot of time, after making your decision, just patching people's wounds and propping up their confidence and their egos.

The Wrong Decision

This is, of course, assuming that you made the "right" decision. What if you did not? This may surprise you, but it probably doesn't matter whether you make the right decision or the wrong one, if you do a good job of working with your artists, staff, students, and administration. The implementation of a given decision is a process that can be tweaked in this direction or in that, depending on changing circumstances. Most decisions are neither 100% right nor 100% wrong. The implementation is critical. By the time you determine it might have been better to have done "Y" instead of

"X," it is probably too late to go back. It is usually better to keep going and make the decision work by modifying the approach.

Every now and then, you do hit the wall, and retreat is essential. You made the wrong decision. Or perhaps it was the right decision, but you didn't do a good enough job of working with the dissenters before trying to implement it. In any case, as soon as you determine that your course of action is not in the best interests of your arts unit, you need to turn it around.

How you do this depends on so many factors, the options cannot be concisely listed. Here are the main considerations:

- The needs of your organization are more important than your ego. Do not stay the course solely because you don't want to admit you were wrong. You made the best decision you could at the time; if there is now more information to indicate a better path of action, you need to get on that path.

- Openness and honesty are central to effective leadership. Admitting you made a decision that is not working out is no big deal. Everybody knows it by now any way. Changing direction openly is far preferable to trying to cover up the problems by a series of quiet back-pedaling moves.

- Heading an arts organization is a decision-making occupation. As long as you usually make the right decisions, an occasional bloop will not be too damaging. If you have to engage in this correction process too often, perhaps you are in over your head. The decision to find a new job may be the best one you've made in months.

Learning to say "No"

Nobody likes to say "No." (Well, maybe two-year-olds like to say "No," but with a little luck you don't have any of those working for you.) A central fact of life in administration is that trying to keep people happy by giving them what they want at the moment may just be inviting them to ask for more. Some people keep on asking until they finally get a "No;" it doesn't bother them in the least, since they are accustomed to going to the limit. They need to find the limit; then, they are satisfied that they have gotten whatever there is to get. When you come across someone like this, learning to say "No" is essential.

Fortunately, these folks are in the minority. Most people are very uncomfortable asking for something they may not be able to get. Sensing this, you find it even tougher to say "No" to them. In this case, you don't have to worry nearly as much about setting a precedent. This person will not make a habit of asking you for things, because it is just too unpleasant. You can bet the topic that brought him/her in to see you is of strong importance. Consequently, you only say "No" when it is absolutely impossible to deliver on the request. Do it! Fast and clean, with the appropriate explanation of your reason. The reluctant beggar will appreciate not having to belabor the issue.

The arguer is tougher yet. The person who does not take "No" for an answer will hammer you until you begin to reconsider. Don't do it! If your initial answer is "No," stick to it. Once people learn that your mind can be changed just by harassing you, your life will become a continual battle. Consider carefully before saying "No," and then stay firm. If you suspect you were a bit premature in your "No," you can work toward a compromise. Based on the new information you have gained by listening to the argument, you may be able to come up with a partial "Yes," that will make the arguer feel (s)he has gotten somewhere by talking to you, but that will sustain your reputation as a strong decision-maker.

The ability to say "No," when necessary, is absolutely critical to good decision-making. Somehow, you need to get to the place where giving a "No" feels emotionally just about the same as a "Yes." Remember, saying "Yes" is probably going to cost you money, perhaps significant time, and most certainly some management effort. "No," while it does disappoint someone, will absolutely save you money, time, and effort. Don't let yourself get too hung up over uttering a "No." Feeling equally comfortable with both decisions will put you in the appropriate position to make rational decisions, no matter what the topic. By the way, it does get easier. After you have said "Yes" a few times, when you most assuredly should have said "No," you will get a whole lot better at uttering the "N" word. Honest!

HELPING OTHERS MAKE DECISIONS

The discussion had been hot and heavy for forty-five minutes. There seemed to be a consensus that the student should be dropped from the program. The chair asked for a motion. It was there. So was the second to the motion. Actually, two people seconded the motion. The call for the vote. Then, suddenly, from the back of the room, "Wait! What if we gave him one more semester?" The discussion started again. The same points raised. More elaboration on the student's personal problems. More discussion on classes missed, work not prepared, poor juries, lack of effort, excuses, minimal progress, questionable talent.

OK. The negatives again appear to be overwhelming. (Timing is everything.) "We have a motion and a second to drop the student from the program. Are we ready to vote?" "Well, I remember seven years ago when we dropped so-and-so, and he wound up at the Met." "Yeah, the same thing happened with Miss Clarinet back in 89." "Maybe we ought to just force him to go to the counseling center." "What if we put him on Final Probation?" "He's already on Final Probation from last semester." "Can we continue him on Final Probation?"

(Believe it or not, there actually is a formal action entitled "Continued On Final Probation" for just such cases. Perhaps, it should be called, "Continued On Almost Final Probation.")

When the vote finally comes, there are eight for dropping the student, four opposed, and one abstention—the private studio teacher—the person who knows the student best, but just can't take responsibility for the decision. Now, the studio teacher will undoubtedly go back to the student and say, "I did everything I could, but the department head was determined to drop you from the program."

It's lonely at the top.

Decision-making with Artists

What's the problem here? Is decision-making really all that different in an arts environment? Let's look at the picture and you decide. The anecdote described above actually happened. What's more, it is typical of the decision-making process I have experienced through sixteen years of arts administration and twenty-six years as a member of an artist faculty. There seems to be enormous difficulty in getting artists to commit themselves to a position—especially a public one.

There are signs of panic on the brink of taking a vote as described above. There are attempts to distance themselves from the decision by claiming it was made by somebody else, usually you. There are struggles to avoid the responsibility for a decision, like abstaining for some creative reason, or making sure to vote against the majority; so if things don't work out, it certainly isn't their fault. People decide, then change their minds at a later date, usually when it comes time to implement their decision. Some particularly devious ones tell other people that they were personally opposed to the decision, secretly sabotaging the process of implementation.

The bigger the decision, the more anxiety and fall-out will occur. If the artists have to be part of the implementation, it's worse—they can't hide or pretend they aren't part of the decision—yet, they will try to do both. Perhaps, their need to be liked transcends their ability to take the heat on a given action. Or perhaps, as creative artists, they are more accustomed to exploring a range of possibilities without having to commit to a single path. Or maybe it's just a universal problem; after all, doing nothing is always easier than taking action.

Bearing the Responsibility

Whatever the reason, when a large number of artists fit this profile of indecision, leadership becomes even more difficult. If you happen to be the person in charge, you will bear the brunt of this malady. Artist Hedger wants to blame all decisions on the boss, yet is the first to complain mightily if the head is "autocratic." Even when things are voted upon, the leader will be blamed for the decision, as though the artists had absolutely no choice in the matter.

Decisions that need to remain confidential are leaked. Indecisive artists will often handle their discomfort over being a part of an unpopular decision by abandoning the ship, whispering to others to get themselves into the safety zone of a group on the side against the decision, whatever it is. Many decisions are undercut by the very people who helped to make them, even before implementation begins. If anything at all goes wrong, and it often does, thanks to their behavior, Artist Hedger will say, "I knew that would happen; I only went along with this because..."

No matter how bad a situation is, doing something about the problem is apparently more stressful than enduring it. Artists will often sabotage change of any kind, probably because they fear it might make something worse for themselves.

Good news: if you can get past all of this and actually get things accomplished, there is a chance people will begin to trust your leadership—provided, that is, you are willing to consult with them extensively, but take full responsibility for everything, and, at the same time, bear the label of "autocrat."

Bad news: The other possibility is to rule with an iron hand. When people are afraid to make trouble, the trouble does decrease, but morale then becomes very low and anxiety goes through the roof. The overall environment becomes charged with tension, like a rubber band stretched too tight, ready to snap back into itself, if the leader lets go for just a second.

Building Consensus

How do you get people on board? In short, how do you build consensus? I suspect a true consensus is a rarity in the arts world. There are just too many strong individualists involved to hammer them into a single shape. Do you even need a consensus? Well, unless you enjoy spending all of your time trying to jam people into doing what they don't want to do, yes, you do need to build a consensus. This doesn't mean absolutely everybody in sight agrees with everything you do.

Webster's College Dictionary defines consensus as: "collective judgment or belief; solidarity of opinion; general agreement or concord; harmony." I take all of those phrases to mean: "Most of the people should agree on most things most of the time." That's my definition of consensus. I am also willing to stretch the application of my definition just a bit further. Sometimes you need to act before you have a consensus. Hopefully, if you were right, consensus will build as the decision is proven to be in the best interests of the institution. If you chose to move ahead without a consensus, you'd better be right!

When do you move without first building a consensus?

- In an absolute emergency. When the alarm goes off, you evacuate the building. Period. Not too many situations fall into this category, even though most things that occur in an arts environment are perceived to be emergencies by somebody.

- When the boss says so. If your budget is cut 5% or your external income falls significantly, you can forget about building a consensus. What's done is done. It's your job to deal with the situation, with or without support from your employees. Surprisingly enough, in these situations, you usually get a lot of support and cooperation, since everyone understands it's not your doing.

- Whenever there are two sides to an issue, with significant support on both sides, and nobody is willing to budge.

Somebody has to make the decision. That's why they pay you the big bucks.

- When a timely opportunity comes along for your arts unit and complete confidentiality is needed to make it work. There aren't too many of these. When you come across one, you will know it when you see it. Advice: always clue your boss in or the chairman of your board, make sure you aren't breaking any rules, taking any legal risks, or spending money you don't have. Then, go for it! If it's as exciting as it sounds, you will have widespread consensus after the fact, except for those who think you should have consulted them first.

By the way, if you can't imagine anything that would fit into this last category, don't worry about it. You are probably a more conservative leader than I am. That's OK. I'll bet you also get more sleep at night.

The Tough Ones

Now that we have covered four areas in which you do not necessarily have to wait for a consensus before acting, let's talk about how to build a healthy consensus all the rest of the time. Remember, we are assuming that a few people here and there will never agree to anything everybody else wants to do. (We are dealing with artists, you know.) It also goes without saying, but I'll say it anyway, that in some cases it will be much more difficult than in others to reach widespread agreement. There are some real hot topics out there.

For instance, you will never reach agreement on spending money. Hopefully, that is a decision-making area that is not too widely discussed in your arts unit. The less said about money, the better. It is important for the artists and staff to trust you to make good decisions regarding the financial management of the arts unit, and it is impossible for everybody to know all the details of the overall budget.

Yet, misperceptions abound. It will probably be necessary to invest some time in giving the artists a sense of the spending parameters. They need to know that the money spent on the new building did not come out of their personal salaries. Or that the money Mr. and Mrs. Millionaire donated to the scholarship fund was not available for buying a new rug for their office. It is so easy to perceive that the institution has money for everything else but "me." It is also easy to believe that whoever is in charge should be directing more funds to "my" area of specialization.

That will be the concern whenever issues of money rise to the surface. Nobody really wants the responsibility of dealing with complex budgets; you probably don't, either. Everybody just wants a bigger slice of the pie, and everybody thinks the pie is a whole lot bigger than it actually is. Consensus in money matters is just not feasible. Knowing that, you will probably want to talk about money as little as possible, unless you want to try to reduce their appetites during crunch times, or unless you just managed to get some more of it, and celebration is in order. Even then, tread carefully. When new money comes in the door, it's usually designated for something very specific. Make sure everybody knows how it has to be allocated or your tires will be slashed when word gets out that you spent it on "that."

Another particularly difficult area for consensus-building is space. There is never enough of it. People have an unbelievable need to own it. Somebody is always going to have more space than somebody else, or better space, or more attractive space. Much of the current status of your arts unit's space allocation has evolved over years of turf wars (and make no mistake, this is war;) any steps you take toward improving this situation will result in amazing battles. If you get even an inch of new space, and it's considered prime space, stand back! The only consensus you're going to achieve on this topic is that everybody wants it.

The renovation of our main classroom was almost complete. That useless corner behind the wall that enclosed the heating system was no longer part of the classroom. That corner had

179

been converted into a much needed storage room for music and instruments. It now had its own lockable door, accessible only from the classroom itself.

My assistant and I were making a final inspection before signing off on the project. The classroom looked great! New ceiling, light fixtures, desks, draperies, black boards—the walls and floors refinished. Beautiful job.

As we opened the door to the adjoining storage room, we both gasped. It was bigger than either of us had envisioned. Stan took the words right out of my mouth:

"You know, this space is big enough for the new conductor. Let's stick a desk in here."

The only consoling part about this topic is that some people understand you personally don't print money and you can't create new space. It is your job to do the best you can to find more of both; and it is your responsibility to assign it if and when you get it. While you can't hope for consensus in either of these areas, you can at least share enough information to convince the logical ones you are attempting to be equitable and that you have the best interests of the overall institution at the forefront of all your decisions.

When You Can, Do It!

In summary, try to build a consensus before moving ahead. This is especially true when making a major change. The bigger the step, the more important it is to have as many people with you as you can muster, not because you are afraid to take the heat, but because the dissenters can create more problems than a do-it-yourself appendectomy. If they are smart, skillful dissenters, they may succeed in preventing the operation altogether. If not, they will at least create more complications than you know how to handle. Ultimately, it is you who will suffer. Think of yourself here. Slow down, and build a consensus.

The easiest approach is to start with the people you suspect will agree with you. If even they come up with concerns, you will know you have to resolve some of these problems before moving forward. Maybe your natural allies can help you think through the roadblocks. As you reshape and reposition your plan, move on to a broader base of potential advocates. Once it appears there would be significant support for such an idea, take it to the rest of the population. By this time, you should be aware of the hot spots, and you should also be prepared to work through them with logic and good sense.

It is vitally important as you move through this process to honor the hierarchy of the institution. In some cases, you need the support of the artists for a proposal before it is taken up the ladder. In other cases, you will be better to get the support of your boss or the head of your board before raising an issue with the artists, so you don't paint him/her into a corner. You never want to marshal the forces in order to pressure the administration above you into taking a particular action. First, it seldom works, and second, you will most likely create some legitimate anger from above that you will live to regret. (You've heard of winning the battle and losing the war?)

In an independent arts organization, consensus building should include all areas of the operation from the artists to the technical staff to the administrative staff. In most educational institutions, the faculty are the main constituency for building consensus. Administrative staff are accustomed to implementing whatever the boss sets out to accomplish; however, it is an enormous help to have them committed to the cause, as well. The student body is the one group that should be consulted, or at least informed of a pending action before it happens, and often, is not. This is an enormous blunder! Young adults have very strong opinions about nearly everything, and they certainly have sharp opinions about the education they are receiving and the environment in which they are living and working.

After working with the faculty and staff, if it is feasible as part of this process, consult with your students. This may be a small group of student representatives, or a specific subset of the arts unit you run, if the decision will affect one group of students more than another. Above all, do not insult their intelligence. If the decision has already been made, make that clear. Tell them your purpose is to give them a deeper understanding of the rationale for making the change, to lessen their anxiety about what's happening and why, and to answer their questions—all of this, before you begin the implementation process.

There was a lot of excitement surrounding the choice of our student orchestra for the Italian television project. The students knew this was to be an international production, featuring three student orchestras—one from Milan, one from Moscow, and one from America. To be considered for the project, we had submitted tapes of previous concerts and lots of written materials about the school; finally the producer and director of the project had actually flown in to hear the orchestra perform live. The students had risen to the challenge; their performance was outstanding.

Then, it began: an excruciating period of written correspondence, telephone conversations, contract negotiations, and person-to-person meetings in Pittsburgh, New York, and even in the terminal of the Charlotte, North Carolina, airport. The whole process took months. When we were finally given the word that our students would be doing the project, everyone was jubilant!

The mistake I made was in announcing the decision to the students. I spent far too much time emphasizing the importance of the national and international visibility we would gain through our participation in this television series. I didn't focus nearly enough on the educational benefits inherent in the project to each of them. From the outset, what attracted us to this project was the opportunity for the students to perform in a professional venue. Perfection was required. And any time you can provide a venue for students to pull themselves up to a higher level of achievement, you have dynamited the learning process.

I knew this; the faculty knew it; but, I did not articulate this to the students, and I should have.

What happened next really threw me for a loop. Members of the orchestra began to request excuses from the project—for one reason or another. The numbers were growing. Even the most cooperative students were appearing unhappy and disgruntled about the whole thing. I began to hear statements like, "So, what's in it for us?" I was absolutely flabbergasted! The entire project was for them.

Finally, it began to appear as though the project was in jeopardy; so, I called an emergency meeting of the students in the orchestra. Fortunately, instead of lecturing them about the importance of this opportunity they were threatening to throw away, I listened. I asked them to tell me the problem. Why were some of them unhappy about participating in this exciting project?

To my amazement, they began speaking about a lack of payment. Here they were, doing a professional job, and we weren't going to pay them. I was horrified! I attempted to stay calm as I explained that they were still students, and that this was an educational experience.

The students, growing more strident, responded with, "But we're not even getting college credit for this!" Then, a bell went off in my head. Incredulously, I asked, "Is all of this about credit? Is that why you are so unhappy?" "Because there's no credit?" They nodded and grew quiet. My mind was racing to catch up to their perspective. Of course, they wanted credit! They were here to take classes, get grades, and earn a diploma. How had I forgotten all of that? I was the one who had lost my way.

If you follow this practice of consulting all constituencies before taking major steps that will affect them, you will build a climate of trust and confidence in your leadership that will maximize your effectiveness across the board. Be prepared for some really good input. If you even once take their advice and reshape your plan because of their suggestions, word will spread that you really do listen to people and you do seem to have their best interests at heart. A supportive, cooperative organization is an extraordinary asset to your leadership. Cultivate it, honestly and directly, with respect for their insight and maturity. You won't regret it.

Fall-out From the Consulting Process

The major down side to all of this consensus building is that information will undoubtedly leak out in the process. If your environment is like most, as soon as word spreads that you are talking about "This and That" with "Whomever," rumors begin to spread. When the topic is especially sensitive, people react with great anxiety—not just to the facts, but to the embellished fiction, as well.

Talk about jumping the gun! If you are discussing the possibility of doing "H, I, and J," it will be only minutes before the talk will include the inevitable next steps: "K, L, and M." Plus, a few creative thinkers will assume that your next steps after that are undoubtedly going to be "X, Y, and Z." I know, I know, that huge leap makes no sense at all, but whoever said rumors had to make sense? People panic in the face of potential decision-making, and they start to take intuitive jumps in every direction. Suddenly, you are busier stamping out the brush fires from these sparks of creative gossip than you are working on the problem itself.

So, how do you minimize the leaking of information and the resultant rumor spreading? The most obvious answer is to consult with only those who can be trusted to keep their mouths shut. Hmmmmm. That may leave a very short list: God and the members of your immediate family. (And on this list, God may be the only one who really cares about the obscure problems you are dealing with.) Accept the inevitable: There will be leaks! To minimize the damage of the extra-curricular activity of rumor passing, whenever possible, provide official reports of the truth. Rumors are created when there is a vacuum of real information; so give them as much real stuff as you can.

Different Levels of Consulting

You may wish to state right up front that over the next few weeks you will be looking at the problem of "H, I, and J." Emphasize that you will be consulting with a number of people on this issue, and that you will make an official announcement just as soon as a decision has been reached—before any steps are taken to implement that decision. Invite anyone who wants to express their views to contact you for an appointment. Surprisingly, you will not be inundated with takers. Most people don't actually want the direct responsibility of influencing an important decision; however, they do want to know what's going on. If you are willing to tell them, it can't be too catastrophic. If you are willing to listen to everybody's opinion, lots of other people will probably carry the right message to you, so they feel better already. They can safely forget about the problem until a decision has been reached. (If it's the wrong decision, you will hear from them, however.)

This strategy is just about the safest, when you can use it. It is especially effective when you are contemplating a change that will have widespread impact. Above all, you have opened the door for those who feel strongly about a given subject to do something. When you don't or can't provide this option, an overwhelming helplessness may set in; anxiety runs deepest when someone else—in this case, you—is able to make a decision that will affect people without their input. If you are willing to accept input, your image as a diabolical tyrant is somewhat softened—but only somewhat. After all, you are the person with the power to do "it"—whatever "it" happens to be.

Unfortunately, there are a lot of times when decisions need to be made in a much quieter manner. You just can't afford to take the time to consult everybody, or maybe the confidentiality of the situation makes widespread consultation inappropriate. Whatever the case, you still need to do as much consensus building as you can as early in the process as possible. This may mean talking with just the people who will be most directly affected by the decision to be made; in an arts department, that is typically one of the curricular areas like sculpture, or playwriting, or instrumental music. You might hold a meeting of the faculty working in that specific option to discuss the matter first; then, when a decision is reached, announce it to the students in a small enough meeting that you can answer their questions and address their concerns.

In other cases, the consulting process might cut across more than one area of the organization. Then, you might opt to consult just studio teachers, or a small group of tenured full professors or just the technical staff. It is critical that your consulting process be viewed as even-handed; it is always a mistake to hand pick a few favorite colleagues and routinely turn to them first. Find a category of people that makes sense as advisors on a given issue, and try to include everyone in that natural grouping. Otherwise, you will be accused of having some sort of underground management team.

As for underground management teams, this approach might be just what you need, but you have to get it above ground to make it work. You may find one or two people who are particularly helpful as advisors. They have excellent judgment, sharp analytical skills, a deep understanding of the people with whom you are dealing, and an unquestionable loyalty and concern for the institution as a whole. Oh, yes, and they know how to keep their mouths shut. Such people are rare, indeed. If you have any, for goodness sake get them into your administration where you can legitimately seek their counsel. Titles such as Associate Executive Director, Operations Manager, Assistant Head, Faculty Chair come to mind. (There may be other titles in your organization.)

As long as it makes institutional sense, having one or two official advisors to turn to when you have a particularly difficult problem to address, to help you brain storm and think through the possible ramifications of an action, can be enormously helpful. It is especially beneficial if these people have very different backgrounds and expertise from yours. Then, you have the advantage of diverse viewpoints right at the outset. This helps avoid the common problem of seeing things only through your own eyes, and continually thinking of your perception of the world as the only view.

Caution: if you are lucky enough to have such help, you still should not depend solely on this small set of advisors. They may be helpful in strategic thinking or in deciding just how to effectively build a consensus for a decision you wish to implement, but consulting with one or two people is not enough. In academic settings, you need the support of your faculty to achieve anything meaningful. In independent arts organizations, you definitely need the support of your artists and probably the staff, as well. So, continue to reach out in as many directions as you deem possible and appropriate to get people on board before you try to make major changes.

This entire discussion assumes that you work in an environment in which you are somewhat flexible in your decision-making. Admittedly, there are some institutions wherein the leader's hands are tied to a much stricter process. If you are working in such a place, you need to follow that defined structure. In this case, you don't need me to encourage you to build a consensus. You are probably not permitted to move forward in any direction without a consensus, because much of the decision-making already lies in the hands of the board or someone above your level. This does not mean you are off the hook, however, You are still the person in charge, and you are the one who has to steer the process toward a resolution, hopefully a peaceful one. The issue doesn't exist that will draw total agreement from a bunch of artists without a struggle.

Resolving Differences

That raises the matter of how to resolve serious differences of opinion. When do you have enough support to move forward? What do you do with the people who begrudgingly get swept up by a decision they did not want to see approved?

First, the problem of when to move ahead. You have those in favor, those opposed. You have talked about the issue until you are blue in the face. Everything conceivable has been said nine or ten times.

Do you table the discussion to let people have some time to think about it further? Or do you move forward with a vote? Or do you just do it? Working backwards, the third one is the easiest: don't do it! Once you bring a topic up for discussion, and everyone's views are aired, you are in no position to pick a side. That is suicidal! Besides, it won't work.

By now, you realize that you blew it. The last thing you want to do is raise an issue in such a way that people get polarized into two different positions. Then, they have no honorable choice, but to dig in their heels and fight for their side. If you are an astute leader, you will know your constituents well enough to be able to anticipate when this might happen. Try to discuss the matter in such a way that people do not make an early commitment to a position. Taking either side first, ask everyone to contribute thoughts on the pro side and everyone to contribute thoughts on the con side. Get all the issues out on the table for everybody to consider. Let them know that both sides have merit, but that you somehow have to come up with a single decision. Encourage people to see the merits of each side of the issue.

Gradually, people will begin to reveal their preferences. It's unavoidable. You will eventually wind up with advocates and opponents, but at least you delayed this separation as long as you could to maximize the possibility of the positions being logical and well-informed. Never ask people what they think, before you have provided the opportunity to explore all the factors involved in making the decision.

If it appears that there is no definitive direction emerging from the discussion, you may suggest the need to collect more data. If you have the luxury of time on your side, postpone the vote until more information is gathered, preferably by someone other than you. Again, this emphasis on facts will help to depersonalize the ultimate decision. You want to avoid at all costs the perception that a vote against my position is a vote against me. As stated several times before, artists have an extremely strong tendency to personalize everything.

By the time you bring an issue to a vote, you want there to be a clear decision, with as few dissenters as possible. You also need to be sure that it will be a decision you, as the leader, can live with. Under no circumstances should you reverse a decision you have relinquished to a group decision-making process. (There is no executive veto in the artistic environment.) If you can only support one decision, make the decision yourself up front and try to build a consensus for that decision. Do not go through the facade of a group vote on issues upon which you are unable or unwilling to implement multiple outcomes. Also, do not assume that you can subtly steer the discussion toward a desired result. People can smell a "fix" from 100 yards away.

OK, they argued vehemently against the proposal, but lost the struggle. Now, here comes the implementation stage, and they are still opposed. Unfortunately, these disgruntled souls will not just dry up and blow away. (We are not speaking of those nightmarish few who are always opposed to everything. Here, we want to consider the problems of the more reasonable people, who just happen to disagree with this particular decision.)

If they really are reasonable, they will take a deep breath and accept the inevitable. They had their say; the group voted otherwise; so be it! That's what you want to see happen. Sometimes, even the reasonable can't quite get there from here. You can help. These are the things that matter:

- The outvoted need to know it was OK to disagree;
- They need to feel their opinions are respected by you and by everybody else;
- They need to be invited and encouraged to join the implementation process, not be ostracized further as a dissenter;
- They need to be thanked for their cooperation and given credit for their support, in spite of their desire for another outcome.

If you do your best to ensure that all of the above steps are taken to bring them on board, it is really up to the individuals to make the adjustments. In those rare instances where nothing helps, it may take some time to ease the sting of defeat. Back off and hope for the best. Finding other ways to support unhappy personnel can help a lot. Remember that folks in this type of situation are fragile; do what you can to prevent other negative signals from coming their way on the heels of their perceived loss of stature. And without wanting to sound like a broken record, the problem does cut clear to the issue of Who's Number #1. Obviously, they're not. That's the real problem.

It seems that the stronger your leadership, the tougher the political fall-out will be. As we discussed in "Implementing Change," people react to change with a lot of anxiety. This anxiety is manifested in a variety of ways—and not always out in the open, where you can see it and deal with it. The attacks and counter-attacks can get pretty ugly. The only way I know to survive is to make sure your opponents are not right.

Hold onto your integrity. Make the "right" decisions, as best you can. Work to build consensus, communicating like mad in every language you can grasp. Above all, keep your vision clear. When the air gets a little thick with smoke, find your own set of windshield wipers to restore your sight.

The Value of the Battle

All of this sounds pretty horrendous. What's the point of even having open discussions and democratic voting, if the result is going to be this problematical? The strange thing is that the process is really a healthy one. The discussion, no matter how protracted and emotional it becomes, is extremely helpful in bringing people together. No kidding! If every decision were made by the leader, no one would ever appreciate the complexity of the situation; they would never understand all the factors involved in making the decision; they would have no stake in the outcome. Therein lies the real advantage of widespread consulting: Buy-in.

You need people to have some vested interest in making things work. Otherwise, they simply don't care enough to help, and their apathy becomes a major hindrance to successful implementation. If, on the other hand, they play a role in setting the process in motion, there is at least the hope of some personal commitment to its ultimate completion. Don't ever forget, you can make all the decisions you want as the leader of this arts unit, but you can't implement a thing without the support and the active help of the artists and the staff. So get them on board and let them vote. One way or another, take time to build a consensus.

Chapter #6   Communicating

The importance of effective communication cannot be overemphasized.

Acclaimed violinist... renowned symphony orchestra... highly skilled French conductor at the podium.

The concert was ready to begin. The house lights dimmed, a quiet hush enveloping the orchestra. Conductor and soloist strode purposefully onto the stage, taking their places to the sound of thunderous applause. It was a full house.

This concerto had a lot of sections. A previous orchestra had marked the parts with red pencil, showing which sections they would repeat. Another orchestra had taken a different set of repeats, and had marked these same parts with blue pencil. This morning in rehearsal, the conductor had chosen the series of blue cuts—all standard rehearsal stuff.

He raised his baton. Luscious music soared from the stage like magic from a genie's uncorked bottle. The musicians and audience breathed as one, swept along with the musical phrases by the interpretive hands of the masterful conductor.

Then, it happened! The soloist, following a red marking, moved on to the next section. The orchestra took the blue repeat, as rehearsed, and went back to the start of the previous section. The conductor heard the error on the second note of the phrase, immediately cuing the orchestra, "Three bars after letter B!"

It was brilliant! He even allowed two beats for the players to respond as their eyes jumped to the new spot. Only a musical genius could have reacted so quickly. It was the perfect fix, initiated so fast no one in the audience had time to detect a problem. Perfect—except for one thing: he said it in French!

The entire orchestra stopped dead in its tracks, the players gasping (in near perfect unison,) "What?"

On a day-to-day basis, the arts leader must be able to communicate effectively through a wide range of approaches: one-on-one conversations, working with small groups, addressing large audiences, even responding to the mass media. This chapter addresses some of the inherent difficulties in doing this well.

Determining The Best Method of Communication

A huge portion of every administrator's day is spent in meetings: lunch meetings, dinner meetings, even breakfast meetings; private meetings, group meetings; budget meetings, planning meetings, on and on and on. Consequently, it's probably a good idea to know how to work effectively through this communication medium, and it is all about communication.

It was a typical day at the office. An early-morning meeting had to be held for the Promotion and Tenure Committee, because scheduling across the various disciplines was nearly impossible. The usual bagels, sweet rolls, coffee and orange juice were provided while we worked.

The rest of the morning went by rather rapidly. A few miscellaneous meetings with individual students, faculty, and an off-campus guest brought the lunch hour around before hunger even had a chance to settle in. Off we went, my assistant and I, to discuss the budget over sandwiches at the nearby deli.

When we returned to the office, I casually glanced down at my schedule for the first time that day. I was due in ten minutes at a meeting of the Strategic Planning Committee. In parentheses, Karen had noted: (Buffet lunch will be served.)

First, let's examine the major premise of this meeting thing. In short, are all of these meetings necessary? Is this really the best way to get things done? Cardinal rule #1 is: don't waste time—yours or other people's. If the business can be handled just as well in a memo, send the memo. If it can be dealt with on the phone, make the call. If e-mail will do the trick, start typing. The fundamental purpose of a meeting is face-to-face communication and teamwork. If you don't need either one of these to accomplish a goal, don't waste people's time. Do it some other way.

WHEN TO CALL A MEETING

Far too often, people call a meeting when it isn't necessary. It is also the case, in this day and age, that people frequently make the opposite mistake—they try to handle matters through e-mail that should be dealt with in person. How do you decide when to write, when to type, and when to meet?

- One factor is the number of people involved. If you have to communicate with 200 people, you obviously need to give a speech. If you have something to tell 20 - 30, you can probably send a memo or a group e-mail message, (that is, if you have a convenient network which everyone accesses on a regular basis.) Personal face-to-face meetings work best with smaller numbers of people, and are most appropriate when interaction is desirable, when group decisions have to be made, or when discussion is the primary goal.

Personal, one-on-one communication is best accomplished face to face, although you have the whole gamut from which to choose: a meeting, a phone call, a letter, a memo, an e-mail message. (Notice, the speech has been omitted from this list; it is always inadvisable to lecture to one person, even though it may be tempting at times to do so.) A meeting between two individuals implies a dialogue. If you find yourself talking more than half the time, stifle your next comment and try a little bit of listening. Everyone will feel a whole lot better.

- Another factor in deciding which mode of communication to use is the immediacy of the problem. How fast do you need to get in touch with the other person(s)? In this age of technology, E-mail is very fast—at least on the sending side. Since everyone does not check e-mail continually all day long, however, it is possible for your urgent message to sit there on a computer screen unread. Unless you are certain the recipient of your message will log on soon, it may be better to use the telephone when time is an issue.

The telephone at least gets you to the person's house or office immediately. The old game of telephone tag with secretaries in the middle has become almost obsolete these days, with answering machines grabbing your message as soon as it arrives and spitting it out to the recipient at the first possible opportunity. (Most of us cannot ignore the blinking light too awfully long without handling the call.) The actual connection of the two people on the phone system can still be frustrating beyond belief, simply because so many people have their answering machines turned on all the time; they seldom pick up the phone when it rings. People keep calling back and forth, each one talking to the other person's machine. When a message is urgent, this process just may not cut it.

So, for the exchange of timely information, none of these modes of communication is ideal, but each has its purpose. All of them beat the U.S. mail, although overnight express mail is certainly a possibility for formal communication that is urgent.

- A third factor in determining the preferred mode of communication is the content itself. How personal is the topic of discussion? There is no question about the best way to handle confidential information: it is definitely person-to-person in a private meeting. E-mail is sometimes read by others; phone conversations can be overheard; but a personal meeting can be controlled and kept as private as you need it to be.

- Yet another factor is the relationship of the people involved in the communication. When the nature of the conversation is such that you want or need to establish a closer working relationship with the other person(s), a meeting is very beneficial. When it is important to communicate your personal concern or support as well as the business at hand, a meeting is preferable. As a leader, you need to consider carefully the relative coldness of all other modes of communication. Nothing can replace the rapport you are able to build in a face-to-face meeting. It is the best way to gain someone's cooperation and support; it is the best format for building consensus; it is the ideal mechanism for getting people on board, heading in the general direction of your institutional mission. Whether this is a private meeting, a group meeting, or even a speech delivered to a large number of people, the in-person approach stands head and shoulders above all the rest in establishing effective relationships with the people you seek to lead. With artists, the personal attention may be the key ingredient to gaining cooperation and support.

• Another consideration is what you hope to accomplish. If you need to ask somebody to do something—take on yet another committee assignment, entertain a campus guest, give a speech, play a concert, organize a special exhibit— you would be well advised to do it in person. It is so easy to say "No" on the computer. Think of the times you have received requests by mail that have just gone sailing into the nearest garbage can, but I'll bet you have been caught off guard more than once by a person on the telephone, asking you to volunteer for something or donate to something. You just couldn't think of a good enough excuse to say "No," and it's even harder in person. When someone, anyone, looks you in the eye with that pathetic expression of beseeching need, well, most of us crumble. Remember that! When you really want somebody to sign on the dotted line, ask them face to face.

My suspicion is, all of us already know this, but sometimes we are hesitant to do it, because we are afraid the person will say "No," and a personal rejection is far worse than one delivered by phone. When the "No" comes in the mail or via e-mail, we barely feel it. So, we have, over time, developed an instinct for self-preservation. Stifle it! If you are the guy doing the asking, and if it is really important, forget about the discomfort of a face-to-face "No." Besides, you are the boss. The odds are definitely in your favor here. (By the way, if the tides are turned, and someone else is asking you to do something, remember there is a real art to saying "No" gracefully. We talked about this in "Making Decisions.")

- The final factor in determining the best mode of communication is just how much time you have in your day. While it may be desirable to meet with everybody in person, it just isn't feasible. The effective leader must make time for strategic planning, thinking, and implementing high-level initiatives. The decision as to how to carve up your extremely busy workday is a tough one, requiring continual fine tuning.

Staying in Control of your Job and your Time

It is important to note that you probably don't have time to meet personally with everybody who wants to have a private meeting with you. For this reason, it is a good practice to have somebody other than you screen your calls, and perhaps even your e-mail. If your assistant has clear guidelines on the type of business you wish to handle in meetings, and what types of things you prefer to deal with by phone, memo, letter, or e-mail, (s)he can then steer people toward the mode of communication you prefer.

Keep in mind that artists will always want a private meeting. It is yet another sign of that need to be #1. Often, their concerns can be met by a quicker phone call. If your assistant is good, (s)he can make the alternative of waiting for free time in your schedule look like a dismal choice; steer toward phone calls whenever possible.

Students, on the other hand, have so little opportunity to talk in person to the head of the arts unit, it is wonderful to open this door as frequently as possible. Unlike the faculty, students will not overdo their requests to see you, primarily because they are usually not particularly comfortable talking to the head of their school. An occasional student may become a pest, wanting to traipse through the door every time the slightest problem arises. It doesn't take long to spot these prima-donnas-in-training. (They are often graduate students, who honestly believe they can help you run the program.) Sometimes, students are just looking for an advisor or a parent away from home. Suit yourself, but keep an eye on the frequency of visits; if a particular student becomes a problem, it is pretty easy to send a gentle message that your time needs to be reserved for the big stuff.

WRITING MEMOS, LETTERS, AND E-MAIL

Memos sent via inter-office or U.S. mail to a group of people are generally one-way messages designed to inform the recipients of something—policies, events, data, procedures, deadlines, even upcoming meetings. Sometimes a response is requested; usually, the memo is just informational. Memos should be used sparingly, since they are an impersonal, matter-of-fact type of correspondence; but they are also an efficient way to communicate information to everyone at the same time. Since people tend to file them, every memo should be written with an eye toward the unknown reader, who may some time in the next millennium pick it up and wonder who wrote it.

Some leaders use the memo inappropriately to announce controversial decisions. Unless you want to be regarded as an autocrat or an unfeeling tsar or any number of other more colorful titles, it is probably a poor idea to launch new directions or present bad news through a general memo. Employees prefer to hear the tough stuff face-to-face. It is far better, when you are forced to bring bad tidings, to give it your best shot, complete with remorseful looking facial expressions and grim determination resounding from your very being. A piece of paper just can't quite accomplish that.

Copying to Others

It is an unwritten code of ethics that if you intend to copy somebody on a memo, that name should be included in the address, right after a CC: This is critically important, especially if you choose to send a copy of a personal memo to someone else. If the primary person to whom the memo was addressed learns that another party received a copy of it, the immediate assumption is that you are operating behind his/her back for some reason. (The typical person is quite creative in coming up with a colorful list of possible reasons for your treachery.) When the invisible copy goes to someone on a different hierarchical level of the organization, you really have a mess on your hands. Don't do it!

Another rule of thumb is that when you are sending a memo to someone over your head, always send a copy to your boss and to anyone else whose job sits between yours and the party to whom you are writing; CC their names and titles right on the memo. If you don't do this, you will be accused of trying to go out around your boss, a practice that is deeply frowned upon in the academic world and in much of the rest of the world, as well. Then, whatever you were originally intending to do with your memo will be absolutely dwarfed in comparison to the fiasco you have just created with your boss.

Sending a Personal Letter

With so many different forms of communication available to us, the personal letter has become almost extinct. In this era of Faxing and e-mailing and telephone answering machines, the letter now holds a position of supremacy. It is akin to the Hallmark Card slogan, "Care enough to send the very best." As an endangered species, the letter, when received, tells the recipient that you were willing to take the time to draft a message just for him/her. When you hand-write your message, instead of using a typewriter or word processor, your message becomes even stronger, because now it is clear that the letter came from you personally, not through some unknown secretary or assistant. So, if you want to have the maximum personal impact, do it the old-fashioned way, write a letter. (Isn't it amazing how we have come around, full-circle?)

Sending E-mail

On the other hand, E-mail is usually a pretty impersonal form of communication. It has the advantage of allowing you to communicate directly with another person, without an intermediary like a secretary or an office manager getting in the middle. Further, the message does go out in your words, and the answer comes back directly from the person to whom you are speaking; but (and it is a huge but) there is always the temptation to send e-mail messages too hurriedly. Since your message can be in the other person's computer just as fast as you can click on the "send" icon, it is easy to make a mistake and send it off too quickly.

So, there is a real tendency to be too casual in e-mail communication. Messages typed in the heat of a bad moment are gone before you have second thoughts about them. Consequently, a lot of people say things in e-mail they would never say in person or in a letter. When you type a letter, it is a bigger deal: you usually proof-read it before signing your name, then you have to address the envelope, lick the stamp and smack it on, and finally, you need to take some steps to mail it. As a result, you probably don't send garbage out via US mail very often.

But, e-mail is often far too casual. People don't seem to worry about correct spelling, or proper sentence structure, or even good manners when they are sending e-mail. It's a lot like the guest who drops in on you uninvited; nobody expects you to have the dishes done and the newspapers put away, because it is just a casual visit, probably by a close friend or relative. E-mail has that same feel to it. It is casual communication. Consequently, people seem to feel it is OK to type e-mail as though they are speaking to the other person.

Misinterpreting your e-mail

The primary problem with e-mail is that it arrives without a clue as to how the sender actually feels about the message being delivered; no facial expressions, hand gestures, or tone of voice to guide the receiver through the communication. Even a telephone call provides information about the meaning of the words through the pitch, tempo, rhythm, inflection, and volume of the speech. E-mail has none of these. Since it is written, it can be examined over and over again by the recipient, just like a letter. Yet, this time, the proper amount of care has probably not been taken to make certain the words are clear and unambiguous. The message has been dashed off in "real time" at the one end, yet is received on the other end as a more permanent form of expression. Humor, in particular, can get lost in the translation. Without the aural clues, remarks meant to be funny can easily come across as cutting, hurting comments. As a result, e-mail should be used with great care in business situations.

RUNNING MEETINGS

Getting Something Accomplished

OK, now that we have explored all the other means of communication, I have to admit, there are still a lot of times when the meeting is the best mode to get something done. Whether you are running a meeting or just participating in it, your primary goal should be to get something accomplished. After all, you don't have extra time to waste on meaningless exercises in organizational dribble, and neither does anyone else. So, before you walk into a meeting, any meeting, make sure you have some idea of what you personally want to accomplish.

> *Everything I ever needed to know about how not to run a meeting I learned from one unforgettable specimen back in the early 70's. Miss Management was in charge.*

> *When I arrived, a few minutes before the meeting was to begin, there was nobody there. I thought I was in the wrong place.*

Just then, another member of the committee came ambling in, a seasoned veteran, fully aware that there was absolutely no hurry. Five minutes after the meeting was scheduled to start, the chairwoman moseyed in the door, chattering away at her companion, a rather disgruntled looking chap, who had obviously been caught en route.

She took charge immediately, looking around the room, assessing the group and declaring, "Well, since nobody's here yet, we may as well have some coffee," at which point she turned and walked back out the door. By now, I was beginning to seethe; I had interrupted some important work of my own just to get to this meeting.

Back she came, stirring her coffee with the end of a ballpoint pen. It was now fifteen minutes past the time we should have begun. A few more stragglers had come in and were in various stages of greeting their colleagues and fetching coffee.

"OK, folks, let's get started," said our fearless leader. At that, we all dutifully took our chairs; some of the rookies in the group, me included, took out a pen and some paper in the hope of accomplishing something. The old-timers just leaned back in their chairs. There was no printed agenda and no discussion materials. Actually, we didn't really have much of an idea why we were here; I guess it was just time for the monthly meeting.

Miss Management rambled on for a few minutes about an item we needed to consider. The discussion was aimless, one noisy, opinionated member of our esteemed company pretty much monopolizing the floor. Twice, new people arrived, apologizing for being late as they took their places at the conference table. Both times, the committee chair stopped everything to "bring the late-comers up to date on the topic being discussed." We were now 40 minutes into the meeting, according to the time it was supposed to have commenced, and we had accomplished nothing.

About then, one of the early birds arose with an apology, saying he had another commitment. During the next ten minutes, four others dribbled out the door. Eventually, Miss Management noticed there were fewer people left in the room than had departed. The meeting was adjourned with the threat of more discussion on the same topic to be scheduled some time in the near future.

When you are in charge, it is your responsibility to make sure the meeting is effective, and that the people who attend go away feeling good about the time they spent there. There are actually some excellent books on the market to help you run a dynamic, productive meeting. My objective here is to spell out the various types of meetings you might be involved in as the head of an arts unit and to provide an overall strategy for handling each.

Informational Meetings

These are meetings in which the leader or a guest speaker conveys data, policy information, new procedures, and major announcements to the membership. This type of meeting involves very little input from the constituents, although there may be ample opportunity for questions or comments from the floor. These meetings are usually large, the speaker utilizing slides, overheads, or handouts to help focus the listeners on the information being presented.

Just a few tips on handling the informational type of meeting:

- Avoid duplicating information. This is insulting to the participants. If you wish to use slides or overheads, don't stand there reading them. Your display materials should be used to help the listeners organize and absorb your message. Make sure they are brief and large enough to be read easily from the back of the room. Your speech should provide in-depth information around these points.

- If you pass out handouts, realize people may sit there reading them instead of listening to you speak. On the other hand, don't just read these written materials to your audience.

Handouts should provide the data you are referring to in your speech. If they need to be studied further, consider passing them out after your talk. If, on the other hand, everything people need to know is contained in the written materials, there is really no need for a meeting, unless you are using that time to elaborate on the information, or convey the rationale behind it.

- If your meeting is designed solely for the purpose of providing information, make sure people know that. Do not pretend it is set up for their participation. Also, make certain that a meeting is the best way to convey the information.

Discussion Meetings

These are meetings wherein the group carries the primary responsibility for exploring a given topic. (One topic is usually all that can be managed, since this type of meeting is very time intensive.)The leader of a discussion meeting must direct traffic and effectively steer the conversation toward an ultimate consensus or decision.

Some advice on running a discussion meeting:

- Avoid stating your opinion. As the leader of the meeting, your job is to ensure a free and productive discussion among the participants. Stating a viewpoint sets the leader up as biased and tilts the meeting toward a pro and con discussion of the leader's viewpoint, instead of an open-ended discussion of the topic at hand.

- Make certain everyone who wants to participate has the opportunity. You may have to invite comments from the quieter members of the group, and keep the noisy ones from totally dominating the meeting. Stifle any attempts to criticize someone's comments; all should be free to speak without being attacked. Likewise, refrain from passing judgment yourself; avoid saying such things as "Good point," or people will begin jockeying for position, trying to get one of those accolades for their comments.

- When the same viewpoints begin to be repeated, move the discussion along toward a vote. If it is obvious that you do not yet have a consensus, encourage further discussion by suggesting some area that has not yet been considered.

- Keep an eye on the time, and accordingly work toward a decision within the time allotted. This may mean moving the discussion along with briefer points, making the participants aware of the time factor; but still a decision should not be pushed through prematurely. A satisfactory meeting is one in which a decision is reached when the people present are ready to make it. That may, unfortunately, have to be at the next meeting.

- Postpone the vote only when it is clear that a better decision could be made with additional data that needs to be collected.

General Business Meetings

These are meetings during which a number of people give reports, share information, and conduct old and new business. Here, the leader holds the responsibility for covering a variety of topics, seeing that all scheduled participants get their turn to present their material, and bringing timely matters to a vote. Such meetings are often the most formal, and are the model for implementing the classic, "Roberts Rules of Order."

There are fewer tips needed for the general business meeting, since it is nearly ceremonial in nature:

- Such meetings need to be very well organized prior to the event. The agenda should be carefully planned so that all elements do take place. This usually means placing the committee reports, etc. early in the meeting, with any business requiring discussion or voting occurring last. Discussion will always fill whatever time is available; by placing it last, the parameters can be set according to the remaining time in the meeting, without bumping something important off the agenda.

- With so many elements taking place, it is probably necessary to avoid any lengthy discussions that may crop up unexpectedly. As soon as it becomes obvious that a discussion is evolving, suggest that this item become a major topic on the next meeting's agenda, or assign the topic to a subcommittee for further consideration.

Setting the Agenda

In all cases, it is of paramount importance to set a clear agenda for your meeting, and whenever possible, to distribute this agenda prior to the meeting. It is also important for the participants to know what type of meeting to expect. That enables all of the players to come prepared to contribute to the meeting's agenda. It also enables everyone to decide what they personally wish to accomplish in your meeting. (Hopefully, there are not too many side agendas; however, you should expect there to be some.)

Creating agendas can be tricky business. An agenda that is too long causes frustration for everybody. People feel overwhelmed by the quantity of business to be covered, and are deeply aware during the meeting itself that they may not get through all of the planned agenda. There is a reluctance to participate, because time is obviously short, given the number of agenda items. There is also a tendency to think about a topic other than the one being discussed at the moment, causing only a part of your membership to be actually with you at any given time in the meeting.

On the other hand, an agenda that is noticeably shorter than the time allotted for that particular meeting signals the freedom to expound— and expound they will! There is always somebody in the room who likes to give speeches. Give the impression there is time to burn, and somebody will surely get out the matches. The ideal agenda is planned carefully to be just the right size for the time allotted. When a group decision needs to be made, there should be sufficient time to mount a reasonably full discussion, take a vote, and reach a decision. When input is needed on a particular subject, there should be time to flush it out from as many participants as possible. When information is just being presented, there still should be enough elbowroom for comments and for unexpected discussions to pop up. As stated previously, whenever this occurs, and it appears that a Pandora's box has just been opened, it is advisable to move that topic to a future meeting for a more complete discussion.

If the planned material has been completely covered prior to the concluding time of the meeting, for goodness sakes, quit early! Nobody will believe their good fortune and you will be proclaimed a hero among heroes. Never try to fill the remaining time with something else. Conversely, if the clock says it is time to conclude the meeting, and you have not finished the whole agenda, end the meeting anyway, with an apology for trying to cram too much business into one session. Make sure there is another time set to complete the work, so that everyone can leave with a clear conscience. Most people hate to be a part of a meeting that does not work.

Keeping the Meeting on Track

If the reason you were unable to complete the business at hand was not too full an agenda, then you must have failed to keep the meeting on track. Perhaps, somebody dominated the discussion and went on and on and on. That's your fault! It's really rude for another participant to say, "Hey, why don't you shut up for a while?" It is not rude for the leader to politely suggest that everyone limit their input to three or four sentences; and then, gently interrupt Professor Mouthy when (s)he exceeds that limit. If (s)he persists, take off the gloves and forget about the word gentle. It is your job to keep the meeting running effectively and open to everyone.

It is equally important to have a set starting time and completion time for every meeting, and to stick to that schedule. Meetings that consistently start and end on time bring the leader a reputation for competency and also demonstrate a healthy respect for other people's time constraints.

Running a Committee

Smaller group meetings generally fall into the category of committees or councils or boards. These are usually working groups set up to plan something, design something, write something, or discuss something with a recommendation of action to be taken. If you wind up in charge of such a committee, keep in mind that the larger the group, the longer it will take to get anything accomplished. Large committees seem to exist solely for the purpose of spawning sub-committees.

Leading a committee is very different from running a large meeting. Here, you need to be one of the group, participating much more on the same level as everyone else. Your role might well be to organize the meetings, schedule them, reserve the space, perhaps select the people to serve on the committee, and make certain the designated work does get done. Beyond that, you should attempt to keep everyone involved in the process to the best of their ability to contribute, even when that process appears to be painfully slow.

Committees tend to live forever. This is because they continually generate more work for themselves. A really effective leader knows when a committee is no longer needed. You will do the world a real favor by aiming toward the ultimate goal of getting rid of your committee just as soon as its purpose has been served. (You will make history if you do this more than once.)

In summary, you probably know the joke about the giraffe being a horse created by a committee? Well, I don't know about you, but I wouldn't miss looking at those giraffes every chance I get. How do they support those incredibly skinny necks? Whoever would have thought that would work, what with gravity and all? So, never underestimate the creative power of a committee; go make a giraffe. The world could really use another one!

A Word About Participating in Meetings

With all this talk about running meetings, it may be necessary to take a moment to consider your role as a participant. After all, you won't always be in charge! And when you're not, it's far too easy to act as though you are. This bossing business can become addictive. So, whenever you are supposed to be one of the troops, instead of the commander-in-chief, save your input for one or two major points. These should be elements that only you can contribute. Resist the temptation to run the meeting from the back seat.

Before the session, you might spend just a moment thinking carefully about your role in this group. How can you be useful? Why have you been asked to attend? How can you help advance the mission of this particular organization? Then, go, and keep your mouth shut, until you see an opportunity to make a meaningful positive contribution.

GIVING SPEECHES

There are a lot of things you need to know about giving speeches. Most of them, you have to learn from experience: how to control your nerves, how to regulate the pitch and the dynamic range of your voice, how to pace your delivery, how to project with or without a microphone, how to let your personality color your words and shine through your presentation, and above all, how to choose your audience.

The first clue that I was in for a very long day came as I got out of the car. The concrete steps to the entrance of the building were edged in bright yellow paint. Two very old ladies were helping each other up the walkway; it was impossible to tell who was supporting whom. (Actually, that one cane might have been the critical focal point.) I suspected the slightest little breeze would blow them both into a heap of polyester and cotton.

As I held the door open for them, my eye caught the scene inside: dozens of tiny old ladies—in wheel chairs, on walkers—people who made these two look like rugged teenagers. The butterflies I usually experience before a speech were instantly replaced by panic. Here I was, in my early thirties, about to deliver a speech on "How to Balance a Career with Motherhood," and the median age of my audience was at least 76.

I approached the podium with dread. After a gooey introduction that stressed all the wrong things, I went at it—too late to do anything else. I spoke as cheerfully as I could, given the circumstances, focusing my gaze alternately on specific faces around the room. One was asleep in her chair even before I began. (She may have been dead.) Five minutes into the speech, more began to nod off. Thank, God, there were a few sprinkled through the group who looked interested, or perhaps they were just sympathetic. I began to count on their smiles and nods of encouragement.

When at last I was finished talking, light years after I had begun, the applause was enthusiastic—probably because I had stopped—waking most of the sleepers. There were a respectable number of questions and appreciative comments before we were mercifully adjourned. A number of ladies dutifully hobbled up to thank me for "my wonderful talk." Then, the duo who had collectively arrived with me that morning slowly made their way to greet me once again. I moved forward to meet them half way, not wanting to be the cause of their demise.

The one with the cane peered up at me over the rim of her spectacles. "I want you to know, dear, I have read all your books," she said in a scratchy voice I can hear to this day. Before I could answer, her partner barked, "Oh, no, Hilda! that's not Erma Bombeck!" "It isn't?" she squeaked, her face crumbling in obvious disappointment and disillusionment. With that, they made a painfully slow U-turn and embarked upon their interminable voyage to the door.

Yes, I've made a lot of mistakes giving speeches and somebody may as well profit from them; so, let's talk about those. First, preparation.

Preparing your Speech

Preparation is everything! Unless you are another Johnny Carson, don't try to wing it. (Don't think for one minute that Carson ad-libbed his opening monologues, either. No sir, people made good money writing those lines.) One of the problems with improvising a speech, beyond the obvious one of babbling like an idiot, is that it takes twice as long to say the same thing. When you prepare your remarks, you prune, rework the sentence structure, select the precise word to convey your meaning. The finished product is much more concise than anything you can come up with on the spot.

The argument to counter all of this is that people prefer to be spoken to more directly, that nobody likes someone standing up there reading to them. This is true. My advice is to prepare your speech, then, spend whatever time it takes rehearsing the delivery. You probably won't have a TelePrompTer, like the kind politicians use in their televised speeches, but that's OK. With a little practice, you can learn to glance up and down as you talk, grabbing entire sentences at a blink, using the commas, the semicolons, and the periods to snatch the next phrase. As a result, you will be able to spend at least half the time looking your audience in the eye, smiling, grimacing, whatever the text requires to emphasize its meaning. Plus, your message will be clear and to the point.

If all of this feels just too stilted for your style of communication, you may be one of the few people in the world who speaks better off the cuff. If so, do it, but watch your time. Always speak less than you think you should. A few casual words go a long way. This applies also to those unexpected moments we all experience, where some fool says, "Oh, there's Dr. So and So. Why don't you say a few words?" In these instances, do just as you are asked: say a few words. Don't kid yourself; you are not Johnny Carson! (And you can bet that Johnny Carson studied his monologue plenty before the "Heeeeere's Johnny!")

Controlling Your Introduction

And speaking of introductions, you need to attempt to control these. People will ordinarily ask you to send them a bio prior to your presentation. Don't do it! I once sent a five-page bio to an organization to pull information from as they chose. The woman who introduced me began at the beginning of my written bio, and to my horror began to read it, word for word. Gradually, my smile turned into a frozen grimace. By the time I stood up to speak, I figured the audience had developed an intense hatred for my very being—those who hadn't already gone home, that is. The only thing I could think of to say was, "Well, you will be happy to know that my speech isn't nearly as long as my introduction." Thankfully, they laughed, and we went on together.

My advice is to send the organizer a list of five or six credentials or brief tidbits that you feel would be particularly appropriate to mention in your introduction. (Fewer is OK, too.) This list may change, depending on the group or the topic you will be addressing. But under no circumstances should you give anyone access to your whole life, and expect them to pick the good stuff. You just may have to sit there while they regurgitate a part of your career you wish you hadn't experienced the first time around. It's tough enough giving a speech, without having to climb a mountain on the way to the lectern.

As for mountain climbing, the tougher the topic, the shorter the speech. Don't expect people to be so interested, that they will be happy to struggle through mountains of data—about anything. They won't. Keep the statistics to a minimum. Avoid using "shop talk" only you and your colleagues understand. (Don't think it's OK to use it, if you define it; if you have to define something, you shouldn't be using it. Speak English.)

Watch the humor. Unless people know you well, the first time you crack a joke, they will be hesitant to laugh. If it's subtle, they will really be in a quandary. Plan to give them some time. If you do want to have some fun in a speech, you need to send your audience some clear signals, especially if the environment in which you are working is ordinarily a stuffy sort of place. Once they understand that you are not going to be stuffy, they will listen for the humor; so, don't disappoint them.

It is absolutely impossible to communicate effectively if you bury your nose in your speech. Whether you read it word for word, or follow a less rigid outline of note cards, look at your audience as much as humanly possible. To avoid major slip-ups, keep one finger on your place in the text. Otherwise, when you look down, you will see nothing but unrecognizable gibberish. In this computer age, it is no longer a problem to have middle-aged eyes; just print your speech in 14 or 16 point bold. You'll be able to see the thing from across the room.

Also, always number the pages of your text. You haven't lived until you drop a multi-page speech and try to put it back together again while talking. If the pages aren't numbered, you may as well leave the whole mess on the floor and just make it up as you go along. By this time, your heart will be thumping so loudly, they won't be able to hear what you're saying anyway.

If you have a printed text, you need a podium of some sort. It just doesn't work to stand there holding several pages of a speech. An easel or a music stand will do nicely in a pinch. You do have to be careful, however, with makeshift equipment.

I remember one particularly infamous speech, where I was using an adjustable music stand. As I spoke, I pushed a bit against my pretend podium and it responded by moving down a notch. I continued to press; it continued to move. Gradually, the text slid further and further from view until I could no longer discern even the color of the page, let alone the print it contained.

Ever so slowly, while talking away like mad, I eased the speech up off the music stand, until it climbed back into focus. For the rest of the delivery, my lectern served only to collect the pages as I finished them. This was not a perfect solution, but it was certainly better than winding up on my knees, groveling around on the floor muttering into my printed masterpiece. I hasten to add that my ploy worked. No one noticed, and when I watched the video, I even forgot it had happened; but at the time, it felt like a vaudeville act.

If the circumstances are too casual for a lectern, they are also too casual for a prepared speech. Either sit down at the table with your audience, or stand up and speak extemporaneously. Don't worry. If you prepared a speech, you will remember the gist of it.

Always find out exactly how much time you have for your presentation. Prepare to speak just a bit less than the time they give you, because your introduction will take a few minutes, and meetings generally run a little late. In the history of the world, nobody has ever complained about a speech being too short.

Try to time your presentation at home. As you rehearse it, keep the following points in mind:

- You will probably speak more slowly out loud than when reading silently to yourself.

- You may have a somewhat faster delivery when you are nervous.

- You need to allow for a little bit of time for laughter, if you expect some, or for applause, if you earn it.

- You may have a tendency to add little asides even in a written speech; ad-libbing always takes more time than your planned remarks.

To be on the safe side, you may want to build in some elastic. To do this, clearly mark a few sections of your speech as optional. Either highlight them with a yellow marker, or put a big bracket around them, so you can make the choice to "say it or skip it" on the spot. If your audience looks bored, falls asleep, or begins to fidget or yawn, by all means, "skip it" even if time is not a problem. If someone in the audience looks at a watch, that's OK; if the person begins to shake it, or hold it up to his/her ear, you are in trouble.

Above all, find a way to put yourself into your speech. People listen best to people they like. They can only learn to like you, if you give them a piece of yourself. As early in the speech as possible, work in a personal anecdote of some sort. If you make a verbal error or your tongue gets all twisted up, don't be afraid to laugh right along with your audience.

I told you I've made a lot of mistakes giving speeches. You will, too, if you do it often enough, and when you do make a blooper, let it go. People will love it! Besides, life's too short to worry about the little stuff.

Using a Translator

You probably can't imagine being in a situation where you are lecturing to a bunch of people in some other country; I couldn't either, that is, until I wound up in Taiwan, doing just that.

There were about 200 junior college students and a sprinkling of faculty, all Taiwanese, sitting in front of me, quietly listening to every word I spoke, probably understanding very little, if any, of it. To my right was a teacher, who spoke both languages; at least, I hope he did, because he was busily telling them what he thought I had just said.

His translation went by so fast, I vowed to say less this time before stopping. How could he possibly have followed that last nervous deluge of information. (The tenser I get, the faster I speak.) At last, we fell into a doable system. I slowed down my delivery; I also stopped after about a paragraph, sometimes two, to let him interpret less in one gulp. Students were beginning to nod and smile in what appeared to be the right places. My breathing came easier.

It's actually kind of nice having time out to watch your audience in between thoughts. I was eternally grateful I had written out my speech, however. I don't know how on earth I could have kept my thought process flowing without a full script.

It is really weird the first time you have to give a speech in two different languages. It also takes a lot of courage. Standing there, listening to that non-intelligible gibberish, you just have to wonder if what you said is actually coming out of the interpreter's mouth intact. Some times, you speak a lot and the translation is really short. Other times, you watch while your assistant goes on and on, gesturing wildly, and you wonder what on earth he is saying to these people. Did you say that? You search their faces to see if the expressions are what you would expect them to be.

Preparing to deliver a lecture or presentation in another culture does not have to throw you for a loop. Just a few extra things need to be kept in mind, most of which were alluded to in the example above.

- Use a written script, so you can hold your message together, in spite of the on-again-off-again style of delivery.

- Speak a bit slower than usual, so the interpreter has a shot at getting it right.

- Use as much expression in your face and in your body language as you possibly can without feeling like a fool; your audience will be studying these signals for help in deriving meaning from your words.

- Look at the audience, not at the interpreter, while you speak. Pretend you are speaking to people who understand every word you are saying, and make lots of eye contact to help bridge the gap between your two cultures.

- Stand quietly during the translation process, looking interested, so you will not pull attention away from the interpreter.

- Either discuss with your translator prior to the speech how much (s)he wishes to absorb in each section, or err on the side of caution: no more than two paragraphs at a time.

- Be gracious. If screw-ups become apparent, and the translator needs another go at a section or two, try to simplify your sentence structure and/or your vocabulary just a bit. "Shop talk" or jargon does not translate easily. Try to handle the problem without causing the interpreter any more embarrassment than (s)he already feels. Apologize for using awkward language and be careful to prune out whatever reoccurrence you might have of the same or similar phraseology.

- Remember to plan your speech for only half the time allotted, to allow for the translation process.

If all goes well, you will not even think twice about doing this again. It's really a lot of fun to reach out to people in other countries. Remember to take good care of your translator. After all, (s)he did most of the work. Keep in mind, not all cultures treat the clock with the same amount of anxiety we Americans do. Let's return to that speech in Taiwan.

I had been invited to present a two-hour lecture to a large group of music students at a Junior College in Taipei. I was understandably more nervous than usual. Two hours was certainly a huge chunk of time to fill trying to communicate with young people of a totally different culture. It was difficult to know what to expect and how I would be able to adjust the message to their various interest levels with an unknown translator working between us; but I was willing to give it a go.

I was traveling with another member of the faculty, a native of Taiwan, and my husband. Our host came to pick the three of us up at our hotel nearly a half-hour <u>after</u> our planned departure time. By now, I was really concerned about having enough time to set up the overhead projector and the *audio playback machine I would need for my multi-media address. It was particularly important that I have time to feel comfortable with all of this equipment in whatever setting I would be working. Time was already growing far too short for any comfort at all.*

As we bounced about in the back seat of his Mercedes, I was wearing out my left wrist, pushing my suit coat off my watch to gaze at the pointer. By the time we arrived at the school, I was a total wreck. Sheila turned to translate, "We have to stop first to meet the Department Head." "But, Sheila," I began, "We don't have time. . . ." Harry stopped me in mid-sentence. "Marilyn, it's OK, we're on Asian time." I knew what he meant. We had to have tea first.

We walked quite a distance to the music department, our guide stopping to show us the art gallery, the science building, the library. . . . When, at last we arrived at the music building, we were ushered into a large office, where we were introduced to several office staff and two members of the faculty. Then, into the Department Head's office. Amid her very gracious welcome, we were escorted to the sofa where an elegant tea service awaited.

What seemed like hours later (probably only fifteen or twenty minutes of Chinese conversation, during which we smiled, nodded, and drank tea,) our hostess stood and insisted we follow her. I asked Sheila where we were going now. Her answer, "She wants us to meet the President of the College." It was now ten minutes after the starting time of my lecture. When I asked about the 200+ students I was supposed to be addressing, Sheila just grinned and said, "Don't worry, they'll wait."

And they did. After yet another tea time with the President, we eventually made our way to the auditorium, where the overhead projector, the public address system, the tape player, audio receiver, mixer, and speakers awaited, along with 200 college students, sitting quietly in their seats. No, I was definitely not in America!

IMPROVISING IN PUBLIC

On occasion, you will have to "wing it." When you do, a whole new set of attributes must pop into the picture—that is, if they are there, inside your being, just waiting to be tapped.

- First, is the ability to think on your feet. It's one thing to have hours, even days, to prepare a speech or write a paper; it's quite another to have to speak extemporaneously and respond on the spot to whatever happens next.

- Second, is a nervous system made of steel. When you happen to be in front of a couple hundred people without a script, the stress can be so thick you are certain the audience can see it in Technicolor.

- Third, is a well-developed instinct for survival. This will be needed to drive you through the thickest parts of the experience.

- Fourth, is a solid foundation of self-esteem. Somehow, you have to believe you can do this without making a total fool of yourself.

If any of these traits are missing in your personality, do whatever you have to do to avoid improvising in public. Now it is rare, indeed, for me to offer advice like that, but I honestly believe that improvising is one of those skills not everyone can develop. At the same time, I also believe if you can do it at all, you can learn to do it better.

We were on the air, live. I hate to ad lib! When I have to give a speech, I always prepare thoroughly. In fact, I probably over-prepare; that's how I've always done it—clear back to the days when I was a pianist. Here we were, chatting away about the new faculty I had just hired. . .on national public radio. . . thousands of people listening. I was a nervous wreck!

Finally, it was over. The interview had gone well, both segments. They were now playing one of the new artist-faculty's recordings as the announcer and I talked privately about graduation, which had just taken place yesterday on the campus. Kurt knew I was full of anxiety about talking on the air; he also knew how to help a guest relax during off-air time.

I stood up to leave, and he interrupted, "Marilyn, could you possibly stay   one more minute? Just to say good-bye to the listeners? It feels strange to have a guest disappear during the music." "Sure, Kurt, no problem." I was feeling good again, having lived through this ordeal without saying anything really stupid.

The music ended. Kurt turned back to the microphone. "That was Mr. Earl Wild, new distinguished artist-in-residence at Carnegie Mellon University. We've been talking here in the studio with Dr. Marilyn Taft Thomas, Head of the Music Department at CMU. Marilyn, you folks had a beautiful day for your graduation ceremonies yesterday, didn't you?" "Yes, we certainly did, Kurt."

"Say, before you go, would you tell our listeners just a little about graduation? I understand the president gave a rousing speech to the seniors?" "Yes, he did!"

"I wonder, what do you tell young people going off into the world in 2007? Could you give us, in one or two sentences, the gist of the President's message to this year's Carnegie Mellon graduates?"

My mouth dropped. My heart pounded. I could feel the blood slowly leaving my head. Yesterday, at graduation, so much stuff on my mind, I hadn't heard a word of that speech."

Let's talk about each aspect of the problem of improvising in public. Thinking on your feet is the toughest part. It requires that all the rest of the attributes listed above are already in place—the iron nerves, the survival instinct, and the self esteem. A weakness in any one of these areas can sink your ship. Assuming for a moment that they are all there, you then have to have the kind of mind that can focus on something and can quickly sift through various options and select a workable path forward, almost instantaneously. This takes an interesting combination of analytical and creative thinking skills. Yet, even people who have both of these, cannot always react quickly enough. Bear in mind, there is absolutely nothing wrong with you if you cannot improvise effectively. It is a relatively rare talent. Some positively brilliant people avoid it like the plague.

What happens when something actually goes wrong in a speaking situation? Terror. Terror strikes like a bolt of lightening, calling upon every part of your being to come to the rescue. Instantly, something from the very depth of your soul cries out, "Survive!" Now, when this survival instinct comes surging to the rescue, it can swallow those nerves in a flood of determination. The experienced performer knows this feeling intimately: the adrenaline is pumping and the head no longer seems to be in charge of the situation. Yet, somehow the body does what it needs to do—the fingers, the lips, the diaphragm, all reacting like finely tuned soldiers, so accustomed to executing their moves with precision, they no longer depend on thought to direct their actions. It is a mutiny of the finest kind. The brain can no longer handle the task, so the ligaments, the muscles, the tendons all take over the situation and make it work. Make no mistake, it is that need for survival that is driving them on.

Actually, the brain is still involved. We know that. But it doesn't feel as though it is. To you, the performer, there seems to be a protective distance between the mind and the body for an instant, as you pass through the point of greatest fear. The survival instinct carries you through the panic and with gritty determination, you consciously regain control as you move on. (My palms are getting sweaty as I type this; the experience is all too familiar.)

After surviving this over and over again, eventually you learn to believe in your ability to perform, no matter what. This self-confidence is the final ingredient of the effective improviser. Without it, your mind is so busy saying, "Geez, I don't think I can do this; I am about to make a fool of myself; what will people think of me?" etc., that there is no longer an essential focus on what is transpiring. With sufficient self-confidence, however, you are able to stifle those thoughts and think solely about the topic at hand, sifting through the options, and pulling out the words that need to be implemented.

So, you see, all four abilities—thinking on your feet, controlling your nerves, calling upon that instinct for survival, and trusting yourself—are necessary ingredients for effective improvisation. If you have them, great! Let's consider how to use them in two different situations: the interview format and the question-and-answer session, better known as Q&A.

Conducting an Interview

Professor Clarinet was ultra-famous. At 75, his performing career had been long and distinguished, and was actually still going strong. In fact, he had just returned from a trip to the Far East, where he had given several concerts and a bunch of master classes. He was a superb teacher! Just about every major orchestra in the country had a student of his as principle clarinetist.

And funny! This guy was as good as any stand-up comedian in the business. You couldn't talk to him without dissolving into laughter. He just loved to entertain.

So, it was a real surprise when he got nervous about talking to the student body. All we needed him to do was to talk about his career. He did this all the time, casually dropping names like Lenny (Leonard Bernstein) and Aaron (Aaron Copland) as if they were everybody's close buddies. His career was a real inspiration to all of us; we just wanted him to share some of his professional experiences with the students who didn't see him on a regular basis.

But he was so nervous about doing this. He kept asking me, "What should I say?" until I promised to sit up on the stage with him. We'd treat it like a dialogue; I would ask him questions, just to keep things moving along. I even took him to dinner the night before to rehearse, and I laughed so hard, I could barely eat. This guy needed no help at all; he was hysterical! Still, he thought he did, so I was happy to agree to the interview format.

I had never done anything like this before, but how hard could it be? My role would be simple: I would just lead him into the stuff he had talked to me about at dinner. Once he got started, his gift for storytelling would take over. My only fear was that his humor might get a little bit off-color. I'd have to watch that, and be ready to steer him out of trouble.

The welcoming applause was deafening as we walked onto the stage and took our places, seated behind our individual microphones. After a brief introduction, which referred to the written bio in the programs, I baited Professor Clarinet into his first topic. I phrased my question just as I had the night before, when he had rambled on for five minutes in delightfully entertaining detail about his early days as a clarinet student. "Professor Clarinet, tell us about how you began your career as a clarinetist?" He hesitated, and replied, "Oh, there's not much to tell, really."

A bit surprised, I immediately followed up with a more specific prod, "Well, how did you first discover the clarinet?" Another hesitation. "Oh, they don't want to know about that." I switched gears, feeding him a more specific question, which he answered with a single, "No. Growing desperate, I reminded him of our conversation the evening before and asked him to tell the students about his first audition for a major symphony orchestra. His answer? "Well, I played, and they hired me."(Does anyone out there have an aspirin? or maybe a gun?)

Now, this painful example just points up the need for careful preparation. I don't mean the person being interviewed is rehearsed—even that doesn't guarantee a successful outcome; but, rather, the person leading the interview thinks carefully about the questions that should be asked before the interview actually takes place.

As the interviewer, your job is to enable the guest to communicate clearly. Ask questions that encourage lively feedback. Try to avoid any that can be answered with a simple, "Yes," "No," or "Not really." Plan questions that will probe into the most interesting aspects of this person's topic and reveal the essence of his/her being. You are in control of the flow of the discussion, but the speaker controls its content. So, you, too, may be surprised, amused, informed, shocked, right along with the audience. That's part of the challenge. Therefore, while you may prepare a list of questions beforehand, you must also be ready to follow through, down unexpected paths. In addition, you must be prepared to steer the conversation back, if the guest moves too far away from the subject you seek to explore.

To accomplish all of this, it is probably necessary to do some in-depth preparation, just to be able to speak knowledgeably and comfortably with your interviewee. Call it research or call it curiosity; you may want to read the book (s)he wrote, listen to some of the music (s)he composed, go to a play in which (s)he starred, study some of his/her art work—anything to give you a better sense of who (s)he is as an artist and as a person. Then, and only then, can you really get to the heart of the topic and hopefully to the person, as well.

Knowing your guest beforehand can be a tremendous help! For this reason, most interviewers attempt to at least talk to their speaker prior to the actual interview. The skillful ones are thus able to determine how much or how little help will be needed to draw out the essence of the person. Even then, as can be seen from the anecdote cited above, there can be uncomfortable surprises. A person may chat easily with you, one on one, but freeze up completely in front of the camera or the live audience. Things that felt perfectly natural to discuss in private may seem inappropriate before a group of strangers. That's apparently what happened to Professor Clarinet.

It is also possible that, taken out of their element, even the most extraordinary performers can feel totally at sea. As an inexperienced interviewer, I failed to realize the vast difference between Professor Clarinet's spectacular performing skills on the clarinet and his improvisational abilities as a public speaker. One of the students in the audience must have sensed the problem. He actually saved the day by raising his hand in the midst of our struggle and asked him to play. This, our guest did in an instant. I had been too nervous (or too stupid) to even notice the clarinet he held in his hand, like an extension of his very soul. I am eternally grateful to Student Sensitivity. Without him, I might be sitting there still, searching and poking for the perfect question that would open up our guest like a flower in spring. No need. The music said it all. I should have known that.

So, sometimes the guest speaker just may not be a speaker at all. You will have that, if you interview enough people. When that happens, pray for a commercial break or the presence of Student Sensitivity to help you on your way.

Living Through the Q & A

You can really get chewed up in a question-and-answer session. In fact, I had such a dreadful experience early in my administrative career, it was years before I permitted myself to be in that situation again. (No, I won't tell you about that one; some things are just too painful to share.) But since that time, I have learned a lot about how to survive these infamous Q&A sessions, which usually follow on the heels of a well-planned, clearly delivered speech.

All goes well until you innocently ask, "Are there any questions?" Usually, this will be met with a brief silence, and then, perhaps, one or two hands move gingerly upward, each one dangling a polite question mark at the ends of their fingers. No problem. Now if, instead, numerous hands shoot up like bullets from a cannon, you are most definitely in trouble.

Anticipating the Questions

Perhaps, you saw this coming. If you knew there would be a strong reaction to your message, hopefully you spent some time thinking about how to respond to a potential outburst. When you have to give bad news or take a controversial stand on an issue affecting a group of people, you know there will be some upset as a result. It is wise to spend some time beforehand trying to imagine the worst-case scenario. Write down anything you can think of that people might ask. "Why?" is a common question. Why are you doing this? Why are you saying this? Why do you think as you do? Even if you have included a detailed explanation of "Why?" right in your speech, that does not preclude someone from asking the question directly. The question may even be framed in a cloud of hostility.

You should prepare to face questions like "Why?" "When?" "What if?" and "What will you do next?" You should also be prepared to acknowledge strong emotions, whatever they are. Think about how you can validate the feelings of the opposition without appearing to reverse your position. If there is flexibility in your message, be ready to emphasize the areas of elasticity; this will help to meet your audience half way.

Never insult the questioner by pointing out that you have already covered that in the address (tempting though this may be;) instead, reiterate your main points as succinctly as you can. The person has just provided you with an opportunity to summarize and highlight your message. Plan to say in a nutshell what you have already elaborated upon in your speech. No need for lengthy responses. (You've had your turn to speak; the questioners now have their turn, and they will probably not be happy to have you hog up all of their time, too.)

Keep in mind, the people who are asking you questions are more than likely trying to tell you something, or else they are trying to tell the rest of the audience something. If they are upset, they will feel better just by saying what they have to say. If they have opinions that need to be voiced, they need the chance to do this. If they just want to impress everyone with their wisdom or their insight, this, too, is a valid use of the Q&A. So, give them some space to emote, and try to keep your answers shorter than their questions.

Be careful, though, not to brush someone off with too short a reply. You should treat each question with respect, answering it with honesty and with courtesy. If you are unable to give a complete response, state the reason—insufficient data, confidentiality, the wrong place or the wrong time—and tell them when you believe their question will be able to be fully addressed. Under no circumstances should you ever ignore a question or turn away from the person asking it until you have satisfactorily dealt with the essence of that point.

Equity is important in a Q&A sessions; people can really get upset when a leader permits one or two people to monopolize the session. If you get into a lively discussion wherein a lot of people wish to participate, politely limit each to a question and a brief follow-up. If possible, set this guideline before Mr. or Ms. Mouthy gets out of hand, so you don't appear to be insulting a specific person. As soon as you see lots of hands in the air, you might say something like, "Since so many people have questions or comments, let's limit ourselves to only one question plus a follow-up." You can always choose to go back to Mr. or Ms. Mouthy after everyone else has had a chance to speak.

Dealing with a Dearth of Questions

It is difficult to know in advance just how much time will be needed for Q&A, and you may have guessed wrong. It is actually better to have the scenario painted above, with too many people responding, than to have your plea for questions met with silence. So, err on the side of too little, rather than too much time.

Now, for those circumstances when you are left holding the bag: nobody seems to have any questions and there is a lot of time left. You always have the option of cutting it short; but if you are convinced that there are questions, and people just need to get going, you might try asking yourself a question. This probably sounds absurd, but some times you just have to prime the pump. Once you get them started, they may surprise you with their enthusiasm and strength of opinions.

If you have spent some time thinking about the questions you might get, pick one—the most controversial—and ask it yourself. Then, perhaps you might answer your own question, good-naturedly, of course, trying to give a bit more information that could inspire discussion. If this fails to arouse a response, you could try asking the audience a question.

The idea is that if they won't ask you questions, you will ask them one; so, ask your question and wait. If you still get no response, poke around a bit. Make your question a little bit more outrageous. Go to the extreme. Eventually, you may push somebody into a response. If so, see if you can invoke a good discussion. If not, then find a way to bring the session to a close without making them all feel as though they have failed some sort of test. You don't want your audience to leave feeling guilty for not participating. If you have saved a good joke for the end of your meeting, pull it out. Thank them for being a great audience and go home. At least, the police didn't have to be called in to quiet an angry mob. Now, wouldn't that be a whole lot worse?

DEALING WITH THE MEDIA

Radio. Television. Newspaper reporters. You never dreamed you'd have to do this sort of thing, but here you are. Your assistant has just transferred a call from an Associated Press reporter, and you are about to say something that will turn up in tomorrow's local newspapers.

Handling the Unexpected Press

How on earth do you deal with this? Nobody teaches you how to talk to the press. Suddenly, you just wind up doing it. Having learned on the fly, like just about everyone else who does it from time to time, let's see what I can share with you about the pitfalls of handling the media—or at least, how not to get manhandled by the media.

Forget everything you know about preparation. You hardly ever get the chance to prepare. An event happens, the press gets wind of it, and they want to talk to you. Also, forget about delegating this one. They want to talk to you, the head of the arts unit, and they want to talk to you yesterday. I know, you've been trying for months to get some publicity for all the great stuff your arts organization is producing, but they want to know about this.

There really aren't that many guidelines on dealing with the media.

- Tell the truth and stick to the facts. If you don't know something, don't try to wing it. Say something like, "I'm sorry, but I don't have that information at my fingertips, but I will be happy to get it for you and call you back." That will give you enough time to collect your facts and summon help, if you need it. Don't worry about sounding dumb. You will sound a whole lot dumber if you give them the wrong information and it shows up in print.

- Never say anything damaging about anybody, not even as a joke. They will quote you—every time, and it won't be funny on paper. They may even inadvertently change one or two words that tilts the tone of your comment ever so slightly further toward the negative.

- Talk slowly and carefully. If you can possibly do it, try to give one or two-sentence answers. The more you talk, the tougher it is for the reporter to capture the essence of your comments. The faster you speak, the greater is the likelihood of a misquote.

- Assume that everything you say will show up in print. Don't be fooled by statements that begin, "Off the record, can you tell me . . ." A good response to that is a laugh and "Sorry, I never say anything off the record!" This will signal to the reporter that you know what you're doing (even though you really don't.)

- Remember, this is not about you. (Unless, of course, it is a story about you.) So, try not to think about how you will look in the public eye or how you will sound to the public ear. This will only raise your level of anxiety and will take your mind off the goal. Instead, concentrate on articulating the facts as clearly and concisely as you can. Your personality will undoubtedly peek through the fabric of the interview regardless. More than likely, your whole conversation will be boiled down to only one or two brief quotes. You need to furnish these as best you can.

- Be as open as you possibly can be. Reporters need to collect information. If you don't give it to them, someone else will. If a reporter thinks there is a story there, you cannot get the idea buried. So, don't even try. Remember, it is your responsibility to lead your arts unit. Anything that shows up in the press or on television or radio could enhance or damage the reputation of your institution. Your objective should be to grab every media opportunity you can get, and try to turn each one into positive publicity for your arts organization.

The Reporter's View

If all of this sounds somewhat frightening, it may be helpful to consider the topic from the other side: the reporters' vantage point. Reporters are in the business of telling people what is going on in the world; to do this, they need stories. To stay in business, they need to get these stories faster and write them better than their competitors. Some reporters are more skillful than others, but they are all just people trying to do their jobs.

When you talk to a reporter, it is really important to keep this in mind, because, sometimes you will feel intimidated (the reporter may be abrasive or extremely pushy.) Resist the temptation to react to the personality at the other end of the line or the other side of the microphone; your reaction can only lead to a less effective job of putting a positive spin on this story. Other times, you may become so comfortable with the reporter, that you will relax and begin to chatter like you would with a new friend. Careful! You may get sloppy with the information and say some things that you will later regret. The reporter is neither friend nor foe; (s)he is just the person doing the job. Keep yourself focused on the goal: to get some good public relations for your arts organization.

Smelling a Story

Once you've been in this situation for awhile, you may be able to anticipate an occasional media blitz before it hits you. If so, get ready. Prepare a one-page summary of facts and related information. Gather up a brief bio of anyone remotely involved in the situation. Research the dates of events leading up to the story—the times, the places, the people. (They always want background information.) Then, step back and think about how all of this relates to the mission of your arts organization. How can this story help advance your institution's reputation in the field?

Jot down one or two key statements you would be happy to see quoted. Wordsmith them a bit. Make sure they are short enough and crisp enough to be quoted "as-is." Then, put your media sheet somewhere handy, so you can grab it if/when a call comes in from the press. If it turns out that you were wrong, and there is no publicity bonanza, file it along with your other media sheets. Who knows? The story may hit in a week or a month or even next year. You'll be doubly glad you have this data prepared.

Working with Professionals

All of this sounds as though you are the only game in town. Hopefully, you have someone on staff whose job it is to handle public relations—a real professional. If so, you will want to get as much of this public relations stuff into his/her hands as possible. After all, (s)he does know what (s)he's doing, and you are an artist, remember? Unfortunately, you will find that the media doesn't want to talk to your publicity director; they want to talk to real people, like you. They also want to talk to the experts—the people at the top. Again, when it comes to the arts unit, that's you. Even if you have a whole staff of public relations people on board, you will still be called upon to speak on behalf of your arts organization.

What you can do is turn to your public relations office for assistance in learning how to talk to the press. They should be able to give you a lot more help with the tools-of-the-trade than I can offer in these few pages of Heloise-type hints. This kind of assistance is best received when things are calm, when the heat is not on. There may be some institutional guidelines, as well, which you will want to know about. If you anticipate having to do a lot of interviews, on radio or television, you may even wish to do a little work developing your speaking voice. Look for an expert voice instructor to help you. Any of this training will give you more confidence, which will undoubtedly translate into more effective interviewing and public speaking.

Getting Press When You Want It

Believe it or not, sometimes you actually want the press around, especially in our business—the arts. We have this whole public side, in addition to our role as leaders, and we need it to prosper. You can only get people into those theater seats, into those art galleries, into those concert halls by telling them what's happening: what, when, and where. Furthermore, they won't come unless you convince them that your event is worth their time and attention—perhaps, even their money. There is a whole lot going on out there. People lead really complex, busy lives. Why should they come to your arts event?

Why, indeed! To you, it's one of the most exciting things that has ever happened. (Well, sometimes, at least.) But when you try to convey the importance of this affair to your public relations rep, your glowing description is received with a huge yawn. Take a good hard look. That yawn is important for you to see, because it is the same reaction everyone else out there is going to have when your event is listed in the newspaper or announced on the radio. Your event will be competing with every other arts event in town, not to mention the local football, baseball, hockey, and basketball teams.

Everybody wants the same bodies you are trying to attract in their seats.

Local newspapers may or may not have their own arts critic. More often than not, major arts events are covered by reporters who know little or nothing about that arts area—that is, if the event is covered at all. Trying to attract significant media attention prior to the event is about as easy as awakening a bear in hibernation. Usually, the best you can hope for is a listing of the concert, show, or exhibit in the arts section of the paper, if there is one. Paid ads are always an option; but advertising costs can quickly surpass the earned income from ticket sales resulting from those ads.

Radio and television coverage of the arts is even tougher to achieve. It takes a really unique event to capture the attention of the live media. Even then, it is an enormous challenge to convince anyone that an arts happening is worthy of prime-time news coverage. Human-interest stories are those warm, fuzzy features that pop up from time to time in the midst of an otherwise dismal sea of "bad news." When the arts manage to grab any media attention at all, this is usually their niche—the human-interest spot. Any time you want some coverage for an arts activity, try to sell the idea on the basis of human interest. Be ready to articulate in one or two compelling sentences just why your event is newsworthy.

You need to keep your expectations for publicity realistic, especially if you are working with someone else, whose job it is to handle the press coverage for you. Everything your arts organization does is not of equal importance. The bottom line is that you and the people in your organization have to do most of the work to build your own audiences. Your public relations person(s) should be responsible for helping with the truly newsworthy events.

Identifying a Story When You Have One

It takes more than a normal performance or exhibit to grab the attention of the press. But, every now and then, you do have a story; so, it's important to know one when you see it.

The ingredients of a happening that just could become a news item include any one or more of the following:

- A national or international celebrity associated with your arts organization. This may be worth at least one feature story in the arts & entertainment section of your newspaper.

- A bizarre event or program. Sometimes this can be "pitched" to an editor or a reporter in a related area—not the arts. Look for a tie-in to the education column, or science & technology, etc.

- Any human interest type of activity.

- The big news items: sex, violence, intrigue, tragedy, mystery, crime. (Hopefully, you don't have a lot of these.)

- Anything that is truly unique or innovative. There appears to be no end to the opportunities here.

- Any story that goes out on the national wire service, which may be picked up by all sorts of media.

When we introduced a new program for bagpipers in our music conservatory program, we became the first school in the entire world to grant a bachelor's degree in music with a major in bagpiping. Stories about this new option appeared on CNN, PBS, NPR, in Newsweek (even the Asian edition,) the Chronicle of Higher Education, People Magazine, Ripley's Believe It or Not, and innumerable press articles all around the world. I even wound up talking to a disc jockey on a radio talk show in Chattanooga, Tennessee, while in the middle of Chicago's Ohare Airport on route to Detroit, Michigan. This story had three different surges of publicity over the span of two years.

The best you can do in these cases is to work through the media, doing your best to maintain the dignity of the arts institution you serve. It is usually possible to maintain a positive image of the overall organization, by making a clarifying point or two in whatever interviews you give. Your goal should be to use the media to enhance the reputation of your arts unit.

Dealing with Bad Press

Brace up: sooner or later, you're going to fall into some bad press. I once got some really good advice from then President of Carnegie Mellon University, Richard M. Cyert. He said, "Don't worry too much about bad press. Most people won't even see it, and those that do, will forget about it a day or so after they read it." Of course, this is not the case with murder or mayhem, but with a little luck, you won't have to deal with too much of that.

The point is, anything that hits the papers about your arts unit will seem like a much bigger deal to you than it does to outsiders. Just keep in mind, it is really hard to get good press. The news media is convinced that people only want to hear about the sensational stuff—the tragedies, natural disasters, and criminal violence—and, oh yes, the sports and the weather. So, getting any kind of news coverage for your arts unit is an achievement. When it is not 100% positive, well, that's the breaks.

> *The Mendelssohn Choir of Pittsburgh was holding open auditions for new members. After receiving several strange phone calls, the Managing Director checked the ad they had placed in area newspapers. It read: "The Mendelssohn Choir of Pittsburgh will hold auditions for sopranos, tenors, and baritones on Sept. 1 by appointment only. Asses need not apply." Result? A record number of singers auditioned that year.*

CHAPTER #7   HANDLING PERSONNEL ISSUES

HIRING

Hiring is a lot more fun than firing, but both require great people skills and clear decision-making. There are a lot of ways to screw up either process—unfortunately, the big mistakes can even land you and your institution in court. So, it's really important to do it right.

"You fired who? Are you crazy?"

Yes, I know, the correct word is "whom;" she should have said, "You fired whom?" But, this mother was furious! I was not about to correct her grammar. Her daughter's teacher had just called to tell her he had been fired, and, boy, was she ever mad!

"I had, indeed, just fired her daughter's private studio teacher. Yes, he was a nationally renowned performer who held a principle chair in our city's highly acclaimed symphony orchestra. No, I could not tell her why on earth I had done this, but I could assure her that it was absolutely necessary."

"Yes, I did realize it was the middle of the year, and that she had sent her daughter to our school specifically because he was on our faculty. If she chose to pull her child out of our program and transfer her to another conservatory, we would certainly miss her; perhaps she might want to wait to see who would be replacing her teacher here before taking that step."

"No, I didn't know who that would be just yet; this whole thing just happened this morning. I would be happy to call her just as soon as a new teacher had been found. . ."

Four days later, I called this parent back to tell her the name of the person we had just hired. Her response was even more incredulous than the first time we had spoken; only this time, she was back on our side:

"You hired who? How on earth did you get him? Why, he's the best in the whole world!"

In this instance, we were able to move fast, because it was a part-time position. Had it been a full-time faculty appointment, we would have had to advertise nationally and go through a long and thorough search process, with the intense involvement of a committee and a lot of input from the faculty, students, and administration. As it turned out, I consulted immediately with the key members of our faculty, master teachers from our symphony orchestra who knew the specific field and who could identify the national leaders in performance and in teaching.

I got lucky—and I certainly needed some luck, given the extraordinary circumstances in which I found myself that morning. Everyone I consulted said the same thing, "Well, you might try so-and-so, and such-and-such, but, of course, the best in the field is Mr. Incredible, but you'll never get him!" It was uncanny. I spent four days talking to the experts. Everyone told me he was the best; and everyone also told me to not even try him, because he was already teaching in two other schools.

I could think of no good reason not to call him first. After all, I had been forced to fire a very prominent performing artist. The only way to prevent being lynched by a bunch of irate parents was to find somebody better; I definitely needed the best teacher in the country—fast!

As it turned out, I got him—with one phone call to his agent. The secret to this success was undoubtedly my opening sentence. I started out by saying, "I need the best horn teacher in the country, and everybody says that's you." This was probably the only thing I could have said that would have gotten Mr. Incredible's attention. He was definitely intrigued. After another ten or fifteen minutes of negotiation, he had agreed to fly in once a week to teach for us—yes, starting next month, right after the holidays.

"Joy, to the world," indeed!

Advertising the Position

OK, so that example is not typical. Let's say, you have an unexpected opening on your full-time faculty or staff, and the key word is full-time. You cannot just go out and hire someone, like I did here, even if you believe that you already know the perfect person for the job. Unless that person works in the institution, and would just be moving from one job to another, you are not free to hire him/her without opening the job to others. The issue you need to be concerned about is anti-discrimination—equal opportunity. There are federal laws, state laws, local laws, and executive orders regulating hiring. So, to stay in compliance with all of these, you must make your job opportunity known to a wide diversity of possible candidates.

Your institution will probably have some written guidelines to help keep you in compliance with the most recent laws. Follow these guidelines to the letter, every time you set out to hire a new person. There may, for instance, be institutional rules about posting job openings—where to advertise, how long the ads must run, etc. Your institution's guidelines should keep you out of trouble.

Once you are fully informed about the correct procedures, design an ad that accurately describes the position and place it in all the venues deemed appropriate by your organization. Checking other ads in these publications and other ads placed previously by your institution can help you determine what information needs to be included in your notice. There will be some costs involved, but these are necessary expenses. The benefits of advertising your position far outweigh the time and effort involved. You will, no doubt, be pleasantly surprised by the breadth of candidates who respond to your ads.

Significant staff time will be involved in screening the applications as they arrive, acknowledging their receipt, and setting up files of candidates. Even if you handle much of this yourself, you will probably need some help—a committee or a staff assistant. No matter how many people respond to your ads, you may still want to reach out to other strong candidates who may need to be actively recruited for the position. Identifying potential candidates is an important aspect of the search process; consult anyone you believe might be helpful in steering you toward "the right person."

Interviewing the Candidates

Once you have screened the applications and have selected a small number of top candidates, you will want to interview each of them. The first time you interview someone, you may be as nervous as they are. No need. Everyone you meet will have the written credentials you are looking for. (You already screened the candidates on the basis of their professional backgrounds.) Think about the job itself, what you actually need from this person. Your goal is to try to look between the lines of their resumes to determine who would go beyond the written job description and really excel in this position.

Draw up a list of questions that will help reveal the qualities you are searching for—things like, their enthusiasm for the type of work required, communication skills, motivation toward excellence, willingness to focus on the needs of others. Look for a good match between each person's life-time goals and the job in question.

Avoid discussions in areas of possible discrimination. (Review the list of danger zones before you begin interviewing people.) For example, even friendly chit chat about a person's national origin, marital status, age, etc., designed to help them relax, may be interpreted as a formal part of the screening process. If the person is not chosen, (s)he may accuse you of eliminating him/her on the basis of this conversation. So, don't do it!

If possible, try to interview all your final candidates on the same day, or at least during the same week. This gives you the best opportunity to compare them to one another and to weigh the pros and cons of each. If too much time elapses between interviews, your orientation changes and it is more difficult to make objective decisions. For faculty positions, when on-campus visits are needed, you may wish to see one person each week until the process is complete. As far as possible, keep the procedures the same. Have the same people meet all the candidates. Try to begin with the same list of questions. Each interview will, no doubt, wind up to be very different, and the direction the candidates take their interviews will help you sense the best fit for the job.

Making the Decision

Collecting other people's impressions of the candidates can be extremely helpful in making a final decision. Always check references, but make certain the candidates know you will be doing this. If they wish to have their application held in confidence, honor this request as long as you can. If you find it necessary to speak to someone in their current place of employment, talk with the candidate first to gain permission to proceed. Sometimes a person will prefer to drop out of the search, rather than jeopardize a present position; so be it!

In addition to the people's names submitted by the candidates, you should contact people they did not suggest. Previous places of employment can be good sources of information, provided you once again inform the candidates that you wish to do this. If there is a risk that such checking will get back to the current employer, you may be limited in your ability to snoop. Ultimately, if you are close to hiring someone, (s)he will need to understand your need to "fish or cut bait." Each situation is unique, but never cross the boundaries set by the candidate. If you can't agree to a reasonable level of inquiry, then move on to a different candidate.

Also, consult with anyone who met the person during the interviewing process. It is not necessary to give everyone an equal vote, but you should follow through to at least collect their opinions. Then, it is up to you to juggle all this input and make a final decision about whom to hire. Realize that you will occasionally blow it. Everybody who hires a lot of people will, sooner or later, choose a person who doesn't work out as hoped. Some people are really good at selling themselves in an interview, and not nearly as good at doing the job. (Checking their references should give you an inkling of this problem. So will a series of short-term jobs on their employment record.) Even when everything looks terrific, the job just may not suit the person. If you make a mistake, try to correct it as speedily as possible, before it turns into a real liability. (More on this in the next section on "Firing.")

Closing the Deal

When you finally reach a decision and are ready to hire someone, realize that person may turn you down. Consequently, don't reject everyone else quite yet. You may want to inform the bulk of your applicants, those you are certain you will not want to hire, that you appreciate their application, but. . . . Hold onto all those who received an interview, plus any that you were on the fence about. Keep on holding them until you have a signed contract. Let me tell you why:

We were down to three candidates for an important faculty position. All three were brought in for campus visits. The search committee unanimously preferred Candidate #1. So did I. So did the students who had met her and the other artist/faculty who had talked with her and had observed her teach.

Delighted to see such a clean process, I called Candidate #1 and offered her the position. She was equally jubilant and accepted the offer. As we chatted, she remarked that she did want to come back to campus one more time to check on housing and other personal things. So, as a courtesy, I agreed to pay the expenses for her second trip.

After completing the call, I sat down and called each of the other two finalists and gave them my most sincere regrets, telling them how difficult the decision had been. We sent off an official rejection letter to all the other candidates the next day.

Three days later, our new professor arrived. We wined and dined her, helped her look for housing, and treated her, in general, like a new colleague. I took her to lunch and we talked in depth about her new job and our hope for exciting growth in her area of expertise. We sent her home with positive impressions all around that we had made a remarkably good decision.

The next day, I received a call from our new professor, telling me she had changed her mind. She had decided that the position would not be the best way to nurture her active research career and that she now knew she was not quite ready to dedicate the kind of time to teaching that we were expecting of the person who accepted this position. I attempted to reassure her of our support for her research, but to no avail. Her mind was made up.

My next phone call was made only after I gulped down two aspirins and pounded the desk a few times. It began like this, "Professor So-and-so, I know when we talked last week I confessed that you were our second choice for this position. Well, would you consider moving on up to first place?" Candidate # 2 laughed heartily, and responded, "Do you mean to tell me somebody actually turned this position down?" I sheepishly responded, "Yep, and I feel like a real jerk having already mailed you a rejection letter." Without a pause, he said, "Hey, that's OK. I accept. Now, what should I do with the reject letter?"

I think I told him to pour champagne on it. I know I welcomed him to the department and then asked if he would like to

> *know the salary. This man clearly knew what he wanted, and*
> *we were really lucky to have him on board.*

So, you see, it's never a good idea to throw away the runners-up, until you have a written contract signed, sealed, and delivered. This example is not all that uncommon. It may seem strange that a person would go through an entire search process and ultimately turn down the job; but there are a number of reasons why this happens. Perhaps, the money isn't as attractive as they originally hoped; maybe their spouse was unwilling to make the move; sometimes the candidate wasn't really interested in the job from the start, but was trying to gain some bargaining power to better his/her position at home. Whatever the reason, you can never be confident a person will accept a job offer until the contract is actually signed. So, hold onto those other finalists all the way to the finish line.

Recruiting the Best

People at the very top of their field do not want to feel as though they must beg for a job—any job. So, they will not apply. If you want to hire one of these folks, you will need to actively recruit him/her. Let's say, you want to entice Professor Wonderful to take a look at your position. (S)he has been nominated by several faculty and by someone on your advisory board. Professor Wonderful is in great demand. You are not the only school trying to recruit him/her.

This can be pretty tricky, since your first overture has to work. I suggest that you find out as much as possible about this person before you call or write. Where does (s)he work now? What can your position offer him/her that (s)he doesn't have already? Then, think of one or two good reasons why (s)he should consider a move to your institution—these may be unique strengths of your program, exciting new directions you are taking with the organization, or even an appeal to autonomy. If you are really looking for leadership to build a certain aspect of your program, the opportunity to make a difference may strike a responsive chord.

Be prepared to reveal the truth. If you are attempting to hire someone to fix a troubled program, say so. Don't try to hide a weakness or misrepresent the institution in any way; this will only lead to disillusionment and unhappiness somewhere down the road—and usually not too far down the road, either. The remarkable thing about strong leaders is that they are often attracted to the jobs with the greatest potential for growth. We tend to think that we have to already have the finest program, in order to recruit the finest artist. But more often than not, the finest artist is deeply intrigued by the possibility of building the finest program.

So your best recruiting tool may be your determination to make the place better. Your vision of a program of the highest excellence should be the driving force in your sales pitch to Professor Wonderful. That and the assurance that the support (s)he will need to build that program is in your hands, just waiting for your new leader to take the helm. Your willingness to pass along the reins and stand by when help is needed just may be music to this person's ears. For the right individual, the challenge to create something wonderful is irresistible.

It is also advisable to be right up front about your reasons for wanting him/her for this position. Convey that you want the best in the business and that everyone you have consulted has advised you that (s)he is that person. Remember that every artist desperately needs to feel (s)he is #1. Don't be reluctant to go straight to this most important point at the very outset of your conversation. It is not false flattery, if it is true.

When you initially approach a person about your faculty opening, (s)he may not be particularly interested in the job; you have to sell this person on the idea of leaving a present position. Which brings us to a vitally important point: never assume anyone is unattainable. You have no way of knowing when a person might be growing discontented in a current post. Just because (s)he has a great job already, doesn't mean (s)he is opposed to moving onto something else. It never hurts to knock on the door.

Checking out the Fit

Keep in mind, you are not offering Professor Wonderful a position just yet. You are trying to engender enough interest in the job to come to campus and check it out. You have already gone through an extensive search process and you and your committee have decided that (s)he is at the top of the list. The people further down have applied for the job; many look OK, but (s)he would be extraordinary. So, you are attempting to get Professor Wonderful into the process.

It is important to handle very, very carefully the fact that you are considering, not yet hiring. Emphasizing the need to check out the fit with the people in your institution is an effective way to do this. Professor Wonderful will know you can't hire someone you've never even met (assuming you haven't met, of course.) (S)he will also be savvy enough to realize that the artist/faculty need to play some role in the hiring of other colleagues. There is no need to feel ambivalent about trying to recruit someone you are not yet certain you will hire. You are attempting to sell your program; whether or not (s)he ultimately joins the faculty, you want Professor Wonderful to know what a great place it would be to work. This won't hurt, even if (s)he doesn't come.

After a lively conversation with you, the interest is piqued. You have opened the door. Now, invite the candidate to campus. State clearly that you want to see if (s)he likes the place and if (s)he would be a good fit for the position. Then, roll out the red carpet and do your best to reveal just how special your organization really is.

Before (s)he arrives, send whatever marketing materials you have for your institution. These are usually glitzy and a bit idealistic, designed to impress people; but that's exactly what you are trying to do—impress someone. So, use them. Also, work with the artist/ faculty, staff and students to prepare them for the visit, so they understand the decision is not yet made, and that they will play a part in determining the outcome. Professor Wonderful should be referred to as "a leading candidate" for the position. When speaking to Professor Wonderful, I would probably use a slightly different description: "The leading candidate." This is a subtle difference, but an important one. It helps emphasize to the artist/faculty, staff and students that the door is still open for their input, while emphasizing to the candidate that (s)he is really #1. Both are true.

In fact, you do need to see if Professor Wonderful is an effective teacher. The campus visit should include some interaction with students, which you can observe, to better assess this aspect. It should also include interaction with the artist/faculty and staff, and a private discussion with you. It may involve meetings with the search committee as a group and with your boss or any other administrators who play a role in the hiring of faculty to the institution. Everyone should be prepared to treat the person as a guest would be treated— with enthusiasm, kindness, and warm hospitality. It should not feel like an examination or a first-degree murder investigation. Let everyone know there will be plenty of time to critique the candidate after (s)he goes home. Then, make sure there is.

One of the biggest sins of the search process is to involve people and then not listen to their input. Students, as well as artist/faculty, staff, and administrators, should all have an opportunity to give you feedback. This may be on a written evaluation form (with ample space for comments) or it may be in conferences with you. All opinions should be gathered immediately after the candidate leaves, so you can move quickly if you want this person; but everyone involved should be given a chance to offer an opinion.

Hiring Professor Wonderful

Then, it's your job, perhaps in consultation with the search committee and/or your boss, to make the decision. If you are ready to make an offer, call the candidate at once. Express your appreciation for the visit (remember, Professor Wonderful is a busy person) and assure the person that your interest was greatly strengthened by the campus visit. Relate some details of other people's support for the appointment and make an offer (s)he can't refuse.

Most of the time, Professor Wonderful will want to think about it, perhaps negotiate a bit, and call you later. Under most circumstances, "later" ought to be soon—no more than a week. If you have done your job well, (s)he will be dying to come! If (s)he isn't, find a way to ease the concerns, whatever they are, or move onto another Professor Wonderful. You won't always get the first one you want, especially at this level of the profession. Usually, a person at the top of the field is too busy to mess around with a job that is not intriguing; so, if you get the individual to campus, you probably have a good shot at hiring this person.

One last comment: at no time in the process should you infer that Professor Wonderful is more wonderful than your institution. Even if you are hiring this leader to build a part of your program, you should be able to illustrate other areas of excellence in the institution. Your vision must not be just a pipe dream. (S)he needs to be able to see the potential for greatness and believe it is achievable in this area. So, reveal your peaks. Introduce the person to your key artist/ faculty, and sell the job with the passion of your leadership and the clarity of your vision.

Rejecting Professor Wonderful

Suppose you decide Professor Wonderful is not right for your program; now, what? Perhaps, (s)he is not a terrific teacher. In spite of extensive expertise as an artist, (s)he may have lousy communication skills. Or maybe (s)he just isn't that interested in building talent. (S)he may be wonderful with the young professionals, polishing those already developed skills; but, with the greener students just beginning to blossom, those who need a lot of help in gaining technical proficiency, (s)he shows little or no patience. Well, this turns out to be the biggest challenge of all: how to get Professor Wonderful back out of the picture after you dragged the person into it? The last thing you want is to have anyone think ill of your institution. This artist is highly renowned. (S)he travels all over the world. Just envision the damage (s)he could do to the reputation of your school, if (s)he decided you were a bunch of bozo's.

Now, if you call and tell the person you have decided to hire someone else, you will be putting Professor Wonderful on the defensive. (S)he will be forced to lash out at the institution, rather than admit that there may be somebody better out there. You need to avoid delivering such a fatal punch. As the wicked witch of the east said in The Wizard of Oz, "These things must be done. . . De-li-cate-ly!"

Call as soon as you know you don't want to hire the person, but do not say you have reached a negative decision. Instead, try to come to this decision together, on the phone. Make it an open-ended conversation at the outset. I would suggest you begin by thanking the individual for coming to campus, and by inquiring about the travel arrangements home. Then, ask how (s)he felt about the visit; what did (s)he think of your program, the faculty, the students (s)he had met?

Now, I am willing to place a sizable bet here that (s)he will give you a real mixed response. The standards will be extremely high. After all, (s)he is at the top of the profession; that's why you decided to recruit this person in the first place. So, there will be some things (s)he didn't like. Listen carefully, and look for a hole in the picture—one you can poke a finger into and make bigger. Pick up on it and say that you were worried about the very same thing. If I lose the bet, and (s)he is totally positive about the visit, be ready to open up your own wound. Indicate your concern that such-and-so problem just may not be solvable, because of insufficient space, money, whatever you can think of to make matters worse than they originally appeared. Make certain the problem you choose as your "fly in the ointment" is not Professor Wonderful's fault or yours. It is just one of those insurmountable obstacles—the kind of obstacle you have been attacking with glee, but (s)he won't know this. You don't have to be dishonest here. There are always problems that can be overlooked or emphasized.

Your goal is to part company with Professor Wonderful with everyone still intact. The collaboration just isn't going to work. The circumstances are beyond everyone's control. Be sure to let the person know how much the campus visit meant to you, to the artist/

249

faculty, and to the students. If it is feasible, you may even want to invite the artist to come back from time to time to give a master class or a guest lecture or whatever. Believe me, it is necessary to be very positive throughout this entire conversation. You want Professor Wonderful to be glad (s)he came and to be comfortable with your joint decision not to pursue the position any further.

A follow-up letter of appreciation can be the icing on the cake. In writing, treat the visit like a guest artist appearance. Do not refer to the job any more. Just focus on the educational contribution (s)he made while (s)he was on campus, and express your hope that this new professional relationship you have carved out will continue well into the future. (Be specific enough that (s)he cannot possibly think you are referring to the original job opening.)

Now, all of this will sound pretty strange to someone not in the arts. Industry certainly doesn't have to worry about the psyche of the rejected executive nearly as much as we in the arts world do. We have no product to sell. We deal in very subjective definitions of excellence, and the reputation of our institution depends solely on the quality of the art we create—that of our alumni, our artist/faculty, and our students. If highly renowned leaders in our profession do not respect our work, our reputation suffers. This, in turn, affects our ability to recruit other top professionals to our institution and the most gifted students to our programs. The effective arts executive knows this and treats people with the utmost care.

Hiring the Best

When you actually succeed in hiring "the best in the field," you need to brace up for a challenging adjustment period. Assume every person you hire is going to be difficult in some way; (a lot of artist/faculty are, you know.) Just make sure each one is worth it. If you need a leader, then be prepared to provide some elbowroom for that person to shape the area (s)he was hired to lead. You will probably have to pump some additional resources into that program and you may be surprised by some of the ideas that surface as the new person takes hold. Don't provide too much freedom, or you may completely lose control of the growth and the direction of a piece of your organization. Do make it possible for that area to be shaped and improved in dramatic ways. After all, that was what you were seeking when you launched this search, wasn't it?

When you are visionary enough to place key people into key positions, the organization begins to grow from the inside out in ways even you may not have anticipated. As this takes place, other areas of your program start to react to these new developments. Leadership might well emerge in some different parts of the organization, leadership that has been lying dormant for some time. Gradually, you discover this elephant of an institution, which you have been trying to push forward from behind its enormous bulk, has evolved into a galloping gazelle, and you are now running after it, trying desperately to make sure it is headed in the right direction.

Don't get too excited. Your gazelle still has elephant's ears and that long, outdated trunk. There's lots of room for improvement in this new animal you have managed to create. At least, now you have some help. Caution: Do keep your eye on this help. You may find your elephant/gazelle developing the neck of a giraffe or the mane of a lion. What on earth will you do with an elephant/gazelle/giraffe/lion type of creature? Not to worry. You are a born leader. You'll find a way to put this unique being on top of a mountain, where all can marvel at its splendor.

FIRING

Professor Exuberant just lit up the room whenever she walked through the door. She was one of my favorite people. I had hired her as a part-time teacher in an area that needed to integrate closely with several others, knowing she had both the people skills and the professional background to do a superb job.

Students adored her. But the faculty teaching the other segments of the curriculum gave her mixed reviews: they,

*too, found her to be a delightful colleague in every respect—
except one—the depth of her teaching.*

*Apparently the specific subject I had hired her to teach was
not her strongest area of expertise. She was doing an OK job
of conveying the information, but the skills of her students
were not developing as well or as quickly as they needed to
in order to prepare for professional careers. It was a classic
case of the wrong person for the job.*

*They say if you stay in a position long enough you begin
to fix problems that you yourself created. Well, here I was,
now scheduled to fire somebody I had hired, and worse
yet, somebody I really, really liked. She would be here any
minute. I was certain she didn't have the slightest clue that
this was the agenda of today's meeting.*

*Karen buzzed, signaling the arrival of my guest. I dragged
myself to the door, feeling as though I had a spear stuck in
my chest. There was no way to do this without hurting her,
probably severely. I knew she absolutely loved teaching in
our program.*

*As I opened the door, in she popped with her four-month-old
baby boy all wrapped up in her arms—a fluffy, blue blanket
covering all but his chubby little cheeks and softly closed
eyes. Professor Exuberant's face was electric with happiness.
She knew I wanted to see the baby, and this seemed like the
perfect time.*

Finishing the Story

Hopefully, you will never have to fire a woman holding a baby. If ever
I needed a sharp picture of the emotional impact of an "involuntary
termination," as they call it in the human resources office, this was it.
It took just minutes for Professor Exuberant to deduce the purpose of
our meeting. As the realization sunk in, her face gradually crumbled
into a mirror image of the anguish I knew was inside her. I knew,

because I was fighting for some semblance of control over my own inner turmoil. I think I remained professional—that is, until the baby woke up, sensing even in his sleep the turbulence of emotion that surrounded him.

Both mother and baby were now sobbing uncontrollably. I could think of nothing more to say, so I wrapped my arms around both of them and just held on until she could begin to deal with it. When the mother quieted, the baby did also, sucking on his pacifier in between spasms, huge eyes fixed on his mother's troubled face. She apologized for falling apart. I apologized for having to give her such rotten news. The baby, of course, had nothing at all to say. The meeting was over. I helped her gather up her things, handed her a couple more tissues, and walked her to the private door that avoided the path back through the reception room.

This was the absolute worst experience I have ever had as an arts administrator. As I closed the door, I dissolved into tears, all the while vowing to never again hire the wrong person. That is, of course, the only way to avoid having to fire someone. However, no matter how careful you are, you can't anticipate every aspect of a job and every aspect of an individual's personality or professional abilities. The reality is, if you are a leader, you will probably have to fire as well as hire, so you may as well prepare to "bite that bullet" (and I do know why they use that phrase so often to describe the process.)

Firing with Compassion

There isn't a whole lot I can say about how to do it. Every situation is unique. But in general, it is helpful to depersonalize the conversation as much as you possibly can. Do everything in your power to convey to the person being fired that (s)he is not the problem; it is a question of not being the best "fit" for the particular job at hand. Focus on the job that needed to be done, the specific circumstances surrounding this job that made it particularly tough to do well, and your recognition that the real problem was a poor match between the position and the person trying to fill it.

You may choose to emphasize in your conference the person's many strengths and some of the aspects of the job that (s)he has fulfilled magnificently well. Your goal should be to minimize the damage to the person's self esteem, while making clear the rational grounds for concluding that a change in personnel is needed. Do not leave the door open for any doubt about the outcome of your meeting. If you have to fire the person, make sure you do it. And make doubly sure you have sufficient cause to do so.

Since involuntary terminations are the targets of a lot of litigation these days, you regrettably should think about a possible lawsuit every time you have to fire someone. In most instances, you will be well advised to accumulate a paper trail to support your action. A written warning of job inadequacies can be very helpful in either correcting a problem or paving the way for an eventual dismissal. So can any written indications of the problem—whether from faculty, students, administrators, or even people from outside the institution. In some settings, you are required to provide a written warning to an individual with a reasonable period of time allotted for bringing about positive change. Even if it isn't required, it's a wise thing to do.

In cases where the position is a one-year appointment, renewable from year to year, you are perfectly free not to renew that person's contract without further procedure. This is technically not a firing; but if the person has been on board for some time, it may still feel like a termination. So take steps to prepare the individual for the inevitable upset. The story related above was an example of such a year-to-year contract. The young mother even knew there were a lot of problems in her professional interaction with the other faculty and their curricula; yet, the outcome was still a total shock. Had I been a more experienced administrator at the time, I would have made certain there were more signals of pending dismissal prior to our actual meeting.

In a similar situation, a few years later, I did meet with a part-time teacher on several occasions prior to ending his contract. In these conferences, we discussed the problems he was having in the classroom with a directness that left no doubt that his position in the program was in jeopardy. These review meetings took place at the end of each semester over about a two-year period. By the time I had concluded that his employment just wasn't going to work out, he knew it, too.

It can be tough to exercise this much patience, especially when students are complaining and other faculty may be pushing for an immediate solution. However, when you weigh the painful consequences to the person involved and the added burden to you of searching for the "right" person yet again, it is nearly always preferable to at least try to find solutions with the employee already on board. (Besides, when you hire someone, you take on a moral obligation to do everything in your power to make it work.)

Separating the Personal from the Professional

One of the most difficult aspects of managing people is the personal element involved. Unless you are a totally remote, isolated administrator, you will have a personal investment in most, if not all, of the people with whom you work. You've probably met their spouses, perhaps even their children. You may be aware of difficult divorces, family tragedies, deaths of parents, even health problems—both minor and serious. Projecting an appropriate level of concern and caring can enhance your ability to lead any group of individuals. You want to have a workplace full of employees who have made a commitment to the institution; it certainly doesn't hurt if they also care deeply about pleasing their boss.

Along with this appreciation for the value of the individual comes the possibility of misunderstanding. I remember one glaring example of this from a class of music theory students I taught several years ago.

This was a course with a well-defined grading system. Students received a written syllabus the first day of classes with the criteria for grading clearly spelled out: four quizzes - 25%; homework assignments - 25%; final exam - 25%;

and class participation/attendance - the final 25%. It was the type of course for which objective grading was both appropriate and possible.

One of the poorest students in the class consistently earned "C's" and "D's" on his quizzes, seldom completed the homework assignments on time, and just barely squeaked through the final exam with a "D. His only redeeming activity was his class participation: he always came to class and offered his input generously with zest and enthusiasm. Everyone liked this guy a lot. He just lifted the spirit of the entire class. (He is probably out there selling something and making a fortune. I suspect he is not a musician.)

When it came time for grades, Mr. Personality was between a "C" and a "D." Since his participation in class had been truly excellent, although his answers were not always correct, I decided to give him the "C." Much to my amazement, he came bursting into my office the day grades were issued with a look of utter shock. "How could I have given him a 'C'?"

Calmly, I asked what grade he had expected to receive. His answer was astonishing, given the reality of his abysmal record of achievement: "Why, a 'B', of course!" "But," I countered, "you didn't have anything higher than a 'C' the entire semester." With a particular kind of logic only an adolescent would find reasonable, he answered, "Yeah, but I thought you liked me."

Make no mistake, feelings can very easily get all mixed up with facts, even in the most professional of work environments. While you probably won't bump into such a striking example of reality shifting every day, you will see a great deal of over-personalizing throughout your organization. When you are forced to make the tough decision to fire someone, a previously warm working relationship with that person can add even more pain to the awful impact of the dismissal. The employee may react in a manner quite similar to the student example cited above: "How can you possibly fire me? I thought you liked me!"

The flip side of this problem is the assumption that "You are firing me just because you don't like me." Herein lies the basis for more than a few messy lawsuits. Unless people are able to come to grips with the fact that it is their work that falls short of the target, not their personal relationship to the boss, it is likely that the firing will feel unjust. A lot of people today pursue their own personal definition of justice just as far as the court system will permit.

You can mitigate this problem somewhat by very carefully articulating a clear separation of your personal from your professional relationship to the employee. It may help to make this distinction explicit frequently as you attempt to work your way through the firing process. If things get messy and you are accused of acting on your feelings rather than on logic, you will be eternally grateful for whatever paper trail you were able to create. Pointing to a written piece of evidence of the problem being discussed is a superb way of focusing the discussion back on the facts. This is also the kindest way to minimize the damage to the person's self esteem.

Timing the Process

Timing is everything. Well, maybe not everything; but it is vitally important in this highly unpleasant business of firing someone. Never jump into the process of termination on the spur of the moment. Think through the problem clearly; make sure you have objective criteria; also be certain that you have on hand whatever papers or documents you will need to support your action.

Choose a time when you will not be hurried. While it probably won't take very long to get to the point of the meeting, it may take quite a while to work through the response. The person you are firing may have a lot of questions; (s)he may wish to argue with some of your data or attempt to talk you out of dismissal; (s)he may want another chance to solve the problems. Naturally, you have already considered all these other options, and you are convinced that firing the person is necessary. (If you are not certain, it is imperative to wait until you are, before beginning the termination process.) In any event, you will not want to have to cut this discussion short; so make sure you have enough uninterrupted time to work through the process in one meeting.

On rare occasions, a person may introduce new information that is a total surprise to you. If this should happen, you will need to think through the ramifications of this news on the spot. Does it change everything? Might it in some way explain the inadequate work and, if so, does it open a new door to the likelihood of future success on the job? Let us say, for example, that just as you are about to dismiss a person, she tells you that she is being sexually harassed by a senior person in the organization. What you have been observing—her unwillingness to participate on committees to which you have assigned her; her difficulty in working with the faculty in her division; her obvious anxiety in meeting the responsibilities of the day-to-day job—all of this, has been directly related to the presence and the inappropriate behavior of another member of the faculty.

What a revelation! You had no idea. This is the type of new information that literally changes everything. You will, of course, want to reconsider your decision to fire her, at least until you investigate fully the situation she has described. Ultimately, it may still be the case that Professor Inadequate is inadequate; but any new information that bears directly on the person's job effectiveness warrants your full consideration.

On the other hand, telling you of some personal problems the employee is experiencing is not an appropriate reason to reconsider the termination. It is quite common for a person being fired to counter with a litany of problems at home, and the promise that once all those things are out of the way, (s)he will be the perfect employee. By the time you move into the dismissal process, you should have already weighed the impact of possible personal stresses. People always have personal problems. You have personal problems. We all do. We also have jobs to do, and have to find effective ways to deal with both. So, it is not heinous of you to acknowledge these regrettable problems with sincere empathy, while continuing to implement the firing. If the person is unable to do the job, for whatever reason, you need to find someone else who can do the job.

In the process, you can also help your employee find the support (s)he needs to cope with the stress of this added predicament. Losing one's job is traumatic—always. So, whatever you can do to assist the person in finding another job or in getting the counseling help that may be needed, you should gladly do. All of this takes time, so clear your schedule of other appointments before you begin this meeting to fire someone.

It is also important to select a time when the employee does not have to rush off to teach a class or critique a student or direct a rehearsal. There is a long-standing administrative custom of firing people on Friday afternoons. This isn't such a bad idea, unless, of course, the person being fired is directing a show that night, or conducting a concert. It is just being compassionate to try to set a meeting time that will enable the person to immediately get out of the place and find solace with friends and family.

Handling a Difficult Case

Firing someone in the middle of the semester is obviously not ideal, so any action that would disrupt the educational process should be considered carefully. If the problem can wait until the end of the academic year, this is ideal. If it can't, then you will need to be prepared to implement some damage control. Any time students are involved, or could conceivably become involved, you have a rather messy situation on your hands. Employees can attempt to get students on their side to pressure the administration to change their minds. You, of course, are the administration. So, you are the target of all the counter-actions.

The difficulty is that you are not free to give the students your reasons for firing their teacher. On the other hand, the teacher may be bombarding the students with his/her side of the story. With only half the picture, the students and their parents may be incensed by your action. Now you have yet another problem, and this one is bigger than the first.

Keep in mind that firing someone is akin to divorcing them, and you know how ugly divorces can get. The nicest people can turn into monsters when they have to deal with serious rejection. Forget about logic. We are dealing with pure emotion here, and a lot of pain. Seeking some reinforcement of his/her personal worth, the individual being fired may flail out in all directions, talking to anybody and everybody who will listen. This unpleasantness will not be easy to absorb. But unless it ultimately leads to a lawsuit, the process will eventually work itself through and the environment will settle down once again. You may need to put on your armor and just ride through the storm.

Keeping your eye on the big picture, you know what you are doing is in the best interests of the institution you serve. Handling the fall-out from an involuntary termination is just part of the job. It is inevitable that things will be doubly difficult for a while. You will have to find a replacement for the person you fired, perhaps in a climate of hostility and pain, and the person you hire needs to be really good. You may have to reassure others that they are not at risk of losing their jobs, too. (Dismissing someone usually sets off fire works of self-doubt and insecurity.) The up side of this issue is that people who have been dragging their feet for some time seem to find renewed motivation and energy from the disappearance of a colleague.

You may have unhappy students, irate parents, even an occasional question from your superiors about the wisdom of your move. If it gets real messy, the upper administration may actually be called upon to step in. In colorful cases, the media enters the picture, and the lawyers begin to reach for their business cards and their accounting books. (That paper trail you kept is beginning to look better and better, isn't it?)

When you can anticipate a particularly difficult situation on the horizon, it is especially important to move the person immediately out of the environment. Firing someone after the semester ends and students have left the campus will help contain the destructive interaction that is likely to occur. You've heard of people being fired in industry and having an hour to clean out their desks and leave the premises. This doesn't usually happen in academia, but in some rare instances it is the best way to minimize the damage that employee is able to cause.

Sometimes the person you must fire is responsible for expensive equipment or costly facilities. One of your concerns then must be to protect the institution's property from theft and/or vandalism. I once had a locksmith change the locks on a computer music facility while the director was out of town, and fired him as soon as he returned. This is really drastic, but some occasions warrant that type of caution. You will always want to recover keys and organizational property as part of the termination process—as gently as you are able to proceed, given the particular circumstances.

Attending to Future Needs

Your chances of having an acrimonious situation on your hands are greatly lessened if you are able to extend some extra levels of support throughout the dismissal process. Giving lots of notice, when possible, is healthy for all parties involved. The person you are firing will need time to find another job and will need some grace period during which (s)he is still receiving a salary; you will need some time to find a replacement. If the employee is able to help with a smooth transition—somewhat unusual in typical firing situations— then, by all means, let this happen. This is much more likely to take place in cases in which another job is clearly on the horizon. Any help you can give to ensure a positive next step for your employee, short of lying about his/her abilities and inabilities, should be taken. This is yet another way to emphasize that the problem was just a bad fit with this particular job, not an insurmountable flaw in the person's character or abilities. It is also in the best interests of the institution to help with the placement process, since your arts unit will be shouldering the unemployment benefits, if they are needed.

In closing this rather difficult topic, I want to emphasize the importance of separating your personal feelings from your professional obligations—not just with the person you are firing, but also within yourself. Once you know you have done everything in your power to make it work, you need to somehow rise above the anxiety and the pain of the situation and work through it as best you can. Don't be reluctant to seek your own support from wherever it can be appropriately drawn.

COPING WITH LEGAL ISSUES

I know, probably the last thing on your mind is suing somebody. After all, you are up to your neck in this job already; you couldn't make time for a legal tangle if you had to. Right? Well, guess what? Somebody's suing your arts organization and maybe even you personally as the head of your organization. You are the guy who has to save the day, and, believe me, you will make time for it. You have no choice.

So, what do you know about law? Nothing, huh? Well, no matter. You'll learn—on the job—just like you've learned everything else. Just in case this book reaches you before the lawyers do, (and hopefully your organization has a team of lawyers ready to help you) we may as well take a stab at preparing for the worst.

We are going to assume you came into this job clean—no major crimes hanging over your head. (Messy divorces and traffic violations don't count here.) You have already learned how to stay out of trouble, by leading a decent, honest life, working hard, trying not to do anybody any harm. Is that enough? Not any more!

In this day and age, litigation is a reality for any business organization. You are a target, because you are in charge of a large and complex organization; you potentially bear responsibility for much of what happens within this organization and you can be sued for many of the things that people say or do to others, while working in the environment; (that includes the faculty, staff, students, contractors, and other agents associated with your arts unit.)

Let's think for just a moment about all the types of legal situations that hit the 6:00 news: murder, rape, theft, vehicular homicide, arson, possession of illegal substances, terrorism, kidnapping, hijacking, sniping, stalking, sexual harassment, assault and battery, forgery, perjury, larceny, plus the attempt to do any of the above. All of these things happen all of the time, and unthinkable as it may be, any of them could happen to someone in your organization. You've probably come to grips with the fact that you could become an innocent victim of one of these crimes; but have you ever considered the fact that you could some day be accused of one of them? Or even more likely, sued because one of these events allegedly occurred on your watch, in an environment over which you are supposed to be in charge? Or to individuals in your environment whose health and safety you are supposed to safeguard? Scary, isn't it?

It isn't just about doing something wrong; today, you can also be sued for the things you don't do. There are all sorts of laws, statutes, and organizational policies pertaining to equal opportunity and to civil rights. These regulations affect the way in which you go about hiring people, firing people, assigning raises, promoting, and granting or denying tenure—all those vitally important personnel issues we have just discussed. Even the perception that you have failed to act in total compliance with one of these laws can lead to a lawsuit.

Staying out of Court

There are some things you can do to minimize your risks, and these actions should permeate everything you set out to accomplish in your job.

- First, document appropriately. Whether you are hiring or firing faculty or staff, counseling a student, rejecting an applicant, advising people in a decision-making situation, you need to keep good records. This doesn't mean writing down everything you say and do. You can't possibly manage that without quitting the rest of your job. There simply isn't time; but you can develop the type of filing system that will help you through an investigation or lawsuit. Usually, you will need to resurrect enough facts to recreate a time line of who did what and when. Nobody keeps all of that miscellaneous detail in their head.

Consequently, I would recommend keeping your appointment books—forever. Stick them in a drawer or file them on a shelf, but keep them. They can at least substantiate when and where you met with the people in question. It is amazing how just looking through your old appointment books will jog your memory. If you keep a day planner with notes about your meetings, this is even better. Looking through these notes can help zap you right back in time. This is exactly what you need to be able to do, in order to recall events that are long past.

Any notes, however you take them, can turn out to be helpful. Unless it's one of those boring organizational meetings, keep all meeting notes. No need to rewrite them. Just throw them into the appropriate files—in any form at all—notebook paper, little scraps of paper, napkins, match-books, whatever you grabbed to hold onto the information at the moment. It doesn't take much time to do this; it just takes a good filing system and probably a really good assistant to keep track of all of the files.

- Watch what you write and say. This is a good time to talk about the nature of your note taking. Never write anything down that could become a problem in court. Just get into the habit of recording facts, not opinions. (You won't forget your own opinions anyway; no need to write them down.) Anything that could be considered personally insulting, slanderous, even mildly offensive or legally inappropriate should not be put in writing—ever. In fact, you shouldn't be thinking or saying these things in the first place or making decisions based upon them. You just can't afford to step even an inch out of line when you hold a position of leadership.

So, when you are on the verge of making a comment you wouldn't wish to hear coming back again, bite your tongue.

- Be careful with e-mail. This has become a rather casual environment for exchanging opinions, as well as information, with friends and associates. Don't forget, it, too, is written material. Someone else may choose to keep it. In fact, you may engage in some e-mail correspondence that you will want to file. Discussions between you and the faculty about a student's overall progress are important. E-mail messages between students and faculty may also be useful documentation. Instruct your artist/faculty to exercise great care in the crafting of their own messages. The ultimate audience may be a lot broader than the intended recipient.

- Know what not to file. Some files need to be treated with particular care: especially those that hold information about hiring, firing, promotion, and tenure processes. Laws supporting people's right to access their own personnel files make these types of records vulnerable to inspection. Inappropriate pieces of paper, like evaluations that may not have been shared with the employee, if kept on file, can be subpoenaed. Confidential letters from outside experts in the field, for example, can be read by the person being evaluated, unless (s)he has specifically waived the right to access these letters. To be safe, check with your legal officers to determine the appropriate way to handle such materials. Private notes, written to yourself as you conduct telephone interviews to check references, should not be kept after the decision-making process is completed.

- Save notes from important telephone conferences. A lot of your conversations with people will take place by phone. Decisions will be made, promises voiced, plans cemented. Be sure to write these down as soon as you can, and file them along with other important notes. Any time you become involved in a difficult conversation, assume there could be problems down the road. When finished with the call, spend a moment or two documenting the gist of the exchange—not the emotion, just the facts. Date it and file it. These are the kinds of notes that can become vitally important if problems escalate.

- Hold onto materials supporting faculty and/or staff searches. People who do not get a particular job may file charges of discrimination. You may have to prove that your institution did attempt to broaden its search to include a diverse pool. You may also have to produce evidence that the person in question was treated fairly throughout the process. Check with your legal advisors to determine how long such files need to be kept.

- Formalize all employment contracts. Documentation is vitally important when legal questions arise. Make certain you have signed contracts with everyone working in your organization, and keep these contracts. Also, keep any written results from formal evaluative processes, which have been shared with the employee. Keep biographical materials and professional vitae of your faculty. Keep special letters of concern or of congratulations, written to employees about their work within the institution.

- Train your staff. Obviously, much of this filing and documenting will be done by members of your staff, not necessarily by you. It is essential, therefore, to train everyone working in the organization to follow the guidelines described above, and the processes outlined by your legal advisors. Laws change, and you need to stay in compliance with current statutes. Remember, as the leader of the organization, you can be held personally liable for the mistakes of your employees.

- Keep everyone fully informed of laws and policies affecting their interpersonal dealings with others in the organization. In particular, make sure everyone is aware of institutional policies on sexual harassment, cheating, academic freedom, and other areas of behavior that may serve as the basis for a future lawsuit.

The challenging part of heading any institution is that everything is so interconnected. Organizations really are complex organisms; so, touching even a segment can set off waves of cause and effect throughout the rest of the structure. Consequently, just about anything you say or do, and nearly everything you don't do, can bounce back to haunt you. This just points up the vital importance of making decisions carefully and rationally, always keeping the mission of the organization at the forefront of your thinking. It also emphasizes the need to take corrective action expeditiously on the problems you encounter. Most legal entanglements start out as tiny grievances. Ignoring something small, even when you sense trouble right around the corner, can be a costly error.

Dealing with a Lawsuit

No matter how careful you are, you may some day wind up in court. Perhaps, you are called upon as an expert witness for a trial of total strangers; you may be asked to testify for or against someone in your own organization; or you may have to defend yourself against charges filed by someone with a grievance toward you or toward the institution you serve. Whatever the circumstances, one thing is certain: this lawsuit is going to take an inordinate amount of your time, right off the top of an already full agenda. It will also hang over your head for months, if not years, to come. Lawsuits seem to last forever; there can be appeals and counter-suits and complicated fall-out from even the smallest of cases. The big ones are a nightmare!

Resign yourself to an unwelcome shift in priorities, and let the legal situation occupy first place, at least until you have collected and organized all the data you need to support your position. Obviously, you have to have expert guidance throughout this process; the institution for which you work will generally provide this. Now is the time to thank your lucky stars if you kept all the right documents, filed all the most important notes, and managed to avoid doing anything or saying anything that ultimately added fuel to the fire. If, however, you screwed up somewhere along the line, well, you probably won't do that again.

Once you've done the best you can to recall the facts and gather the data, you really need to do only three things:

- give this case your full attention, whenever it surfaces;
- tell the truth, no matter what that means;
- and avoid making matters worse.

Making Matters Worse

Here are some things you definitely don't want to do:

- You don't want to talk to the press. Now, you may have to talk to them, but you don't have to tell them anything. If you even smell a lawsuit coming, get legal advice on what you should and should not say about the case, in the event a reporter shows up on your doorstep. (We did discuss the topic of "Dealing with the Media" in the chapter on "Communicating." You may want to take another look at that section now, since it certainly applies to the subject at hand.) "No comment" is the safest answer to most questions pertaining to pending lawsuits; however, you may be able to say a little more than that without getting into trouble. Do be careful, and do take the advice of your legal counsel and public relations folks. Talking to the press is the best way I know to make matters worse.

- Don't get all emotional. This is definitely one of those times when "keeping your cool" is essential. That's tough to do, especially when you are being publicly accused of doing something wrong or not doing something you should have done. Either way, you are going to feel attacked, and your instinct will be to strike back. You can't, of course. Stay focused on the institution you lead. Try to remember, this is all about that organization, not you. You are responsible for maintaining the integrity of the arts unit you lead; in the process of doing this, you will uphold your own integrity, as well. So, keep your head. Getting all stirred up about this will only make matters worse.

- Don't gossip about the case. Lawsuits make great material for conversation. You, too, can be the hit of the party with your latest legal entanglement. Don't do it. This is one of those times when keeping your mouth shut is essential. Saying the wrong thing in public can definitely make matters worse. Keeping quiet may be toughest when the people around you begin to suspect that you have handled things badly. You generally cannot share all of the details of this situation with your faculty, staff, or students; so, they don't really know the facts. When they speculate, you can bet they'll place at least some of the blame in your lap, (where it may or may not belong.) Toughen up. Your shoulders can always grow a little broader, if they have to.

- Don't try to hide the facts. You know, our national government has opened more "gates" than we ever thought possible, just by trying to cover things up. Hey, if it happened, it happened! Your job is to provide information that will show why and how it happened, and hopefully prove everyone's innocence in the process. Most situations are fraught with all sorts of shades of gray. Very few are totally black or white. Your job will be to provide the facts to your counsel so that, together, you can establish that you complied with all legal and policy obligations.

Testifying in Court

When it finally comes time to step into court, review the materials carefully, be yourself, and go in there and tell "the truth, the whole truth, and nothing but the truth." The courtroom will be intimidating, the judge imposing, the lawyers terse, and the jury just a bunch of people like you. The whole process can scare the stuffings out of the most stalwart individual. (The judicial system is designed to be somewhat frightening.) You will, no doubt, wonder, "How on earth did a person like me wind up in a place like this?" It's all part of the job, my friend.

The stenographer was typing away like mad—just inches from the railing separating me from the rest of the world. The imposing profile of the judge was up there to my left, behind a massive desk. The jury sat attentively, two straight lines of them, reaching off diagonally to my right. The ceilings stretched up forever.

The attorney for the plaintiff wore the only familiar face in the court. He was clear across the room, standing at the podium behind a fence of dark wood—like the massive carved mahogany of the whole place. Other people were sprinkled throughout the courtroom, but they were a blur.

I was answering the question, ever so carefully, weighing each word as it came out—hardly daring to breathe as I spoke, lest "the truth, the whole truth, and nothing but the truth" would be somehow tarnished by the extra oxygen. Suddenly, in mid-sentence, a voice from center court barked out "Objection! Hearsay!" Another voice, to my left, snapped "Sustained."

I panicked! My head darted from the objecting lawyer, to the judge, to the jury, back to my lawyer. My heart raced. What had I done? What did I say? Totally rattled by this unexpected turn of events, I lost every ounce of "coolness under pressure" acquired through years of performing, public speaking, running meetings—every bit of confidence just vanished, instantly. I had screwed up, right here in the middle of the justice system.

Then, I heard my own voice uttering all the wrong words, "What do I do now?" The lawyer broke into a grin. "That just means to stop."

"OK." That, I could do.

CHAPTER #8   WORKING WITHIN THE SYSTEM & BEYOND

MOVING PAST THE ROADBLOCKS

Anyone can go to work and just get through the day. The real leader is not satisfied with that; (s)he has at least one eye on the future of the arts unit all the time. In order for any organization to become better than it is today, roadblocks have to be removed, and there are always roadblocks. Oh, you can kid yourself into believing that things are just fine the way they are, that nothing big needs to be changed. If you do feel this way, you are obviously not seeking to push the institution to a higher level, and as a leader, that should be your primary goal. It can always get better.

You can't accomplish this goal by yourself. It takes a lot more than brute strength to push an organization forward; it requires analysis, creativity, energy and gritty determination. If you have all four, great! Let's get started. If you lack one or two, you need to reach out for some help. There is a fifth requirement, as well, which we will discuss in this chapter: resources. You may need additional space or equipment to move ahead. You may also need new people to accomplish your goals. You will most definitely need money. But, let's begin with the identification of the task itself: where are your roadblocks? How do you find them? How do you move past them?

Finding Your Roadblocks

On the surface, this may appear to be easy. After all, the serious roadblocks ought to be visible to everyone. Right? Wrong! Often, the problem lies much deeper than the most obvious obstacle. Yet, there is some comfort in pointing to one of those typical scapegoats, saying, "If only we had more money, we could do XYZ. If we had more space, we could do . . .We can't do BCD without more computers, more instruments, more equipment. . . " In fact, the primary obstacle is probably the people, not the resources, and believe me, resource problems are a whole lot easier to fix than people problems. but we need to come to grips with the tough issues—the real roadblocks to improvement.

Professor Scapegoat had a million excuses for not presenting full-scale student ballet productions. She headed the dance program, which was definitely suffering from a serious malaise: student applications were dropping, the finest students were transferring to other programs, the students currently in the dance option were disappointed, disillusioned, and generally miserable.

They came here to become professional dancers, and they needed to perform. The in-house dance programs were fine, but they just weren't enough. Dance majors were crying out for opportunities to put their talent on the line, to be forced to pull up by their bootstraps (or, in this case, by their toe shoes) and perform better than they were capable of performing, because they had to—the public required it of them. But, these experiences were not being provided in the dance program as it was. "Why not?" they asked. Why not, indeed!

I scheduled yet another appointment with Professor Scapegoat to talk about this. Once again, I endured her litany of excuses: we don't have a stage big enough to mount a full ballet; we don't have enough money for costumes, scenery, lighting; we don't have the musicians to provide even a small orchestra; we don't have the time in the students' schedules to rehearse a fully-staged production; and besides all of this, who would make the posters, sell the tickets, and handle the publicity?

This time, I was prepared to move forward at any cost. So, I invited Professor Scapegoat to give me all the roadblocks. She rose to the challenge, digging out from that storage place deep within her even more problems like: not enough men in the program to balance a production; competition with the professional dance companies in the city; lack of audience interest in a student production. It took a lot of time and patience to wade through all the problems, but finally she wound down to a summary statement, "So, you see I would love to do fully-staged ballets, but we can't."

Little did she know, that I had acquired the funding. By renting a facility off campus, by scheduling time in the dance students' curriculum for productions, and by assigning the instrumental majors to perform one or two ballets a year, we could solve all the problems that she had listed with the help of the new allocation in our budget for ballet productions.

When I delivered this spectacular news to Professor Scapegoat, I naively expected her to be jubilant. She wasn't. Instead, she managed to dig up a few more problems we hadn't yet considered. I assured her that even those could be handled. I was committed to eliminating all the roadblocks that had been preventing her from doing what I assumed she was desperately anxious to do. After all, she was the one who continually complained about the roadblocks that were preventing her from providing the pre-professional experiences her students had to have.

What I didn't realize, and probably should have, was that Professor Scapegoat actually needed these excuses. Without them to hang onto, her own insecurities came bubbling to the surface. Now, her work would be judged on its own merits, without the protection of those roadblocks effectively preventing her from putting it all on the line. She couldn't deal with that risk. So, we spent yet another year not doing ballet productions, even though we now had the resources to move ahead. She provided a whole litany of new issues, and just stonewalled her way through the academic year, presenting another season of in-house student recitals.

It finally became clear that we had a people problem, not a resource problem. It took a major reassignment of faculty to solve this problem, but I learned a lot about roadblocks in the process.

This anecdote is not an unusual one. A lot of people have hang-ups, and most people are really good at hiding them. All that is required is to have some visible roadblock to take the blame for their lack of achievement in a specific area. The important thing to realize is that for these people, the roadblocks are necessary. They have to have something to hold onto that protects them from potential failure; and often the potential failure lives only in their minds and in their insecurities. These are usually very gifted people, who would succeed, if only they allowed themselves to take some risks. They won't, and in truth, they probably can't. The most supportive way to help is to move Professor Scapegoat to a less stressful assignment.

Changing Personnel

You won't always know you have a people problem until you remove all the other roadblocks; but sometimes it is so obvious, that you can begin right on target by finding the right person for the job. It can be a tremendous asset to have on board a new person with huge expectations. (I don't mean expectations for personal rewards, but expectations for organizational excellence. The world is populated with people of the first type—not so full of people of the second type. If you find one, grab him!. . . grab her!)

Whenever you are attempting to do something that has not yet been done in your arts environment, or at least not within the recent past, it may be necessary to reach out for Artist Live Wire. If (s)he has done it before, somewhere else, (s)he isn't afraid to do it again. If (s)he hasn't done it before, but is really hungry to do it now, (s)he will be a tremendous help in moving forward. It is probably unrealistic to expect people, who have been in the environment for a long time, to be able to envision things as they could and should become. Change is difficult, as we have discussed. There will be a predictable tendency for everyone in the arts unit to hold on for dear life to the status quo. Things just could get worse for them personally, and who wants to take that risk?

If resources aren't available to add personnel, you may be able to juggle people around enough to get somebody else to pick up the reins. Either way, when the person you have in charge cannot climb the mountain, you need to know that your people problem is your primary roadblock to progress.

Making the Case for Resources

Even when resources seem to be the fundamental roadblock, you may still have a deeper problem: inadequate communication. While recognizing that there may be real limits to the money, the space, and the equipment ultimately available to an arts unit, it is true that you have to be able to effectively sell your needs to whomever holds the key to the vault. If your arts unit is part of a larger institution, somebody is in charge of the distribution of resources. Perhaps the allocation of budgets and of space lie in two different offices. It may appear that you have little or no control over either one of these processes. In reality, you can probably accomplish much more than you can imagine, just by making a strong enough case to the right people.

The important issue at hand in this discussion of roadblocks is that the resources themselves may not be the fundamental problem. You need to have a very clear image of a future without roadblocks, and you have to be able to articulate this vision to the right people—the people with the power to help you move forward.

This requires clear analytical and sharp data gathering skills. Whether going to a major foundation for funding or to the head of a larger arts institution, chances are you will be making your case to someone who is not an artist. Your whole area of work may be somewhat mysterious to this person; this may make it easier or it may make it more difficult to articulate your unit's needs, but passion is everything—or very nearly everything. If you are absolutely convinced that your arts unit is stuck at a level below its potential, and that with the right amount of help, you can remove the obstacles to future excellence, then you have to be able to prove this to those who can help you. Words aren't enough. You need good data.

Several themes are guaranteed to ring wake-up bells quite effectively:

- Competition. Maybe you can demonstrate that the other arts organizations in your field, who are known for their excellence, all have whatever it is you are attempting to acquire. Further, you may be able to show that even the mediocre programs out there have more of this than you do. Statistics on just about everything are contained in reports compiled at the national level by accrediting agencies for each of the arts areas. These reports are available to you for the asking, or for a minimal charge. Colleagues from other arts programs might also be willing to share specific data with you, if you nurture friendly relationships with these leaders. However you choose to get it, arm yourself with data before attempting to talk to your potential funding source about the competition.

- Attrition. Everyone worries about attrition these days, probably because it is one of the factors used to rank schools nationally. If you are running an arts school and suspect you are losing students, because you do not have certain essential resources, again, you need to find a way to prove this to the people who can help you get those resources. Perhaps a survey could be sent to every student who leaves your program, asking some open-ended questions about their reasons for transferring or quitting. An exit interview with you might also be a mechanism for determining the cause of your particular attrition problem, if, indeed, you have one. Being able to demonstrate a tangible difference between the attrition rates in your weakest option and attrition in the rest of your department or school, may help you acquire the resources you need to fix that option in trouble. (But, be prepared; the administration may prefer to eliminate the option, instead of fixing it. Consider this, and be prepared to articulate the reasons for fixing the program, not dumping it.)

- Visibility. Sometimes the resources you need can help make the arts program more visible on a national and/or international level. With this increased visibility rides the reputation of the entire institution. Being able to itemize the specific activities you could implement with the needed resources just might be the key to attaining them. The impact has to be obvious; the splashier, the better. In today's international arena, everyone needs to worry about their world-wide image. If your arts program can help advance the image of the institution around the world, you have a real good chance of getting lots of support from the powers-that-be.

- Innovation. Most institutions care about being the first or the best at something. If you have one of those "something's" in your bag of tricks, it may be fairly easy to sell the people who hold the resources on the idea. Obviously, you have to be capable of succeeding in this venture, and that usually involves taking some risks—maybe even big ones. But, if you are a good salesman, and have a track record of delivering on your promises, you should be able to gain their confidence. The people at the top of a vibrant, exciting arts environment will probably jump at the opportunity to lead the pack.

These four themes: competition, attrition, visibility, and innovation, are the likeliest candidates for attracting support, if you are not a freestanding arts unit. There may be others. What matters most is your approach. It will just not be enough to say that you want to do such and such. You need your employees on board, so if respected artists are asked, they will spout off precisely the same needs you have voiced. You can also use the help of your advisory board or your board of directors. If they are convinced that you need something, they can do a lot to influence others to fund it.

Avoid trying any of the more aggressive approaches, like getting a bunch of artists to write a petition to the executive, or having a group of faculty show up on the provost's doorstep, demanding action. These types of pressure will just make everybody mad, and will probably fail to gain the support you need. Proactive presentations of data and logic are most effective. Prepare your case, and then look carefully for the right opportunity to present it.

Presenting Your Case

This is going to sound strange, indeed, but I am about to tell you that there will rarely be an opportunity for a single meeting, a single grand presentation, wherein you ask for and receive resources. It just doesn't work that way, 99.9% of the time. So, put away the slides you were crafting and cancel the marching band. What you really need here is a very watchful eye and a well maintained speedway running directly from your brain to your mouth. No kidding!

For opportunities to make the needs of your arts unit known will pop up in all sorts of places, often when you least expect them. Let me provide a few real-life examples:

My first experience of this sort came only six months into the job. I attended a speech to the faculty given by the President of the university. Sitting in the back of the hall, I was there to listen, to learn, and to observe. Looking around the room, I noted who came and who didn't; not surprisingly, the people who had already surfaced as strong, influential leaders on the campus were all there. Most of the people I knew to be whiners and complainers were not.

The presentation was a bit dry; but I forced myself to listen. In the process, I discovered the key issues that were currently on the mind of our President. (That's really important information. Something you may be trying to accomplish just might fit into this key agenda.) I also got a sense of his funding priorities, again from the general direction toward which he was steering the institution, which issues he chose to discuss with us.

Following the speech, there were questions. I listened carefully to who asked what questions and how the President responded to these inquiries. (You can learn a lot about a person's comfort level with various types of people just by observing such interactions.) It became clear to me that this President appreciated strong people; he interrupted when questioners "beat around the bush." He probed for problems, and expected people to be direct and to the point. He never ducked a tough issue, but seemed to relish these. He gave the impression of intense eagerness to attack the problems and put them to rest—like a hunter's excitement in spotting his prey.

A reception followed. A lot of people left. I stayed—just long enough to exchange small talk with a few associates and, oh yes, to bump into the President, who was mingling with the guests. We shook hands. I commented specifically on something I had learned in his speech and thanked him for the information. He zeroed in on me, and with steely eyes, asked "How is the Music Department?" I muttered the usual polite response, as you would when an acquaintance on the street stops and asks, "How are you?" He shook his head impatiently and said, "No, I mean how is it, really? What's your biggest problem?"

I was stunned, but managed to articulate in two or three sentences our desperate need for new leadership in the string program. He asked why I didn't launch an international search for such a person? I responded that I didn't have the elbowroom in the budget. He nodded and said, "Go ahead; I'll cover it." With that, he turned away from me and began talking to someone else.

The next morning, when my mouth had finally closed and my breathing restored to normal, the President's assistant called my office and asked how much I needed for the search and what account number should she use to transfer the funds? From that moment on, I vowed to never be without a succinct answer to the question, "What's your biggest problem?" This preparation has served us well in all sorts of situations.

I have often been accused of going out around the system to gain resources for our program. Now, the secret is finally out. This is how it happened, every single time. I never once scheduled a meeting or wrote a memo to a superior without the express knowledge and approval of my immediate boss. Yes, we did gain a lot of support through these chance encounters with a President who liked to work at parties. They don't all, however. So, I certainly wouldn't suggest you try this, unless you are specifically asked to respond, as I was. Nevertheless, you definitely need to have your act together at all times, just in case you get an opportunity to make a pitch on the spur of the moment.

Another example, this time another era, another President, a totally different style of leadership:

The President and the Provost came to the department to talk directly to our faculty. It was an information exchange— a chance to inform a small group of faculty of the upcoming development campaign and an opportunity to listen to a subset of the university, to hear their concerns, and to bridge the gap between their individual needs and the university's mission. A wonderful chance to get to know the administration and for them to get to know us!

The meeting went very well. Both the President and the Provost spoke to us about the university's direction, its mission and goals, and their appreciation for the work we were doing in the arts. Faculty, in turn, freely expressed their concerns about space, scholarships, and a variety of other pressing issues. It was a highly productive meeting and a cordial one.

As we wrapped up, the President said some positive things about the leadership of our department, and how relentlessly we pursued resources on behalf of the department. Then, he unexpectedly turned to me and asked, "So, what should I brace up for next? Give me a sneak preview of what you have cooking now?" He said it with a good-natured laugh.

I was really astonished, since this President did not ordinarily probe for problems. Nevertheless, I was ready. I launched into a one-paragraph summary of a new idea we had to present "Distance Master Classes," wherein performance faculty in Mexico would teach, via satellite, string students here in our department—long distance, in real time, through extremely high-speed computer transmission. I knew the idea was very expensive, but it was right on target with the President's new focus on distance learning.

He looked surprised, but nodded thoughtfully at the exciting prospect of being "first" to demonstrate the feasibility of such an activity. The seed had been planted. Months later, in a university-wide meeting with faculty, we were asked to each propose an innovative idea we could implement if we just had the discretionary funds. It was an exercise in visionary thinking. Again, I presented the idea of the "Distance Master Class." After the meeting, the President approached me and suggested I write a proposal for internal funding to the new Technology in Learning Committee.

I followed through with the proposal. It was funded. Another six months later, we actually presented the first such demo, and it worked brilliantly. A different President, a slower process, but again the goal was met through chance opportunities to float an idea in casual encounters.

This discussion is not intended to imply that you never present your requests for resources in a normal manner. Of course, you do! You will still have to write proposals, craft strategic planning documents, respond to requests for supplementary data, and participate in all sorts of allocation processes. It's just that there are also these brief opportunities to plant seeds and insert ideas all over the place. If you are quick on your feet, you can utilize these to catch the attention of the people who really can make a difference. In an arts organization, it isn't easy to get your needs onto someone else's agenda. Be prepared to cheerfully nudge yours into the picture every chance you get, all the while being careful not to turn yourself into a stalker. (They arrest people like that, you know.)

Advocating for Your Unit

There will always be too many requests for the available resources. You know this from your own job. Most people hate to say "No," especially when the request is a reasonable one. Neither of these truths should deter you from being the strongest advocate you can possibly become for your arts program. After all, the artists are all counting on you to do whatever it takes to provide a supportive environment for their artistic work. That's your job.

So, when thorny problems arise that require expensive solutions, or when creative vision leads directly to additional resources, it is your responsibility to at least try to get more money, or more space, or more equipment—whatever is needed for the continued development of your arts unit. The answer may ultimately be "No," but you have to at least try, and in so doing, you just may find a way to make it happen.

It is in this situation that the temptation to conjure up the "Us against Them" attitude creeps into the picture. Don't let it. It's fine to make a passionate case for the needs of your arts unit, but avoid at all costs getting caught up in the personal side of the argument. It's your job to ask; it's your boss's job to say "Yes" or "No." If your need is compelling, and if the resources are there to support it, you will probably get the funding. If not, you won't. Hey, that's life!

Now, all we can really do is maximize the odds for success. (Keep in mind, if the money isn't there, it won't make a bit of difference how good you are at pleading your art unit's case.) That said, let's consider some of the factors involved in effectively advocating for resources on behalf of your organization. We will assume you are going to ask your boss for support in person.

Any of these following points really can make a difference in the outcome:

- Be sure to do the necessary research and prepare your case carefully before setting up the appointment.

- Be upbeat, optimistic, and energetic. Nobody enjoys having a moaning, groaning, complainer in their office; so, don't be one of those.

- Present your request clearly and directly. Don't beat around the bush. If you need money, say so. Don't make the executive sit there wondering exactly what you are eventually going to ask for.

- Describe the problem or the project; provide your best estimate of costs and how much of a shortfall you currently have; outline the possible results of not moving ahead vs. the expected results if you do.

- Bring supportive materials with you. Offer to provide more data, if needed.

- Once you have dealt with all the questions and have given it your best shot, shut up and wait for an answer. If your boss is unable to provide one on the spot, (s)he will probably indicate when you can expect an answer. If not, politely ask, and then leave. Don't wait to be thrown out. Everyone appreciates a person who shows concern for their time.

- No matter what the outcome of the meeting happens to be, go out the door as cheerfully as you came in. That's important. Shake hands. Thank the person for the time (s)he gave you. Smile if it kills you, and go!

Some times you will be asked to put your request in writing or to take it to another person. If so, do that, but be certain to keep your boss fully informed of the process every step of the way. Don't go elsewhere without your superior's prior knowledge and support. Even if you manage to get the resources, you will lose your boss's trust, respect and support. That is vitally important to your future in the institution and to the continued health of the arts unit you represent.

Accepting the Limits

Some things just can't be done, but not very many of them. Knowing when to back off and regroup is a really important skill. Notice, I did not say to forget it. If your arts unit really has a legitimate need, and if that need is blocking your path toward a higher level of excellence, you can't throw in the towel altogether; but you may have to ease up a bit and wait awhile. The hints to do so are really pretty clear:

- Somebody over your head has said, "No," not "maybe," or "we'll talk about this later," but "No." This is a pretty clear message. Time to hang it up—at least, for now.

- You have become aware that there is no more funding, or no more space, or no more of whatever it is you need. If there isn't any, you can't very well get some, now can you? That doesn't mean there might not be some way to expand the pie, but give it a rest until you can put together a whole new approach, with at least a potential solution to the resource problem built into the request.

These are really the only two instances in which I would advocate crying, "Uncle." Even then, I would do so silently, or in a whisper. You don't want to officially accept this position of defeat; after all, your arts unit still needs what it needs. That hasn't changed; but you are understanding of the circumstances that block the resolution of the problem at this point in time. Tell them you understand. Thank them for their time, and go back and start working on some other approach to the problem. Do not argue with a "No" or a lack of resources. Accept the reality of the situation and give everyone a break.

The creative leader can always think of yet another way to address a problem. Provided you give it some time to rest in peace, you can probably resurrect your request for resources at some future time, when circumstances have changed or when you have thought of some new angle. Make sure before you try this that the reasons for saying "No" have been addressed or that the once limited resources now have some hope of being expanded. If nothing has changed, don't harangue people with the same old stuff. They will start hiding behind trashcans when they see you coming.

Sacrificing Yourself for the Cause

It is the rare case, indeed, that is worth risking your life (which in the professional world means your credibility) for the cause. But occasionally, this happens. You know for a fact that standing up for a certain position is going to cause you big problems. Perhaps, you will be swimming up stream, against the tide of the institution's current direction. This is big trouble, because here you risk being seen as a real foe to the system. Much better to be perceived as an overzealous advocate for your arts unit. That is a risk worth taking. The former one is not.

If your opponents are strong, influential leaders within the institution, you really have your work cut out for you; and it may get ugly. Some may consider you courageous, others may see naivete or, worse yet, stupidity. If you have to wear a badge on this issue, make sure it is a badge of courage, not a badge of lunacy. Gauge carefully the risks and the possible benefits to your arts unit before you go off on a crusade. Sometimes, there are no benefits on the horizon, but doing nothing will ensure a seriously negative outcome for your program. Tough call. It's your job to keep your arts program out of harm's way; so, do what you have to do.

When all the risks are personal, and all the potential benefits are for the organization, you know you should do it. That's the real stuff of leadership. Usually, you can weather the personal storms that result. Occasionally, you can't. If your credibility or your effectiveness as a leader is seriously damaged by the stand you feel you had to take on behalf of your organization, well, that's that. You are a hell of a leader!

Make no mistake, I am not advising you, nor would I ever advise anyone to put their job needlessly on the line in the middle of a battle for resources or anything else, for that matter. That usually smacks of soap-opera behavior. You can always resign later, if you really find that necessary; but throwing in threats like, "If we don't get this or that, then I'll quit!"—well, that's a chip you just don't want to play around with. After all, if you are as big a "pain-in-the-ass" as it appears, they just might welcome your resignation, in spite of your confidence that they can't live without you. Don't make their day! Hang in there for the duration. If, in the end, you still lose the battle, retreat. Time heals hot tempers.

Whatever the circumstances, stretch the limits as far as you can stretch them. Your job is to take your arts organization to the highest level of excellence possible, operating within the structure of the institution to which you belong. If you don't bump into a wall from time to time, you aren't trying hard enough. But if you find you can't even take a step without crashing into brick, you have probably gone just about as far as the institution will let you go. If you have the arts unit where it needs to be, great! Just keep the fires burning. But if your vision takes it beyond this point, and you've now got those bricks right in your lap and on top of your head, it's probably time to pass the torch to someone who is satisfied with managing a really good arts organization. You need to move on. And, by the way, it's nobody's fault, really.

DEALING WITH INADEQUATE SPACE & EQUIPMENT

Space Needs in the Arts

The space requirements of an arts organization are massive—so extensive, in fact, that few arts institutions feel they have enough room, even those with multiple buildings. Consider the visual arts: every artist has to have space to create. Maybe not an entire attic loft, but certainly a well-lit space large enough to house an easel, plus a large table or flat working surface, and all the materials used in creating art: paints, pastels, clay, a source of water, and a variety of objects to serve as subjects for the canvas.

In a music school, with each student receiving a private lesson every week, the need for studio space can be a real problem. Since most of the part-time studio teachers are actively working as performers in symphony orchestras or chamber music groups, and many teach privately at more than one institution, the scheduling of lessons is built around external elements, unique to each individual teacher, and are very difficult to plan in advance. To further complicate matters, it is not at all unusual to have large numbers of people needing to teach on the same day of the week, especially when a major symphony orchestra in the city is the primary source of teachers. A day off for the symphony frees everyone to teach, a fact that taxes even the most spacious of facilities.

Practice rooms are a major problem in music, although they can be quite a bit smaller and basic in their accouterments. A room big enough for a piano and a music stand is the primary requirement, but issues of temperature control, humidity control, and sound absorption are critical to the quality of work that can be accomplished in these spaces. With an average of six to ten students sharing a music practice space, and serious students practicing on the average of four hours a day, it is not hard to envision the wars that can ensue over who uses what room, now! Most music schools feel they need twice as many practice rooms as they currently have, no matter what the number.

The President of the University was taking piano lessons from the head of our keyboard program. Most of us knew about this and we had tremendous respect for his willingness to explore a totally new educational arena so late in life, especially with all the pressures of his staggering position. What a tremendous role model for the rest of the campus!

I came out of the office on route to a luncheon meeting when our office manager Karen stopped me, solely with her eyes. They were bigger than I had ever seen them. With total professional calm in her voice, she said, "One moment please," and turned to me with a look of astonishment.

"It's the President's office on line #72. The President is on his way over to our building. He wants to practice. Where should I put him?"

> *With a grin that must have looked diabolical, I answered,*
> *"Put him in the worst space we own; how about that practice*
> *room in the back with no window and no ventilation?"*

(Hey, there's more than one way to make a pitch for better space!)

Every educational area needs classroom spaces, but arts programs also require exhibition space, rehearsal spaces, and performance spaces for orchestras, dramatic productions, wind ensembles, art exhibits, jazz bands, multi-media presentations, choirs, operas, chamber music, and faculty and guest artist recitals. These are, by necessity, large spaces with a myriad of specialized and expensive equipment, ranging from recording facilities to grand pianos, from percussion instruments to motorized lifts; and, of course, seats for the audience, rest rooms, box offices, etc.

All practice and performance spaces require temperature and humidity control, specialized lighting, and sound separation. Fighting poor acoustics or poor lighting can be a nightmare. Good acoustics in rehearsal and performance spaces are vital to the success of a music or theater program; superb lighting is essential to the visual arts and theater programs.

Equipment Needs in the Arts

Equipment to realize the educational mission of the arts unit as well as to support the public performance/exhibition element is a major area of concern for anyone heading an arts program. Sets must be constructed and installed into the performance space. Every costume, every prop must be acquired, stored, and implemented into the production with no margin for error. This requires complex management and highly skilled labor.

Mounting an art exhibit also requires the transportation of precious artwork, often fragile and easily damaged, either during the move or while hanging. Specialized skills are required to assemble, organize, and display a room full of individual artwork. The management of this process, while running a full educational program, can challenge the most gifted administrator.

Large instruments like harps, timpani, double basses, celli, must be moved from rehearsal halls to practice rooms to concert halls. These instruments are large and fragile and expensive. Many belong to the students; some are purchased and kept by the institution. Storing them safely with adequate access for the students who must use them requires specialized space and careful management. Moving instruments requires a van or truck. Maintenance of institutionally owned instruments and monitoring their use is yet another organizational nightmare not faced by the head of a math program.

The River City Brass Band needed a new set of timpani, and the funding was in hand. That was no small achievement, since the cost of a set of "Clevelanders," was upwards of $20,000. We had been granted the funding through our last proposal to the Allegheny County Regional Asset District, a government council that supports public parks, libraries, and cultural arts through a 1% tax on the citizens of the region.

The RCBB already owned a set of timpani, but the players had convinced us, and ARAD, that it was time for a quality upgrade. The plan was to keep the old set for use in outdoor concerts, especially those held in inclement weather. This new set would be used in all the regional subscription series concerts, held in seven different venues, as well as on tour to cities throughout the USA.

After a long wait, the instruments were transported to Pittsburgh, but we also needed a set of travel cases. A good set of hard cases was apparently essential in preventing damage to these fragile instruments as they were transported from place to place in the Band's tightly packed percussion truck. So, we ordered a set. These protective cases were being hand crafted by a gentleman in Cleveland, who was known for his skillful, high-quality work. It would take several months to *finish them. The cases would cost us another $2,000, but this expense had been included in the funded proposal. Since we were already using the new timpani, with only soft coverings for protection, everyone was really nervous about moving them around without firmer cases.*

At last, the custom built cases were ready. All the bills were paid, the final report with receipts was mailed to ARAD, and the timpanist was sent to Cleveland to pick up the cases. Finally, I could quit dealing with all the issues surrounding timpani. We had our new timpani; we had the cases; now, all we had to do was figure out where to store the old set, which was currently housed in the timpanist's apartment.

The phone rang. It was the timpanist. "We have a problem. (I have come to hate that sentence.) "The timpani cases don't fit." "What do you mean they don't fit?" I asked, through clenched teeth. "Well, they take up so much room in the truck, we will never be able to get all the other percussion instruments in there, too."

"Now, wait a minute. We've been using the new timpani for weeks. They fit in the truck, don't they?" "Well, yes, but the hard cases are a lot bigger than the soft ones."

OK, so the saga of the timpani had only just begun. Of course, we tried to return the cases. Too late for that, although the artisan did promise to let us know if he heard of someone else who might want to buy these from us. (Fat chance of that! Those people would be his next customers, and his next set of custom-made timpani cases.) So, we embarked upon a crusade to find a new home for a brand new set of useless timpani cases. Oh, by the way, these cases would only be useful with Clevelanders—the most expensive of available timpani. We had to find somebody who owned a set of Clevelanders, and did not yet have cases for them. Great!

Meanwhile, what were we to do with these cases, that would not fit on the truck, unless it was empty? After much brainstorming, we came up with the solution. We would store the cases in our office complex until they could be sold. That solution lasted only till the next phone call from our much beloved timpanist.

"I'm sorry to tell you this, but the largest of the cases won't fit through the door of the office building." "What? How is this possible? How could they make a case that won't fit through a normal door?" "Well, they usually go in through a loading dock."

Naturally, we have no loading dock at our rented office building.

Now, this story does have a positive ending.

The Concert Manager knew somebody. She was the Vice Principal of Penn Hills High School, the school Cindy had attended. This V. P. had become a friend of Cindy's, and she loved the Band. In fact, we were in the process of collaborating with her on an outreach concert for children, to be held at their school. Their auditorium was huge; so was the back stage area. Yes, there was plenty of room to store timpani cases in the very back, where nobody would bother them. We could keep them there, free of charge, until we found a buyer for them.

This was certainly a better solution than we had come up with to date. We were about to rent a storage building, which would have cost more than we could justify spending on the problem. We had jokingly considered turning the cases into homeless shelters for a family of four—or three plus a dog.

Happily, after putting our Operations Manager on the problem, along with significant help from Google, he had managed to find a buyer. The buyer even picked them up at

Penn Hills High School and carted them away. Fortunately, we never heard from those ubiquitous cases again.

However, without protective cases, we did have several injuries to the new timpani—each one costing several hundred dollars and a trip to and from Cleveland for repairs, before we gave up, and purchased yet another solution—a three-wheeled dolly to move them around. We had a two-wheeler, but it was not stable enough to keep the big timpani out of harm's way.

As for the old set of timpani? Well, after juggling those in and out of our timpanist's second-floor apartment more times than I want to remember, we eventually took them to a music store that rents instruments. They now store them, free of charge. We go get them whenever we need them for an outdoor event. In the interim, they rent them out, and RCBB gets a portion of the rental fees. No, I don't ever want to hear the word timpani again!

Much of the complexity of the space and equipment needs of the arts unit is due to the dual missions of even the smallest arts program: there is usually the educational mission plus the public performance/ exhibition mission. These two distinct areas of activity interweave in a most essential manner, causing tensions at every corner. The leader of an arts program must struggle continually to balance the conflicting needs of each.

Dealing with Inadequate Space

Since space is not one of those things you can just snap your fingers in order to get more, chances are you will need to maximize the use of the space you already have. Here are some suggestions from arts leaders who have operated outstanding programs in severely limited spaces.

- Use classrooms for chamber music rehearsals, acting scenes rehearsals, student art projects, etc. when they are not needed for classes. This will mean students are given access to these teaching spaces after hours; so expensive audio/video equipment should be secured and some means of monitoring the use of these spaces enacted.

- Utilize teaching studios after hours as practice rooms. This will require locking file cabinets and desk drawers, and making sure faculty minimize the amount of personal belongings left about. It will also require some control over who uses these spaces; perhaps faculty studios could be made available only to the more mature graduate students. A system of scheduling time and of signing out a key for each night of usage could be put into place. Granted, faculty would prefer not to share their studio spaces, but it may be the only way to open up enough rooms for students' individual work.

- Develop a policy that nobody owns space. Expect faculty to share their studio spaces. This is really tough to do, but once established, such a philosophy can more than double the available space, because nobody works all the time. Visiting faculty can be juggled so that they don't all "visit" on the same day. Faculty who are accustomed to working off-site one or two days a week, can be "encouraged" to schedule this time out, so you can utilize their spaces on these days. Try to have two to three faculty sharing studio spaces all the time, and then squeeze in the visitors wherever you can. We once had a renowned faculty quip that "Teaching here is like working in the Holiday Inn. As soon as you walk out the door, somebody else moves in." Now, that's full utilization of space.

- Cooperate with other departments. When a physics professor (who did have his own office space) went on sabbatical for a year, he graciously permitted his office to be used as a guitar studio. The science faculty in adjoining spaces quickly adjusted to their new neighbor, and came to enjoy the quiet music coming from room A67. Ever since, we have been tracking faculty leaves like a bunch of vultures, and the guitar teacher has moved happily to a different home every year. (This obviously wouldn't work with trumpets or tubas or timpani.)

- Use performance spaces for multiple purposes. Performance spaces require some extra care, because they are ordinarily outfitted with expensive equipment, and need to be kept presentable for outside audiences. Yet, even these spaces can be used for rehearsals. Whoever manages the hall, or his/her assistant, will need to be responsible for the space around the clock; security will have to be maintained, in spite of the heavy usage. This does raise the cost of managing your facilities, but it may be considered one of those essential expenses.

Security vs. Usage

There is no question: facilities can best be kept secure by limiting their usage, but a balance has to be struck. A perfectly secure, locked space will probably last forever; but if artists are standing out in the snow, with no place to do their work, that closed up building isn't serving much of a purpose. On the other end of the spectrum, it doesn't make a whole lot of sense to permit a group of visual artists to paint a set in a concert hall with wall-to-wall carpeting and upholstered seats.

When space is at a premium, every inch of it should be optimized. This usage needs to be controlled, so that spaces continue to function for the purposes for which they were designed, so that the wear-and-tear on the facilities is minimized. In the long run, increasing the use of space will most assuredly increase the need for maintenance. It may also result in more acts of theft and vandalism; so, with an increase in usage, there must be a requisite increase in security. No facility will ever be 100% safe as long as people are using it; but with the right level of monitoring, a place can be humming with productive activity nearly 24 hours a day.

The epitome of space sharing was illustrated during that international television project, which was described in Chapter #3.

Somehow, we had to find a space for the visiting conductor from Russia, who would be working around the clock for three to four weeks. The space had to be in the arts building, near his rehearsal space. He needed a piano (preferably a nine-foot grand), a desk with a telephone, and some comfortable furniture. The space had to be large enough to film some behind-the-scenes interviews and to stage some tutoring sessions with conducting students. It also had to be acoustically fine and spacious enough to house stage lights and cameras, and it had to look good on film.

We had no such space. In fact, most of our faculty would have killed for a space like that—for themselves. We once toured a new facility renovated for the English Department and one of our professors was amazed at the spaciousness of their Xerox room. He just shook his head and remarked, "Gee, if we had a space this big, we'd put three faculty in it." He was right. (We are the same people who stuffed our renowned conductor into a closet, and he loved the space, because he knew he wouldn't have to share it.)

Still, the Italian producer insisted that all of these requests were necessities. The solution? Our resourceful Assistant Head discovered that the art gallery adjoining our orchestra rehearsal hall just happened to be dark during that particular month The gallery had cathedral ceilings, track lighting, and a gorgeous wooden floor. With the permission and incredible cooperation of the art department, we turned this space into a temporary office. Furniture was bought from the budget for the television production, which would later be moved to a new faculty room. A Steinway grand, which had just been purchased as part of our major fund-raising campaign, was delivered to the art gallery before being moved upstairs to a chamber music room. A few plants, a bowl of fresh fruit, a floor lamp, and a small decorative rug added to the overall ambiance. It was perfect!

By the time the conductor arrived, he had accommodations more elegant than the people running the university. The day he left, everything was immediately moved back out. The room once again stood empty, ready for the next art show to be installed. The only remaining hint of the creative deal that was struck that January was the huge basket of flowers delivered to the head of the art department.

BUILDING AN UNDERSTANDING OF THE ARTS

Translating between Disciplines

We don't like to think of the very institution we serve as a possible roadblock to achieving a higher level of excellence in the arts, but sometimes it is. If your institution is made up of all sorts of educational units, the upper administration is probably not full of artists. For one thing, there are not many artists out there with the organizational skills and the analytical strength to run large organizations of any sort. Nor do many of them have the desire to do so. Consequently, the artists who do emerge as leaders and managers are typically scooped up by arts organizations, which are desperate for strong leadership.

That's, of course, putting the most positive spin on the situation. It is also true that artists are perceived as very focused individuals with narrow areas of specialization. Those arts leaders who do have a desire to broaden their base can have great difficulty gaining credibility from scientists, humanists, and business-oriented professionals; so, large educational institutions are generally run by people trained in these other areas.

For the leader of an arts unit, this presents a special problem: articulating the needs of the discipline to people from very different areas of specialization—people who have the power to allocate funds to those areas they deem important for the institution as a whole. Making a strong case for an arts program often requires the arts leader to act as translator between two very different cultures. People who are not trained in the arts tend to be mystified by them and to consider artists as folks one or two steps removed from reality. (Sometimes that's true, of course, which doesn't make the task any easier.)

Nobody ever says it out loud: "The arts are unimportant!" I almost wish they would. It would be so much easier to debate right out there in the open, where everyone could see the issues and weigh the facts. Instead, you get bits and pieces of evidence flying around like shrapnel from an explosion. Deep inside, you know they don't get it. Here are some of the signs:

- When the president of your institution refers to your arts program as the "jewel in the crown of the university" or the "icing on the cake;"

- When somebody, anybody, says, "Oh, I didn't know your institution had arts programs, too;"

- When a parent remarks to an admissions director, "My son wants to be an actor, but we can't see paying tuition for that!"

- When a highly acclaimed sculptor is up for tenure and the committee asks for her record of research and publications;

- When a candidate for provost is considered too narrow, because he just heads a music school; whereas, the head of a metallurgical engineering department is deemed to be highly qualified for the job.

This chasm of misunderstanding should not be underestimated. The arts leader's first and most important message to the world must always be the vital importance of the arts to society. If the leaders of your institution fail to grasp the value of what you are doing, there will always be other areas that gain priority for their attention and their support. So, your primary concern needs to be the validation of your discipline at home. Depending on your surroundings, this concern may permeate everything else you seek to accomplish within the institution. I hope not, but often this is a major hurdle.

As callous as this may sound, you may have to "sell" the administration on the compelling need for your arts area in their educational environment, and the quickest way to accomplish this goal is to make sure the excellence of your organization shines forth for all to see and hear. As you well know, the arts are capable of lifting the spirit and enriching the life experience of every one they touch. As the commercials so eloquently state, "Reach out and touch someone"—preferably, the leader who sits at the very top of the hierarchical ladder of your institution. Do whatever you have to do to engage this person in the work of the arts.

It is then just a small step to illustrating the impact superb arts programs can have on potential major donors to the institution. This is a straight path to the consciousness of every administrator in higher education today. Arts activities lend themselves quite naturally to impressive ceremonies, presentations, and entertainment for even the most prestigious guests to the campus. They are an ideal mechanism for extending the reputation of the institution well beyond its borders and expanding the visibility of the place worldwide. It's really tough to do any of that with a mathematics department or a psychology program, however outstanding they might be.

Use your art to represent itself. Words are never going to cut through the mystique, no matter how eloquent. Rest assured, once you have reached them, really reached them, you will no longer have to try to explain your discipline or its importance to the "powers that be." Then, and only then, are you ready to seek their support. Yes, I know, even I have fallen into the "them" vs. "us" type of thinking here. However, once you have won their respect and their support for your arts area, the chasm between you and "them" will melt away like a snowfall in April.

Doing Your Job

Respecting your arts program and respecting you are not the same thing at all. In order to be a strong advocate for your program, you need to establish personal credibility with the administrators above you. This is easy. All you have to do is perform brilliantly—that is, do your job in a way that exceeds all expectations. In particular, here are a few things the people above you will most assuredly be looking for in their arts leader:

- the ability to deliver a balanced budget. Make no mistake: This is Number One!

- the people skills to manage the arts organization without a whole bucket full of problems spilling over into their offices;

- a real understanding of the big picture, and how the arts unit fits into the institution as a whole.

Of course, all the qualities of a strong leader are also on the list, but I fear they are icing on the cake in the eyes of the upper administration. They need you to handle your department without overspending, without causing them daily grief, and without asking for the impossible. If you do all of that, and more, you will earn their respect and their trust. Once you have that, you may even be able to ask for the impossible, and occasionally get it. A good administrator appreciates the fact that strong leaders are active advocates for their units. So, don't be afraid to make your needs known. Admittedly, it does take courage to go to the mat over the important stuff— especially when you're wrestling with the boss.

Advocating for Inclusion

It's not just about resources, either. It is also your responsibility to head off at the pass any new policies or procedures that will adversely affect your arts unit. It is your responsibility to remind others of the arts any time they are overlooked in important issues of governance. You cannot expect someone from the sciences or engineering or business or the humanities to understand all of the ramifications for the arts unit of a certain action affecting the institution as a whole. That's your job. Keep your eyes open, and stay informed about the overall organization. If you see a decision on the horizon that will be a problem for your program, speak up.

There are so many facets to this type of discussion, it is not possible to create a laundry list of all potential problem areas. But let me try to provide a few examples, just so that we don't get too general to be useful.

> *The university president is deeply concerned about the retention of students. The data shows too many students transferring to other institutions after their first or second year. Steps are about to be taken to monitor each department— to track the number of students leaving each program prior to graduation.*

> *The problem is that a significant number of students enter an arts area without realizing how focused that type of study actually is. They may choose it as a major initially, because they enjoy it; then, they discover art is a lot of work when it becomes a profession. Helping such students change to a different major is a real success story in skillful advising and early counseling intervention.*

> *You see that there is no plan to track where the student goes when (s)he leaves a department, so you advocate an additional step be taken to avoid counting students that stay within the university as a whole. Sounds obvious, but without your participation in the process, the statistics would have been compiled according to bodies in—bodies out of each specific department. The data would have distorted the real picture of retention in your department, among others, and would have seriously damaged the administration's perception of the effectiveness of your arts program.*

The time to act is before or during the implementation process of a new policy or procedure, not after it has already had an adverse effect on your arts unit. In this case, after the data is already in, your explanation will appear merely defensive—that is, if you even get the opportunity to offer an explanation. Keep an eye on data and how it is collected and interpreted. Somebody will be studying that data and making judgments about your arts program based upon it.

That's one example. Here's another:

The faculty senate is considering instituting a formal review process for all part-time faculty. Most departments only have a few part-time employees; your department has a million of them, some of whom only teach a few private students each week. You know there are not enough hours in the day to carry out the type of review that is being considered for so many employees. You would never get anything else done, and neither would the faculty committees charged with the task of assessing these faculty.

You bring this problem to the attention of the senate. Ultimately, it is decided that part-time faculty teaching fewer than a specified number of hours per week will not be included in the review process. Whew! That was close. If you had been asleep at the wheel, the ensuing chaos would have made the rest of your job look like a day at the beach.

Some times, you have to look pretty deep to find a time bomb. Consider this example:

The admissions office changes its application form for admission to the university. One of the subtle changes in wording requests that students check all their areas of interest. (It used to say, "Check the area(s) you are considering as your major.) High schoolers, hoping to impress the school with their breadth of interests, check drama if they have even seen a play in the last four years; the same with music and the visual arts.

Result? All those applications which have an arts area checked off are, as has always been the procedure, sent over to the specific arts department to arrange an audition or portfolio review. Suddenly, according to the statistics, the number of applicants to these programs has tripled. Nobody knows why. If you or somebody else doesn't stop and take a look, here's what happens:

Everyone involved in the admissions process grows more selective. They have to. If they usually accept one out of every two who apply, for example, they need to ease up a bit—take one out of every three this year; otherwise, all things being equal (which they never are, by the way,) the school will wind up with far too many freshmen majoring in the arts. They won't have enough teachers, enough space, enough beds, enough equipment. . . you get the point.

But, wait! What happens next? As the various arts offices begin to telephone the applicants to schedule their auditions and portfolio reviews, they begin to discover that a whole lot of their applicants aren't applicants at all. In fact, they had no intention of majoring in the arts. They were just interested in the arts. In the end, the total number of real applicants to the arts programs turns out to be just about where it was last year and the year before and the year before that. Only, this time everyone operated with the wrong numbers, and accepted too few students in the arts. Take three deep breaths and prepare for a tiny freshman class.

How could this have been averted? By someone, and it may as well be you, looking deeper to try to discover why the data looked different this time around. Learn to ask why. Don't trust the numbers, unless they make perfect sense.

Institutions of higher education rarely make changes without a lot of warning. As the leader of an arts unit, it is your responsibility to keep one eye on the big picture. Step back to assess how institutional policies and procedures are affecting your program, how changes in these might impact your mission in the future, and how you can influence the direction of the institution in matters of greatest concern. Obviously, you can't poke your nose into every little thing, nor do you have the time to do this. But staying informed and staying involved in the workings of the institution to which you belong is just plain smart. Failure to be informed, or the reluctance to influence the process as it is taking shape, can result in an environment that is not conducive to the effective functioning of your arts program.

When we consider all of the potential roadblocks in our quest for an exciting future for our arts unit—ineffective personnel, limited resources, inadequate space and equipment, and an institutional lack of understanding regarding the needs of high quality arts programs—by far, the most critical is probably the last one on the list. None of the other problems can be successfully addressed without the enthusiastic support of the leadership in the home institution. The effective arts leader appreciates the importance of working within the system, and does everything humanly possible to project to all who will listen (and even to those who try not to listen) the magnificence of an environment rich in artistic excellence. That, after all, is the ultimate goal.

EPILOGUE   MAKING A DIFFERENCE IN THE FUTURE OF THE ARTS

WHY YOU?

As if you don't already have enough on your plate! Am I now to suggest that you worry about the rest of the arts world, too? Well, yes, I suppose I am. There are some really good reasons for you to look beyond your own arts organization and do what you can to help the arts in general: your visibility in the profession, opportunities to speak out, and the desire to make a difference.

Visibility of the Arts Leader

Whether you like it or not, people know who you are. Not everyone, of course, but a significant number of people recognize the name and often the face of the leader of the arts organizations in their community. Why? Because the arts operate in the public domain, and whenever and wherever art is presented by your institution, you are the official representative of that arts organization. You may attend the event, your name may appear on published materials supporting the event, you may formally introduce the event or host a reception following the event, you may be interviewed by the media in conjunction with the event—whatever the circumstances, if you stay in the job long enough, people will begin to recognize you as the leader of your arts organization.

Now, this is a good thing. For the more visible you become, the better able you will be to "sell" your program to the community. And at least part of your job is to help get the work of your artists out there for all of the world to experience—or at least, that part of the world willing to get involved in the arts. We should stop for a minute to admit that we are only speaking here about the artistically curious segment of the population—that fraction of the overall community that is willing, hopefully eager, to sample the arts from time to time. These are the people who will come to know your name.

As the head of an arts program, you are also a natural source of information pertaining to the arts. The media may turn to you when they are looking for background data on a story about the arts. You may be asked for an opinion or a comment on any number of topics: the recent death of a prominent artist, (especially if that artist was an alumnus of your institution or worked for your organization;) the development of some new trend in the arts; a newsworthy arts "happening," whether associated with your institution or not; anything taking place in arts education—either good or not so good, etc.

News reporters need to anchor their stories on facts; if they don't have enough of these, they may turn to you to dredge up a few. One or two strong quotes from an arts leader may be just what the doctor ordered to clinch a story. Obviously, if you don't know the nature of the story or the fundamental slant that reporter is taking, you could be used to prove a point you would never in a million years support. So, caution is definitely in order here! But do expect to be contacted from time to time; your expertise in the field is obvious from the position you hold. You can be sure it will be tapped.

Your stature in the profession will also prove to be highly attractive to non-profit organizations seeking new board members. In fact, it is not at all unusual for an arts leader of one organization to be tapped by a dozen others to serve as advisor. Some even go as far as to say they don't care if you are too busy to come to meetings, just as long as they can use your name as a member of their board. If your institution is highly regarded, the prestige of your title can greatly enhance the credibility of a smaller arts organization. However, nine times out of ten, the organization does want more from you than your name; they also want your time and your money. So, proceed with your eyes wide open.

Opportunities to Speak Out

If you have a talent for public speaking, you can be sure you will be asked to speak in public—a lot. If, on the other hand, your strongest skill lies in the written word, you will have numerous opportunities to express yourself on paper. You may be invited to give a talk or present a paper at district or national conferences of leaders in your field; you may be asked to speak to area arts organizations or to serve as honored guest at important arts functions; you may be interviewed by local radio or television announcers. You can expect to have your professional knowledge tapped frequently on behalf of the artists with whom you live and work.

With each new step out into the community as a representative of your arts institution, your visibility spreads, and so does the reputation of the organization you lead. So, choose your opportunities carefully, and watch every word you say in public. Consider your leadership position a megaphone permanently attached to your mouth. Know that whatever you say will be amplified and broadcast far wider than you can ever imagine. Your actions will be scrutinized, your opinions exaggerated. Even a casual comment can be magnified into a major statement having far-reaching effects. It doesn't take long to discover this. You only need to screw up once or twice to realize that you'd better weigh your words as carefully as a scientist operating in a lab. If you don't, others will.

The positive side of all of this is that your leadership position lends great credibility to all that you say or do; spend this credibility wisely and you will discover the power to make a difference. Effective leaders don't have to wait to be asked. If you feel strongly about a recent development in the arts, speak up. Your voice will be heard.

Desire to Make a Difference

All of this assumes that you want to make a difference. I honestly believe that most of us do—at least most people who wind up in positions of leadership. The opportunity to have a positive effect on an institution that is destined to continue into the future, hopefully well beyond your own life span, adds a level of urgency to a job that might otherwise feel oppressively demanding. Remove this ability to make a difference in the organization and you are left with a management position only. While this can still be a challenging and rewarding position, it pales by comparison to the impact you could be making if you really step up to the plate.

It is unlikely that you will ever make a lasting impact on the organization you run merely by getting through the day, reacting to whatever falls apart. Making a difference demands that you step back and view the big picture. Whatever appears to stand in the way of your vision for the future of your arts organization becomes a major concern. This is one of the criteria that draws you toward what may appear to be unrelated issues and causes. Problems on the horizon, which you may be able to alleviate, can actually be central to the mission you are attempting to accomplish with your local arts organization.

Figure out how to move beyond the present; head toward the future, and in so doing, you will help to define that future. Leadership requires action when you don't really have to act, speaking up when no one has asked for your opinion. Leadership is all about moving past the gate, pushing the boundaries out of the way, forging ahead in spite of perceived road blocks—and, oh yes, carrying an organization full of skeptics, hopeful followers, and a few die-hard opponents right along with you.

ADVOCATING FOR THE ARTS

The voice of an arts executive from an institute of higher education or an independent arts organization has enormous impact. A letter to the editor from you will be printed, and it will probably make a difference. A speech given in support of the arts, an appearance on a panel of experts regarding the state of the arts, even a phone call to the president of a school board where arts funding is in jeopardy— any of these acts can make a tremendous impact, and none of them take an enormous amount of time.

Whether we like it or not, we have the responsibility to speak out wherever and whenever the arts are threatened. We have the obligation to support the efforts of other arts leaders who are fighting for expanding arts education in the schools, for strengthening the

National Endowment for the Arts, for including the arts in media coverage. If each of us in arts leadership positions today vowed to do just three things this next year on behalf of the arts in the USA, we could collectively make a joyful noise that would be heard around the world.

Getting Involved

Getting involved is usually not a problem; there are plenty of people out there looking for your help. Choosing the causes you wish to serve can be the real trick. You have to believe the work is vitally important or it is not worth the time you will have to commit to it. Sometimes you see a cause so critical, you sign on without even being asked. Yet, volunteering can be exceedingly difficult, not because the opportunities are lacking, but because you have so little discretionary time. It is a sacrifice to get involved in things you don't have to take on—things that other people could and should be able to handle. But the "could's" and "should's" of life would fill the Grand Canyon many times over. What the world needs now is a lot more "will's."

Are you needed? You bet, you are! Because you will do what you set out to do. Every time you get involved in a common cause, you learn a great deal; you also forge valuable new relationships. The knowledge and the people added to your life will more than compensate for the contribution you make to that cause. Remember: the real reason you got involved in the first place was to make a difference.

Now, getting uninvolved can be the most difficult part of this whole thing. The fact that there is no word to express it more succinctly (like exvolved or outvolved) tells us something, doesn't it? The door often swings only one way. So, how do you extricate yourself when you have contributed what you came to give? Just say so! "Hey, guys, I really think what you are doing is important, and I wanted to help. But, now that we have done XYZ, I'd better get back to work on some other things. I've really enjoyed getting involved, and will continue to support your cause from a distance," etc. A good rule of thumb is to always contribute what you alone can offer an organization. Then, if there are others around who can do things as well as or perhaps even better than you can, well, that's the signal to slide back out the door. Look for other places where you might make a long-term difference with a short-term effort.

Serving on Boards

Boards can require just the opposite: a long-term effort to make a short-term difference. This shouldn't be the case, but more often than not, membership on boards of non-profit organizations can be extraordinarily time consuming, primarily because the leader does not use the board members as effectively as (s)he should. My advice is to choose your organizations carefully by examining the leadership as well as the mission of the group. Once on a particular board, if your time is being wasted, make as quick an exit as is prudent.

Some responsibilities are absolutely a must. Boards need to be kept up-to-date with complete information about the organization—financial, operational, and philosophical. Yet, this information does not have to be communicated through long and frequent meetings. Written reports can be read at home in a fraction of the time it takes to go to a meeting. However, board members are always expected to attend board meetings, even if the leader initially tells you otherwise. So, it's a good idea to find out when and how often these meetings are held before agreeing to serve.

Unless the board is actually running the organization, quarterly meetings should be sufficient to exchange new information, discuss pressing issues, and make governance decisions. If you wind up on a board that meets too frequently or suffers from long, rambling board meetings, figure out when the heart of the discussions usually takes place and arrange to be there for just that portion of the meeting. Slipping in late or leaving early is also a subtle hint to the leader of that organization that your time is valuable, and so, by the way, is every one else's.

Whatever expectations there are for board members to support the organization outside of these meetings should be made clear at the outset. Attendance at special events sponsored by the group is frequently a key responsibility. Sometimes the board's primary role is to provide financial support—either through their own generous donations or by soliciting help from others they know. Again, if this is the expectation, new board members should be told this as they are being asked to sign on as members.

Why join an organization as a member of its board of directors? The noble reason is because you care deeply about the work of that group, and because you feel you can make a unique contribution to its growth and development. The real reason is probably because somebody you care about asked you to serve and you couldn't think of a good excuse not to say "yes." Hey, that's OK. Lots of great service to organizations begins that way. Once on the board, you will hopefully learn to care deeply about the work of that group, and you will find a way to make a unique contribution to its growth and development. If not, say a polite "Good-bye" and chock it up to experience.

STAYING INVOLVED IN THE PROFESSION

Every profession contains an element of networking, and in the arts, this activity is especially important. Composers need to know and be known by conductors. Visual artists need some personal associations with curators. Actors need to interact socially with producers and directors. So, keeping your toe in the field as a practitioner also entails staying in touch with other professionals; yet, you are probably not going to have time to stay fully involved in the community of artists to which you once belonged. Still, it is important for your own artistic career, if you wish to maintain it or return to it at a later time, to try to keep alive some of these links into the profession. Time will be your greatest problem.

The good thing about this situation is that some of the opportunities you used to have to create for yourself will begin to come your way, just by the nature of your leadership position in the field. This means you will no longer have to work so hard just to be heard or seen or taken seriously as an artist; the leadership position you have attained in the profession will lend added credibility to your own artistic work.

You can decide for yourself whether or not you wish to practice your art through the institution you run; this may be appropriate, it may not. Some feel it would appear to be too self-serving to display their individual artistic work through the organization they seek to lead. Others find this a valuable method of staying in touch with the rest of the artists in their department, and maintaining their own credibility as an artist leader. Whatever your choice, the networking time you have lost through your intense administrative responsibilities will be more than compensated for by your increased visibility as a leader in the field.

Your own colleagues can be a tremendous resource. Each of them holds a place in the professional world. Spending quality time with the artist/faculty is an excellent way to enhance your effectiveness as a leader of the arts unit; it is also a dynamic way to expand your knowledge of "Who's Who" and "What's What" in the arts scene. If you can't be out there yourself, you can at least listen carefully to those who are. Encourage them to talk about their work and how it fits into the current world of the arts. In the process, you will learn a lot about changing trends and evolving problems.

Attending Things

Perhaps you once frequented all the right places and attended all the important artistic events. You may still be able to do this, but now as a representative of your arts organization. You may even assume a leadership role in some of these arts organizations—whether you want to or not. It is amazing how the tentacles of responsibility reach out in all directions once you take on a leadership position. You will have to use some discretion here, and be able to put on the brakes when too much comes your way. My advice is to select those professional activities that will also keep you growing as an artist, not just those which could use your name or your position to help their organization move forward. Be selective! You don't have to do it all.

Annual conferences of arts leaders or university administrators can be wonderful sources of collegiality and artistic growth. Any opportunities to interact with other leaders in the arts can greatly expand your vision and your artistic knowledge, while keeping you informed of what's what in your profession—especially if you don't spend all of your time together commiserating about your jobs. Learn about your colleagues as artists. Find out what the arts scene is like in their locale. Show interest in the artists with whom they associate, and ask what is new in the arts in their region. In short, grab onto these events and participate as fully as you are able—both in the formal sessions and, probably even more important, during the breaks, after the sessions, in the restaurants and cocktail lounges. It is not a waste of your time; it may well be some of the most valuable time you will spend.

That brings us to just a touch of philosophy: it is far too easy to get stuck in the "doing" part of your job. Stepping out of your office to meet with others in the profession is essential to your organization and especially to your own artistic growth. Besides, never fear, the big stuff will wait for you.

Reading to Stay Informed

Staying well informed in your arts area by reading newspapers, journals, and books is admittedly difficult when you are running an arts organization, because your responsibilities are so diverse. You can no longer focus solely on your own area of expertise, but must be concerned about and informed of professional developments in a much broader range of arts activities. As the leader of an arts unit, you may be expected to know about anything and everything that is going on in the world pertaining to the arts; since nobody has time to meet this standard, you will just have to do the best you can to stay informed.

To make matters worse, you will, most likely, be inundated with other documents that must be read and acted upon. Your daily mail alone probably looks like a full day's work and sometimes is. So, finding time to read professional journals and newspapers can be a tremendous challenge. Most arts executives find that the pile of things they should read grows faster than the weeds in their garden, assuming mountainous bulk in just a matter of days. It's really tough to throw things away after you have set them aside to be read later. But that "later" can easily turn into some other year, when the pile of reading materials begins to eclipse the ceiling light in your study or office. Somehow, reading things later defeats the purpose of staying informed; timely information is of little value when it ceases to be timely.

In this technological era, you can sign up for focused news via e-mail, by requesting that all news pertaining to the arts be sent directly to your e-mail address on a daily basis. This entails your selection of the arts section of specific newspapers and/or news publications. You can also access professional journals on line. Having this ability to target your news is a great way to make sure you don't miss something major in your field of concern.

Another suggestion is to find a valued associate who has time to read, and ask him/her to clip things for you—anything of real interest in the arts, for example. Tapping into the daily material of the voracious readers (if you can find any in this day and age) is a tremendous help in learning about interesting tid-bits in the profession and beyond. And it will save you from the time-consuming act of having to scan multiple newspapers and journals for articles of importance.

The most important thing is to organize your reading material in such a way that you actually get to the reading material you really want to read, as well as to the stuff you should read. I keep two piles: one marked "Want to Read," the other labeled "Have to Read." When I'm in the mood to be stoic, I reach for the "Have To" pile, but when I am sick of the whole mess, I read something from the more appealing stack. Incidentally, I throw away anything that does not belong in either pile, and that's a lot of the stuff that comes in on a daily basis. You can choose to throw it away now or wait till later, when it begins to grow interesting looking fungus. Personally, I prefer clean garbage.

Giving Speeches

We have already talked about how to deliver effective speeches in the chapter on "Communicating." Now, let's consider briefly the content of those speeches when arts advocacy is the topic.

First of all, your message needs to be visionary in content, not glued to the needs of your own organization. You are here to step out of your specific job and address a broader issue affecting the arts in general. Holding the position you do is probably what qualified you to be a speaker on this topic; so, your expertise is assumed. Now you must seek to use this stature in the field for the greater good of the profession. Think broadly and speak in global terms.

Any time you set out to help the cause of arts organizations beyond your own, it is vitally important to leave yours at home. Do not refer excessively to your own arts institution or your entire message will feel like a self-serving commercial. It is certainly important to establish your credentials up front, so that people who listen to you will take your ideas and opinions seriously; but this can be done in your introduction. After that, everyone will assume most, if not all, of your thoughts are based upon your experience in your own arts organization; you do not have to remind them with frequent mentions of your group by name. The effect of doing so is to destroy your credibility on the topic you are supposed to be addressing. People will just not believe you actually care about them; it will appear that you are there merely to raise the visibility of your own institution.

Second, don't be afraid to use your crystal ball. Everyone in your audience is capable of seeing the facts, as they stand today, without a whole lot of help from you or anyone else. They are looking to you as the expert (speakers are always viewed as experts) to provide your own personal insight into this situation. So, it isn't enough to just lay out the facts as you see them; try to move beyond these. If you are discussing a problem, take a whack at some possible solutions. Outline steps that could be taken to address this problem. If you are attempting to raise peoples' consciousness about the need for action, make sure you suggest realistic actions that can be taken. Even if you don't know any more about the future than anyone else does, spend some serious time thinking through some possible scenarios. Imagine that you personally are in charge of the outcome; what steps would you take now to position your organization for this uncertain future? Articulate these.

Third, lift people's spirits, inspire them to do something. There is nothing quite so depressing as a speech full of gloom and doom without any hope of avoiding the disasters ahead. So, if your speech is all about problems in the arts environment, make sure you have some suggestions as to how they (each person in your audience) can help improve the situation. It's OK to inform people of the challenges, provided you inspire them to meet these challenges head on. It's fine to tell them the facts; just give them the means to move forward with these facts. The very subject you are addressing, arts advocacy, implies going to bat on behalf of the arts. That should be your purpose. It takes a real leader to raise people's eyes and to lift their spirits. In short, it takes vision and charisma to inspire people to act. You probably have both. Plan to use them every time you move out into the world of arts advocacy.

Using the Media

Too many of us look to the news media for information, without realizing that the media is looking to us for this same information. On a daily basis, they dig around searching for news. They try to be "there" whenever something important is taking place, so they can show it to us, describe it for us, tell us about it. They also depend on us to tell them what's important. If they believe we want to know about high school football games, guess what? That's what they give us. Can you imagine the 6:00 news covering all the area high school band concerts? Once again, we arts leaders have a responsibility here—the responsibility to help the media see the arts as news. This is not an easy task,

The fact of the matter is, most of what we do in the arts will not fit the news media's criteria of "what people want to hear." Ratings drive the process. If station managers really believed people were eager to hear about the arts, you can bet the opening segment of every news broadcast would feature the arts. The gloomy truth is, people probably don't care all that much about the latest breaking arts report. (The only time I can remember hearing Leonard Bernstein's name on local television was the day he died.) Perhaps, the reason for this dearth of arts news is that we just don't try hard enough to raise the consciousness of those in charge of the news formatting. I am convinced we could do better if enough of us worked on this problem.

Arts advocacy through the media takes time, imagination, and gritty determination. You might try an occasional letter to the editor, or an opinion piece (known in the trade as an "op ed" column.) If there is a current issue facing the arts, and no one seems to notice, write about it yourself and submit it to the press. If something really exciting is coming up in the arts, and you can't seem to get the media interested in it, offer to go to your local radio station to talk about it on the air. Classical radio stations depend on listeners' support; they welcome live guests during their once or twice-a-year pledge campaigns and often in between, as well. So, be ready to capitalize on any and all opportunities to speak up on behalf of the arts. If enough of us demand better news coverage of the arts, the media will eventually respond.

Donating Your Time and Money

This topic is the toughest of all—because you probably don't have much of either. Very few of us have extra time on our hands; and fewer still have significant discretionary money to donate to worthy causes. Most of the time we just react to whatever organization manages to capture our attention and our dollars. When the right person asks us the right question at the right time, we sign on. Sometimes, we regret this spontaneous decision-making as we look back on our use of time and money.

Periodically, it can be a great help to just sit down and prioritize. Think about the best use of your time and your money. As a leader in the arts, a significant amount of your attention should go to the furtherance of those organizations you deem to be important for the future of the arts in your community and beyond. Choose carefully, and decide up front where you wish to place your discretionary resources.

Then, follow through. There will always be a large number of groups competing for your interest. If you have given significant thought to the best use of your time and money, you will probably have the strength to say "no" to the others.

Leading a Charge

Occasionally, a topic emerges from the depths of everyday life and begins to gnaw away at your consciousness. No matter how hard you try to ignore it, that issue gradually strengthens and begins to eat into our problem-solving mechanism, all the while crying out for action. Some of us are much more susceptible than others to this virus called "Do Something!" If you are among the vulnerable, you may as well give up. Once that topic grabs a hold of you, there is no escaping the need to get involved.

Jumping into a problem head-first is usually not the best approach. Most causes require the concerted effort of a multitude of people, not just one. Your first act should be to marshal the forces. Find others to join you in your mission—whatever it is—and spend some important time up front planning your strategy. As in most issues affecting a large segment of the population, the further you go toward solving a problem, the more people you will need to involve. Think of your effort as a huge funnel, perhaps beginning with you, the small opening at one end, but ending with a blast of activity spewing forth in all directions form the massive circle of people at the other end.

Engaging others in your quest will undoubtedly dilute your personal influence as the starter of the engine, but that's not important. Holding onto the issue as your own defeats the purpose. If you can manage to enable others to unite for a common cause, you have achieved the highest form of leadership. If the cause you embrace is bettered as a result, your reward is assured.

There is plenty of room for work in the area of arts advocacy. Most people today, we are told, do not care about fine art, music, poetry, dance, theater. Yet, we know that a significant portion of our society is absolutely zealous in its support of the arts. Find these people. Connect to them. Work with them on behalf of the arts, and we may well succeed in greatly expanding the role of the arts in our society throughout the next century.

ACCEPTING THE IMPOSSIBILITY OF IT ALL

Ok, let's be honest: your job is undoable. Now, you're probably wondering why I didn't tell you that in the first place. Well, if you had known that at the outset, you wouldn't have read this book, now would you? After all, if the job can't be done, why worry about it?

I guess the answer to this is that you have a great opportunity to make a difference in the development of an entire arts program and the people in it. Furthermore, by the very nature of your highly visible leadership position, you have a shot at influencing the future of the arts in a much broader sense. That's a mission well worth your finest effort, don't you think?

Even your finest effort is going to feel like a failure, if you don't accept the impossibility of the task at hand. To do your job perfectly, you would need ten times the hours you presently have in your day; and I just don't think you're going to find those. So, you need to come to grips with reality.

What's it Really Like?

- First, you will rarely go home at the end of a day with your To-Do List done. I don't care how well organized you are or what system of day planning you adopt, there is simply more to be done in a day than you can accomplish, ever.

319

This probably goes for any leadership position. If you have set your sights high, you have created your own gauntlet. Even as you are preparing to jump that first hurdle, everyone else in the organization is coming at you with their goals, their needs. Your personal agenda for the day can rarely be carried out, because of all the demands on your time from faculty, staff, students, prospective students, parents, alumni, administrators, major donors, prospective donors, and all the rest of the world. Learn to live with loose ends; you will have a zillion of these all the time. Some days, you will feel as though you accomplished nothing. Yet, you know you worked your butt off.

- Second, people will be unhappy, no matter what you do. Most of them will blame you for their misery. It is the nature of the position to be held responsible for anything that isn't quite right. After all, it's your job to run the place, and every person in it has very specific ideas about what that means. You can bet each of these concepts is based upon the person creating the image; you can also count on each of these people to be the center of that image, because everyone's perspective is shaped around their own egos. (Remember all those squiggly circles you are trying to keep moving in the same direction?) Learn to live with overt and covert criticism. The more sensitive you are, the more deeply you will feel its tentacles. Criticism will actually swallow you up, if you let it. Don't let it!

- Third, there will be some parts of this job you just won't get done. Deadlines will pass, and you will realize as you sort through mountains of overdue paper work, that a lot of that stuff didn't really need to be done anyway. We all have the best of intentions when it comes to the day-to-day trivia. When there is just too much of it, some has to go into the trash. It's your choice: you can either throw it away when it arrives, or you can save it, with the hope of finding time to do it, and then, ultimately throw it away—probably with a little less guilt. Whichever makes you feel better is the way to go. Let's face it: you won't find the time. Further, you shouldn't find the time, because you really do have more important things to do. So, don't wallow in guilt; dump the small stuff, and congratulate yourself on knowing it when you see it.

- Fourth, sooner or later, you may hate this job. The feeling may be fleeting, interrupted by periods of satisfaction and fulfillment. That's great! It may even happen to you nearly every day, but, again, be surrounded by small and not so small personal triumphs. Again, terrific! It takes a special type of resiliency to "go at" anything day after day after day. You may be able to sustain this commitment for many, many years. As long as the personal rewards outweigh the frustrations, you are probably in the "right" job; but if the balance shifts for long periods of time, and if you begin to feel depleted—physically, mentally, and emotionally—Bingo! That's the signal it's time to make a change. In short, if you actually stop liking it, stop doing it! Leadership requires a certain amount of passion and zest. You can't fake either one.

Knowing When to Quit

Nothing lasts forever. And you don't want to be like those old vaudeville entertainers, who had to be dragged off the stage with a hook. (If, however, you're too young to know about vaudeville, you are probably too young to retire.) It may be time to do something else. Knowing when to move on is one of those life-time skills we seem to have to learn as we go. I really don't think there is anything like a quitting gene, although the geneticists may discover one any day now.

How do you know when it's time to leave this job? As my uncle, who was a minister, once said, "You will know it in your bones."

Well, if your bones don't speak to you, here are a few other recognizable signals:

- A better job comes along.

- Somebody over your head tells you to empty your desk.
- You can no longer remember why you wanted this job in the first place.
- You are having trouble getting out of bed in the mornings.
- Your advisory board recommends new leadership.
- You feel a growing urge to punch somebody. (If it's your boss, quit today.)
- You can't think of anything that needs to be fixed. (Geez, you'd better quit fast! You've really lost your vision.)
- Your psychic tells you to do it.
- Your spouse tells you to do it.
- YOU tell you to do it.

How to Quit

Transitions are important in these types of jobs. It may feel terrific to walk out and slam the door, but it will certainly not help the arts organization you are leading. Planning your departure and helping with the orientation of your successor is the classy way to go. So, unless they have to carry you out feet first, do it right. Make your last hour in this job your finest.

Some people just have to burn a lot of bridges behind them as they leave a position. This is never a good idea. No matter how much you want to spout off to the people who drove you nuts in this job, you've stifled the impulse this long, so keep it swallowed permanently. Ideally, you will leave the post before people begin mixing the tar and collecting the feathers. If so, you will have time to wrap up your own loose ends and to say your good-byes in a spirit of mutual respect and collegiality, with maybe a bit of love sneaking into the proceedings now and then. With a little luck, you might even rediscover all the reasons you loved this job, as you work through the process of leaving it.

I had resigned—a tough thing to do. But, it was time to move on. Now, so many groups of people had to be told. I was determined to do this thing right. It had taken ten days to actually resign: two separate meetings with the dean, one with the provost, several phone calls. But we were finally done with all of that.

Then, it got tougher: an emotional early-morning meeting with the faculty; the difficult announcement to the students at noon; a wrenching private meeting with the staff.

Letters had already been written; now, they were mailed:

- *Formal resignation to the administration: brief, professional;*
- *Official letter to the campus community, expressing the mixed feelings of leaving the position;*
- *Letter to the parents of the undergraduates, assuring them of a smooth transition with no interruption in the educational process;*
- *Another letter to the alumni, doing much the same;*
- *Letter to our advisory board, inviting their help in finding a new Head;*
- *Letter to the other heads of departments in the arts, thanking them for their collaborations.*

Notification to the public relations office. Calls from reporters. An article in the local paper. Another in the campus news. Then, the telephone calls, e-mail messages, and letters pouring in. It was horrendously difficult, getting through it all.

Coming home from work that night, I was completely drained. As I sifted through the mail on the kitchen table, I told my husband I thought I was finally finished resigning. I couldn't believe how many constituents had to be informed. I felt as though I must be working for everyone!

Exhausted, I tore open an envelope that had come from the Music Office. It took a moment to realize that I was actually

*reading my own letter, which had been sent to music alumni.
Since I was an alumna of the department, I, too, had received
a copy.*

Staring down at the letter, I dissolved into uncontrollable laughter.
"Well, I must be done; I just resigned to myself!"

ABOUT THE AUTHOR

Marilyn Taft Thomas is Professor of Theory and Composition in the Carnegie Mellon University School of Music, and an active composer with works for orchestra, choir, brass band, piano, voice, and chamber ensembles. For the past twenty years, she has been unable to avoid leading various arts organizations, from the Headship of the Carnegie Mellon School of Music, to the Executive Directorship of the River City Brass Band, with a number of non-profit organizations sprinkled in here and there. A prolific writer, it is this depth of administrative experience that has led her to author a book on *Leadership in the Arts: An Inside View*. Dr. Thomas resides in Pittsburgh, Pennsylvania, with her husband Harry. Together, they have three grown children and six very active grandchildren.

Printed in the United States
201664BV00001B/1-84/P

9 781434 368881